Key Word for Fluency

Upper intermediate
collocation practice

learning and practising the
most useful words of English

George Woolard

HEINLE

Australia • Brazil

3302919062
d States

HEINLE
CENGAGE Learning™

Key Words for Fluency
Upper Intermediate
George Woolard

Publisher: Christopher Wenger

Director of Product Development:
Anita Raducanu

Director of Marketing:
Amy Mabley

Developmental Editor: Jimmie Hill

Intl. Marketing Manager:
Eric Bredenberg

Production Manager: Sally
Cogliano

ELT Production Controller:
Tom Relf

Illustrator: Bill Stott

CoverlText Designer:
Joseph Sherman

Cover Image: © Anna Macleod

Acknowledgements
I am grateful to Michael Lewis for his help and support, in shaping this book in its early stages.

I should also like to thank those colleagues and students at Stevenson College, Edinburgh whose comments and feedback proved invaluable during the development of the material.

Finally, I am particularly grateful to my editor, Jimmie Hill. The final shape of this book owes much to his careful guidance and to the many insights, suggestions and examples he provided.

George Woolard

The Author
George Woolard is an experienced ELT teacher and trainer who has worked in Greece, Malaysia and the UK. He now teaches at Stevenson College, Edinburgh. His publications include **Lessons with Laughter** and **Grammar with Laughter** (*Thomson ELT*).

For permission to use material from this text or product, submit all requests online at cengage.com/permissions.
Further permissions questions can be emailed to
permissionrequest@cengage.com

Heinle, a part of Cengage Learning, is a leading provider of materials for English language teaching and learning throughout the world.
Visit Heinle at **http://elt.heinle.com**
Visit our corporate website at **www.cengage.com**

ISBN: 0-7593-9627-2

Printed in China by RR Donnelley
4 5 6 7 8 9 10 - 13 12 11

Contents

Introduction

What are collocations?

Collocations are common combinations of words. If you want to speak and write English well, you need to know them. For example, verb + noun, adjective + noun, noun + noun, noun + preposition + noun combinations. Collocation is a major key to fluency.

Look at these sentences containing the word 'problem':

1. There is a great deal of indecision over *how to tackle the problem.*
2. I believe that traffic congestion in large cities is *an insurmountable problem.*
3. We must get to *the root of this problem.* We need to discover the cause.

You can see that problem collocates with the verb tackle, with the adjective insurmountable, and it forms a noun expression with the root of. And these are only a few of its collocations!

Learning vocabulary

When learning vocabulary, it is not enough just to know the meaning or translation of a word. You also need to learn its collocations if you are to use it correctly and naturally when speaking or writing.

**Learning new vocabulary is not just learning new words;
it is also learning familiar words in new combinations.**

Becoming more aware of collocation

It is important that you develop an awareness of collocations and begin to notice them more and more.

Task 1

Underline the collocations of the word ability in these sentences.

1. She was so shocked by the accident that she lost the ability to speak.
2. She has exceptional abilities as a musician.
3. Tiger Woods may be the best golfer in the world, but the Open Championship next week will be a real test of his ability.

To check what you think and find out more collocations of ability, go to the first unit in this book. You also need to know which words do **not** go together. You need to be constantly aware of the fact that words with the same meaning do not necessarily form the same collocations. The following task demonstrates this.

Task 2

Cross out the wrong collocations for progress in these sentences.

1. Fallen trees are stopping / holding up the progress of the rescue.
2. There has been fast / rapid progress in computer technology in the past few years.
3. We are making slow but steady / constant progress.

To check and find out more collocations for *progress,* go to page 108.

Key Words

This book provides practice in learning the collocations of some of the most useful words in English – the **key words** you need at your level of English. These key words are the nouns we use to talk about a very wide range of topics – very general nouns like *ability, change, effect, progress, responsibility, views* etc.

Nouns are the most important words in a sentence because when we talk about something, we usually name it with a noun. Furthermore, studying nouns is a very efficient way of learning vocabulary because the noun will naturally take us to the verbs and adjectives that combine with it. For example, in the sentence *My mother holds very strong views on the subject of marriage,* a focus on the key word **views** leads to the adjective **strong** and the verb **hold.** This means that you are learning expressions, not single words. In this particular case: *hold strong views on.*

How is the book organised?

This book is divided into two sections. The main section consists of 145 one-page units, arranged alphabetically, each of which focuses on a single key word. The second section consists of 20 important nouns which are followed by 'of'. For example: a series of, a lack of, a great deal of, etc.

> **Task 3**
> **We talk about** a lack of help, a lack of funding, a lack of support.
> **Can you think of more ways of completing the phrase** a lack of . . . .?
> **To find out more, go to page 154.**

Each unit consists of a series of exercises which help you to notice and practise the most common collocations of a key word. The exercises usually focus on verb, adjective, preposition and noun combinations. Notes are also provided to give further details on other common uses of the key word.

Some of the key words have different meanings. For example, *chance* means *opportunity* or *possibility*. Exercises usually treat the different meanings separately.

Sometimes the collocations of a word are different if it is singular or plural. Pay particular attention to this in the exercises and notes.

When you finish the exercises for a particular key word, you will have learned at least fifteen new pieces of information about that word. So remember, you may be focusing on only one word, but you are learning other words at the same time and learning groups of words in useful combinations. The collocations of the 165 key words in this book amount to around 2,500 vocabulary items!

How to use this book

There is simply not enough time to learn all these collocations in class, so this book is designed for self-study. It will supplement and add to the work contained in your coursebook, enabling you to develop your vocabulary quickly and independently. You can do the units in any order that suits you.

For speaking and writing
You can use the exercises when you have to write an essay or discuss something in class. For example, if the lesson in your coursebook is about Extreme Sports, then it makes sense to look at **risk** and **danger**. For example, this will allow you to say:

   If you don't wear a helmet while mountain biking, you run the risk of serious head injury.
   It's important that you are fully aware of the dangers of climbing in this area.

For reading and listening
The more collocations you know and can recognise, the easier you will find it to understand texts and to understand films and people when they speak to you. This is because you won't need to listen to every single word, but will recognise longer expressions.

To prepare for an examination
Collocation practice is one of the best ways to prepare for the FCE, CAE, CPE, IELTS and similar examinations, especially for the speaking and writing sections.

Keep this book!

When you have completed the exercises in this book, you should keep it as a reference book. It is like a dictionary – a book that you return to again and again. It is a well-known fact that if you practise new language, you will begin to speak and write English more fluently and naturally. So, think of this book as a kind of 'lexical gym', in which you give yourself regular workouts!

George Woolard, Edinburgh

ability

1 Verb + ability

Use the correct form of these verbs:

affect	assess †
overestimate	lose
doubt	show +

1. Examinations are not the only means of . . . . someone's ability. There are other ways of measuring potential.

2. At first I questioned his abilities, but he has done the job so well. I'm now ashamed that I had so little confidence in him and that I . . . . his abilities in the first place.

3. It is a well-known fact that even small amounts of alcohol can . . . . your ability to drive safely.

4. She was so shocked by the accident that she . . . . the ability to speak.

5. Although Peter . . . . a lot of ability as a teenager, he just wasn't good enough to go professional.

6. I had to give up half way through the race. I had obviously . . . . my ability to run a marathon.

Go back and underline all the verb collocations with *ability*.

2 Noun + preposition + ability

Use these nouns in the sentences:

confidence	best
lack	reflection
test	use

1. Tiger Woods may be the best golfer in the world, but the Open Championship next week will be a real . . . . of his ability.

2. Raymond is very clever, but he doesn't make full . . . . of his abilities.

3. I was surprised when he failed his examinations. His results are certainly not a true . . . . of his abilities.

4. He's extremely competent and will do the job properly. I have every . . . . in his ability.

5. He said that he would try to do the job to the . . . . of his ability.

6. I believe he lost confidence. His failure was not due to a . . . . of ability.

Go back and <u>underline</u> all the noun + preposition + *ability* collocations.

3 Common adjective collocations

Use these adjectives in the sentences:

average	considerable
mixed	natural
incredible	proven

1. Most of us have to work hard to learn to play a musical instrument. However, there are people who are born with a . . . . ability and who learn effortlessly.

2. The students in my class are of . . . . ability, so I teach them in groups according to their level.

3. I have no doubts that he has . . . . ability, but I don't think his personality is suited to this kind of work.

4. We need somebody who has done this before – with the . . . . ability to do the job.

5. I'm not a genius and I'm not stupid. I would describe myself as being of . . . . ability.

6. I don't know how she does it, but Annie Lennox has this . . . . ability to electrify her audience.

Go back and underline all the adjective + *ability* collocations in this exercise.

Notes

1. Here are three ways to describe 'great' ability:
   She has a remarkable ability to recall long poems after only reading them once.
   She has exceptional abilities as a musician.
   His examination results are proof of his outstanding ability.

2. Remember that an adjective collocation can come before or after the noun:
   She has remarkable ability.
   Her ability is remarkable.

3. Notice the use of 'best' in 2-5. 'Best' is usually an adjective, but it is used as a noun in the expression to 'do something to the best of your ability'.

4. We can talk about specific abilities:
   musical ability   *physical ability*
   linguistic ability   *technical ability*
   artistic ability   *acting ability*

5. When we talk about very intelligent children, we often call them 'children of above average ability'.

---

account

1 Verb + account

Use the correct form of these verbs:

accept	*differ*	*corroborate*
provide	*keep*	*listen to*

1. The priest . . . . the old woman's account of the death of her child with compassion.

2. I'm going to . . . . a detailed account of my travels in India. I'm going to write a book when I get back.

3. The diaries . . . . a full account of the writer's experiences in prison.

4. Do you think we should . . . . his account of events? Can we really trust him?

5. The police only believed me after an eye-witness . . . . my account of the accident.

6. There were a number of accounts of the assassination of President Kennedy which . . . . considerably from the official version of events.

Go back and underline all the verb + *account* collocations.

2 Common adjective collocations

Use the following adjective collocations in these sentences:

blow-by-blow account	*clear account*
conflicting accounts	*fascinating account*
full account	*graphic account*

1. I didn't know who to believe. The two witnesses gave . . . . of the incident.

2. We only wanted a brief account of the incident, but he insisted on giving us a . . . . of everything that had happened.

3. Our new director gave a very . . . . of his plans for the future of the company. They were well-expressed and easy to understand.

4. Her new biography gives a . . . . of her travels in the jungles of Africa.
   >Yes. It's very interesting. There's a scary account of how she was almost killed by a tiger.

5. The refugee gave such a . . . . of his torture that I thought I was going to be sick. How can human beings do such terrible things?

6. The Prime Minister is expected to give a . . . . of his meeting with the President to Parliament this morning.

3 Adjective + account

Use the following adjectives in these sentences:

eye-witness	*faithful*	*hair-raising*
humorous	*sketchy*	*moving*

1. I think last night's programme was just what we needed. It was a . . . . account of the events leading up to the plane crash.

2. According to an . . . . account, the robbers escaped in a blue car.

3. She gave a . . . . account of her escape from a pack of wild dogs in the Australian outback.

4. The speaker gave us a . . . . account of life at university. He had us all in fits of laughter.

5. We only have a . . . . account of the accident at the moment. We can't say if anybody has died.

6. The book provides a . . . . account of the suffering of ordinary people in war-torn Eritrea.

"An eye-witness account!"

Notes

1. In 2-2 a 'blow-by-blow account' gives all the details, missing nothing out. Notice these similar examples.
   He gave a comprehensive account of his movements on the day of the murder. It was a very detailed account.

2. If you experience something yourself, you can give a *first-hand account* or an *eye-witness account*.

3. When *account* means *report*, you can use *glowing*:
   We were really proud. All our sons' teachers gave glowing accounts of their progress.

4. The expression *by all accounts* means *according to what people say*. For example:
   The mountain villages are really worth visiting, by all accounts.

action

1 Verb + action

Use the correct form of these verbs:

condone	*demand*	*explain*
put into	*swing into*	*take*

1. Shopkeepers in the town centre are .... tougher action against the vandals who continue to damage their shops at night.

2. She will have to .... her actions – and defend them before the disciplinary committee – if she is to get her job back.

3. We've had enough talk! We need to ...... these ideas .... action as soon as we can.

4. Air traffic controllers are threatening to ...... industrial action if their pay demands aren't met.

5. The emergency services are always on standby and ready to .... action at a moment's notice.

6. There's no way that the college can .... the actions of these students. Throwing eggs at the Queen is not an appropriate way to protest.

2 Common adjective collocations

Use the following adjectives in these sentences:

disciplinary	*drastic*
evasive	*joint*
prompt	*whatever*

1. If the manager hadn't acted so quickly, the whole factory would have been destroyed. It was his .... action that prevented the fire from spreading.

2. The army has been given full powers to take .... action is necessary to restore order to the streets of the capital.

3. The company cannot continue to lose money at this rate. The situation calls for .... action.

4. .... action will be taken against any member of staff who is found using the internet for personal matters.

5. Britain and the US agreed on .... action to combat the threat of world-wide terrorism.

6. The pilot of a commercial jet had to take .... action yesterday to avoid a mid-air collision with a small military plane.

Go back and underline all the adjective + *action* collocations in this exercise.

3 Expressions with prepositions

Use these expressions with prepositions below:

plan of	*course of*	*need for*
implications of	*result of*	*responsible for*

1. We realise that the situation is critical and we fully appreciate the .... immediate action.

2. When the settlers cut down all the trees, they failed to consider the wider .... their actions, so the area became a desert.

3. People who are mentally ill cannot be held .... their actions.

4. How are you going to deal with this situation? What's your .... action?

5. The surgeon was to blame. My father's death was the direct .... his actions.

6. They're planning to build a dam across the river. However, experts disagree whether this is the best .... action to take.

"Taking evasive action!"

Notes

1. Note the following:
   They say he's a good player. I've never seen him in action.
   He is out of action due to an knee injury.

2. We talk about *taking industrial action* when we mean going on strike.
   We talk about *taking military action*.

3. Note the common expression:
   He's a typical politician – all talk and no action.

4. An *action group* is a group of people who get together with a common aim to do something positive, eg to help homeless people.

---

activity

1 Verb + activity

Use the correct form of these verbs:

avoid   be involved in   monitor
do   organise   support

1. Our yoga group . . . . a number of activities throughout the year. Our monthly newsletter gives you an update on our current activities.

2. The police suspect that he is . . . . some kind of illegal activity, but they can't prove it yet.

3. This is a simple activity you can . . . . with mixed ability classes.

4. It is important that you . . . . any kind of sporting activity for at least three weeks after your operation.

5. Charities depend on people like us to . . . . their activities. Otherwise, they would not be able to function.

6. A national committee has been set up to . . . . the activities of the police. It is important that they are answerable to the general public.

2 Common adjective collocations

Complete the sentences with these adjective collocations:

frenetic activity
outdoor activities
pleasurable activities
strenuous activity
worthwhile activities

1. You're wasting your time playing computer games. You need to redirect your energies into more . . . .

2. For me, one of life's most . . . . is going for a long walk in the countryside.

3. I hate being inside. That's why I love . . . . like mountaineering and sailing.

4. You can do some light exercises, but avoid any kind of . . . . if you want to recover from your injury quickly.

5. We worked night and day to meet the deadline and after two weeks of . . . . the job was finished on time.

Go back and underline other interesting collocations in this exercise.

3 Types of activity

Use these adjectives in the sentences:

criminal   economic   extra-curricular
leisure   political

1. A shorter working week means that people today have much more time for . . . . activities.

2. A friend of mine was arrested and imprisoned for his . . . . activities. He refused to accept the government ban on public demonstrations.

3. Apart from its academic programme the school offers a wide range of . . . . activities, including swimming, drama, cycling and archery.

4. There's been an increase in . . . . activity in our area in recent years – mostly drug-related.

5. In third world countries agriculture remains the main . . . . activity.

4 Noun + of + activity

Use these nouns in the sentence:

bouts   flurry   hive   signs   variety

1. The whole of our house was a . . . . of activity on the day of my sister's wedding. Everybody was rushing around preparing things.

2. The new sports centre offers a wide . . . . of activities including tennis, swimming and squash.

3. There was a sudden . . . . of activity when Madonna arrived, then the photographers sat down and waited for the next star to arrive.

4. Doctors tell us that regular exercise is better than occasional . . . . of strenuous activity.

5. The plants in the garden are finally showing . . . . . . of activity after the long cold winter.

Notes

1. These expressions mean a lot of activity:
   The hall was a scene of constant activity.
   The place was buzzing with activity.

2. Note these verb collocations:
   Lots of activities were laid on for the children.
   What kind of leisure activities do you enjoy?

---

advantage

1 Verb + advantage

Use the correct form of these verbs:

give	*have*	*outweigh*
take	*stress*	*weigh up*

1. I think we should go ahead with the plan. The advantages far . . . . the disadvantages.

2. He had no trouble finding a job because he . . . . the advantage over the other candidates of speaking fluent Spanish.

3. I haven't decided yet whether to emigrate or not. I'm still . . . . the advantages and disadvantages.

4. The Prime Minister was at great pains to . . . . the advantages of the new system.

5. His height and long arms . . . . him a huge advantage over other boxers.

6. While we stayed at the hotel, we . . . . advantage of its excellent leisure facilities.

2 Common adjective collocations

Use these adjectives in the sentences:

mutual	*main*	*added*

1. Not having to travel far to get anything you need is probably the . . . . advantage of living in the city centre.

2. The plan is to our . . . . advantage. We will all benefit greatly from it.

3. The new plan will improve living conditions in the villages, and it has the . . . . advantage of bringing much-needed employment to rural areas.

distinct	*great*	*unfair*

4. Some people object to private schools because they give an . . . . advantage to children from rich families.

5. His enormous height is a . . . . advantage when playing basketball.

6. The . . . . advantage of the euro is we don't need to keep changing money every time we go to another country.

Here are three adjectives with similar meanings to some of those in the exercise. Which of the above sentences would they fit in?

additional	. . . .
considerable	. . . .
obvious	. . . .

3 Advantage + preposition.

Complete the sentences with for, in, of, over, to:

1. There are a number of advantages . . . . . studying English in the UK or America.

2. There are distinct advantages . . . . . a more radical approach to this problem.

3. Government subsidies give these companies an unfair advantage . . . . . their competitors.

4. Discuss the advantages and disadvantages . . . . . travelling abroad on your own.

5. The bird's huge claws are an obvious advantage . . . . catching its prey

"It's not fair! I feel your height gives you a distinct advantage!"

Notes

1. In 1-6 'take advantage of' means 'make use of'.

2. Note the expression in 2-2 – to your advantage. It means something is in your interest. For example: *It's to your advantage that you speak French fluently.*

3. In 2-2 it is natural to say that something is to our mutual advantage. You can't say that something is to our mutual disadvantage.

4. Note the use of 'over' when making comparisons. *Digital cameras have lots of advantages over conventional ones.*

5. Note the following common expressions with disadvantage:
   The fact that he didn't speak English put him at a disadvantage during the visit to London.
   It is clear that children of poor families are at a disadvantage when it comes to getting into university.

6. Notice this common structure:
   There are a number of advantages in (doing something).

---

advice

1 Verb + advice

Use the correct form of these verbs:

give   ignore   take   turn to   welcome

1. If you had . . . . my advice, you wouldn't have lost all your money.

2. Can I . . . . you a piece of advice?
>Sure. Any advice would be greatly appreciated.

3. Matt knows what he's talking about. He has a lot of experience in dealing with this kind of situation so we can't afford to . . . . his advice.

4. We're not sure if our plan to start up a new fast-food restaurant in this area is likely to succeed or not and we would . . . . your advice on the matter.

5. Jim had no close friends, so he had no one to . . . . for advice when he needed it most.

Mark the following sentences:

I   if it means 'ignoring advice'
G   if it means 'giving advice'
T   if it means 'accepting advice'

1. He simply won't listen to any advice from me.
2. He just follows his parents' advice blindly.
3. They just completely disregarded my advice.
4. My offer of advice is still open.
5. Sam's 16 and is actually very good at taking advice.
6. Heed my advice – or take the consequences!

2 Prepositions with advice

Use the following prepositions in the sentences:

against   on   to

1. He went back to work . . . . . . the advice of his doctor. He should have stayed off longer.

2. I bought some technology shares . . . . . . the advice of my brother, who's an accountant.

3. We went to India in July . . . . . . the advice of all our friends who told us to wait till February when the weather would be cooler.

4. Can you give me some advice . . . . . . where to find a good hotel in Rome?

5. My advice . . . . . . you would be to go and see your solicitor first before doing anything.

6. Here's a leaflet with some good advice . . . . . . starting your own business.

Go back and underline all the complete prepositional expressions.

3 Common adjective collocations

Use the following adjectives in these sentences:

contradictory advice   friendly advice
impartial advice   professional advice
sound advice   unsolicited advice

1. The legal system is so complex nowadays that it is often impossible to understand it without . . . .

2. I often ask my teacher for advice when I have a big decision to make. He's full of . . . ., based on common sense.

3. I've been given . . . . by two different financial advisors – one told me to sell my shares while the other told me to hold onto them. What am I supposed to do?

4. I wouldn't say anything to him. He doesn't like . . . . He'll just tell you that if he needs your advice he'll ask for it!

5. It's really difficult to get . . . . nowadays, but your solicitor is bound by rules to give this kind of help.

6. You might not want to hear this, John, but as somebody who knows you well and cares about you, can I give you some . . . . – I really don't think Mary's the right woman for you.

Notes

1. In 2-4 and 2-6 'about' is also possible.

2. In 3-2 you could also say 'good advice'.

3. You can 'ask' someone's advice or 'ask for' advice:
   Ask Stuart's advice about where to stay in Paris.
   I wouldn't ask him for advice on where to eat!

4. Note these expressions about giving advice:
   I'd appreciate any advice you can give me.
   Let me give you a piece of advice.

5. Note this more formal expression:
   Before you write to your landlord, you should seek proper legal advice.

6. We use the expression 'a word of advice' to warn someone:
   A word of advice. I'd keep away from Susan. She's trouble! Take it from one who knows!

---

agreement

1 Verb + agreement

Use the correct form of these verbs:

break	*cancel*
get	*honour*
reach	*sign*

1. Make sure you look closely at the details before you enter into any agreement. Never . . . . an agreement without reading the small print first.
2. We reserve the right to . . . . this agreement if you fail to make the regular monthly payments.
3. You'll have to . . . . your parents' agreement if you want to go on the school trip.
4. When we make an agreement with someone, we always . . . . it. Our reputation depends on the fact that we adhere strictly to any agreement we make.
5. After hours of talking the two sides failed to . . . . agreement. They will meet again tomorrow in a final attempt to come to some sort of agreement.
6. By going on strike they . . . . the agreement they made earlier with their employer. They could be fired for breaching the terms of the agreement.

2 Common adjective collocations

Use the following adjectives in these sentences:

amicable	*binding*
tacit	*general*
unanimous	*verbal*

1. It's best to get things in writing. . . . . agreements often don't stand up in court.
2. Nothing was said at the meeting. There seemed to be . . . . agreement that the subject of the manager's expenses wouldn't be discussed.
3. My wife and I came to an . . . . agreement when we split up. She got the house and I got the money. It worked out really well.
4. There is . . . . agreement in the medical profession that pregnant women shouldn't smoke.
5. It was not a . . . . agreement in their view, so they feel they can break it without penalty.
6. There is . . . . agreement that a new airport is needed. Nobody disputes that, but there is fundamental disagreement over where to build it.

Go back and underline the collocations.

3 Verb + disagreement

Use the correct form of the following verbs:

cause	*express*	*have*	*resolve*

1. Protesters marched through London to . . . . their disagreement with government policy.
2. My wife and I don't . . . . many disagreements, but when they do arise, they tend to be over the best way to spend money.
3. Management and unions have been trying to . . . . their disagreement over proposals to reduce the workforce, but after three days of talks there is still no sign of an agreement.
4. I think the new timetables are certain to . . . . disagreement amongst staff.

"We're not protesters! We're only expressing our disagreement!"

Notes

1. Notice the differences in meaning in the following examples:
   We are in complete agreement.
   (We agree about everything.)
   We are in broad agreement.
   (We agree about most things.)

2. We use a number of adjectives to describe a serious disagreement:
   There is considerable disagreement over the safety of genetically modified food.
   There is profound disagreement on who should become the next leader of the party.
   There is fundamental disagreement about the best way to fund the health service.

3. You can say there is 'considerable' or 'fundamental agreement', but you cannot say 'profound agreement'.

---

aim

1 Verb + aim

Use the correct form of these verbs:

achieve	*clarify*
have	*set out*
pursue	*support*

1. You'll need to . . . . the aims and objectives of your project. Make sure you state them clearly at the beginning of your report.
2. Our organisation is committed to . . . . its aims through peaceful means. We totally reject violence as a means of political change.
3. Some companies . . . . their aims in a very ruthless way – with no thought of what they are doing to the environment.
4. I . . . . the aims of animal rights activists because I want to see a ban on using animals in experiments.
5. He's just drifting. He seems to . . . . no aims in life at all. Would you talk to him?
6. All parents receive a booklet which . . . . the school's aims and objectives before their children start their first term.

In which examples above could you also use:

fulfil   *sympathise with*

2 With the aim of

Complete the sentences below:

awareness
dependency
homelessness
employment
relations

1. My sister went to Valencia last year with the aim of finding . . . . in the hotel industry so that she could improve her Spanish.
2. This booklet has been produced with the aim of increasing public . . . . of AIDS.
3. A new scheme has been set up with the aim of reducing people's . . . . on the welfare state.
4. The police regularly visit schools in run-down inner-city areas with the aim of improving community . . . .
5. A new charity has been set up with the aim of tackling . . . . among young single men.

Go back and underline the full expressions.

3 Common adjective collocations

Use the following adjectives below:

broad	*clear*
common	*underlying*
long-term	*sole*
laudable	

1. Before you start this project, it is important to have a . . . . aim in mind. You really need to know where you're going.
2. Increasing the state pension is a . . . . aim, but I don't think the country can afford it.
3. Promotion to the first division is the . . . . aim of the club, but our immediate aim is to win our next match.
4. I sympathise with the . . . . aims of the party, but on this particular issue I'm afraid I have to disagree.
5. Although the President is here on an official visit, I think the . . . . aim is to promote trade.
6. He's a selfish sort of person. His . . . . aim in life seems to be to make money.
7. This company will only be successful if people work together with . . . . aims.

Notes

1. In 3-4 you could use 'general aim'.

2. Look at this common expression:
   We're paying so much attention to the details of the plan that we are in danger of losing sight of our original aims.

3. Notice these adjective collocations used to talk about very important aims:
   In his speech he said that the ultimate aim of the party was to get rid of poverty.
   The chief / main aim of the course is to familiarise you with the uses of the internet.
   The principal aim of education must be to encourage young people to think for themselves.
   The overriding aim of US foreign policy at that time was to prevent the spread of communism.
   The primary aim in sumo wrestling is to knock your opponent right out of the ring!

4. Notice *short-term, medium-term,* and *long-term* aims or goals.

answer

1 Verb + answer (meaning reply)

Use the correct form of these verbs:

demand *give* *need*
be *receive* *wait for*

1. Did you .... an answer to your letter?

2. We sent a letter of complaint ages ago. Three months later we're still .... an answer.

3. The managing director .... an answer. He was furious and wanted to know why things had gone so badly wrong.

4. The Prime Minister promised to .... a written answer to the MP's detailed question.

5. We .... an answer immediately. If you can't give us one, we can't get on with the job.

6. I rang the bell several times, but there .... no answer.

"I'm sorry, you've got the wrong answer – again!"

2 Common adjective collocations

Use the following adjectives in these sentences:

correct *detailed*
final *honest*
immediate *short*

1. I don't expect an .... answer. Think it over and let me know by the end of the week.

2. Just give me a straight and .... answer, and stop trying to evade the question, will you?

3. Is that your .... answer? If it is, I won't trouble you much longer.

4. The .... answer to your question is NO!

5. They really were very helpful, taking lots of time to give us clear and .... answers to all our questions.

6. Very often some of these questions have more than one .... answer.

3 Verb + answer (meaning solution)

Use the correct form of these verbs:

arrive at *come up with* *guess*
have *know* *provide*

1. If I .... the answer, I'd tell you!

2. Yes, we are aware of the problem, but unfortunately we do not .... the answer.

3. You'll never .... the answer in a million years! Do you want a clue?

4. We're in trouble if someone doesn't .... the right answer soon.

5. The new accounting system will .... the answers you need in a matter of minutes.

6. We .... the correct answer by a process of elimination. We rejected the choices one by one until we only had one left.

4 More adjective collocations

Use the correct form of these verbs:

wrong *simple* *long-term*
definite *obvious* *only*

1. There is no .... answer to the problems facing the economy. It's a very complex situation.

2. Food aid may provide temporary relief to the people of Eritrea, but it is not a .... answer to the problems facing the country.

3. I think you've put the .... answer for number 3. It should be 5.25, not 5.52.

4. We are unable to treat this condition with drugs. An operation may be the .... answer.

5. I don't see what the problem is. If we can't hire a bus, the .... answer is to cancel the trip.

6. It's too early to give a .... answer. We won't be in a position to do so for a couple of days.

Notes

1. Note the following more formal phrase:
   In answer to your enquiry, we regret to say that we have no vacancies at present.

2. If someone thinks they know everything we often say that *they think they know all the answers.*

3. If a child *answers their parent back,* they are being rude.

apology

1 Verb + apology

Use the correct form of these verbs:

give   *demand*   *expect*
make   *offer*   *owe*

1. We weren't looking for any compensation for the delay, but we did at least . . . . an apology.

2. Don't you think you . . . . your mother an apology for the way you behaved at Jo's wedding?

3. I'm really sorry we can't come to dinner on Saturday. Something really serious has come up. Please . . . . our apologies to your wife.

4. My wife was so angry with the way she had been treated that she marched up to the manager and . . . . an apology for the bad service.

5. I have an apology to . . . . I'm afraid I think I've just broken that pen you lent me.

6. What more can I do? I . . . . her an apology for my appalling behaviour at the party, but she wouldn't accept it.

2 Common adjective collocations

Complete the sentences below with the following:

belated   *full*   *sincere*   *formal*

1. Please accept our . . . . apologies for the error in your flight booking.

2. The newspaper was forced to publish a . . . . and detailed apology to the pop star for making untrue allegations about his personal life.

3. The Minister had to stand up in Parliament and make a . . . . apology for his unfortunate remarks on immigration.

4. I'm just e-mailing you to apologise for not turning up for last week's meeting. I was abroad and didn't hear about it – so . . . . apologies.

Now cross out the adjective which does not fit:

5. Look, it was a mistake. Please accept my hearty / heartfelt apologies.

6. The hospital wrote to me personally with a profound / professional apology for their mistake.

7. When a politician makes a mistake, they really ought to make a public / publicised apology.

8. Even the most abject / object apology isn't enough when you are caught stealing from a colleague!

Go back and underline the adjective collocations.

3 Of + apology

Complete the sentences below with the following:

full   *letter*   *way*   *words*

1. Following our complaint about our hotel room, we received a formal . . . . of apology from the management and a voucher for a free weekend for two!

2. As usual Andy was . . . . of apologies for what he had done. But I know his apologies mean absolutely nothing!

3. He sent me some chocolates by . . . . of an apology. He obviously finds it difficult to apologise face to face.

4. After I told him I didn't want to marry him, he muttered a few . . . . of apology and left the room. I felt so sorry for him I almost changed my mind!

"Don't you think at least you owe someone an apology?"

Notes

1. Note the following idiom:
   Getting an apology out of my boyfriend is like getting blood from a stone!

2. We send apologies when we can't come to a meeting. For example:
   The headmaster has sent his apologies. He's had to go to London.

3. Look at this example:
   I make no apologies for what I said to her. She deserved every word!
   You say this when you feel strongly that you were right to do or say what you did. You feel that no apology is necessary.

approval

1 Verb + approval

Use the correct form of these verbs:

give   meet with   need
seek   show   win

1. The board of directors talked over the proposal and decided to . . . . it their approval.

2. My plans for the new house are complete – now all I . . . . is approval to build it.

3. The audience . . . . their approval by calling for encore after encore, then giving them a standing ovation.

4. She desperately wants to . . . . her father's approval.

5. We'll have to . . . . approval from head office before spending any more on this project.

6. The council's plans for new traffic measures have . . . . the approval of local residents.

2 Common adjective collocations

Choose the correct adjective in the following:

1. Most guarantees on anything you buy now state that if the goods do not meet with your . . . . approval, you may return them within 30 days of purchase – as long as you still have the receipt!
(full / detailed)

2. You need . . . . approval from the local council before you can build a garage in your garden.
(official / legal)

3. Much against his wishes, the founder of the troubled company was forced to give his . . . . approval to the takeover plans.
(reluctant / grudging)

4. Last night's committee meeting gave . . . . approval to your plan for a new day centre for elderly people. There wasn't even one vote against.
(complete / unanimous)

5. The constitution of the USA requires the President to seek the . . . . approval of Congress for any kind of military action.
(previous / prior)

6. Incredibly, the proposed changes to the voting system have met with . . . . approval. There have been very few objections.
(majority / widespread)

3 Noun + of + approval

Use these nouns to complete the sentences:

nod   roar
seal   sign

1. Last week the government gave its . . . . of approval to the deal.

2. There was a . . . . of approval from the crowd when Nevin was replaced by Beckham.

3. The children longed for some . . . . of affection or approval from their mother.

4. I was pleased when I saw my teacher in the audience giving me a . . . . of approval.

4 Preposition + approval

Complete the sentences with these prepositions:

on   without
for   in

1. The architects sent the designs of the shopping centre to the planning department . . . . their approval.

2. When we suggested spending £10,000 on new computers, several people at the meeting nodded . . . . approval.

3. I'm sorry, I can't agree to anything . . . . my partner's approval.

4. These goods are supplied . . . . approval. That means you can return them if they are not satisfactory.

Go back and underline the full prepositional expressions.

Notes

1. The phrase used in 3-1 is a common thing to say in speech. For example:
   Are we going to have the meeting in London or Leeds?
   > Well, Leeds would definitely have my seal of approval.

2. Notice the large number of adjectives which mean full approval: *total, 100%, unqualified, wholehearted, overwhelming, unanimous, universal, widespread.*

3. A decision which has not been fully passed can be *subject to the approval of,* for example, the board, the council, the government etc.

area

1 Verb + area

Use the correct form of these verbs:

avoid	cover	develop	destroy
know	police	tour	

1. I'm sorry I don't know where the high school is. Ask Jane. She . . . . the local area very well.

2. Buxton is very central and it makes an ideal base for . . . . the area.

3. The National Park . . . . an area of some 2000 square kilometres.

4. Following the rise in crime, there are calls for more money to be spent on . . . . the area.

5. Heathrow does its best to make sure planes . . . . flying over residential areas at night.

6. The introduction of a good public transport system is essential for . . . . that area of South Africa.

7. Fires have . . . . huge areas of forest around Sydney for the second year running.

2 Verb phrases with prepositions

Complete the sentences with the following:

to	in (x2)	off	outside
from	into	over	

1. A lot of new people have moved . . . . . . this area recently. It's meant a big rise in house prices.

2. Wreckage from the crashed plane was scattered . . . . a wide area.

3. When an old Second World War bomb was discovered in a field, the police cordoned . . . . . . the area with tape. People couldn't go back to their houses till it was made safe.

4. I know someone who has a house in a very select area of the city, but he chooses to live . . . . . . one of the most run-down areas of town!

5. A man answering the suspect's description was seen . . . . . . the area on the night of the crime.

6. The government is desperately trying to attract industry . . . . this area.

7. Thousands of refugees are fleeing . . . . . . the war-torn area.

8. Although the murders were all in and around Manchester, we know from his Welsh accent that the murderer comes from . . . . . . the area.

3 Common adjective collocations

Use these adjectives to complete the sentences:

built-up	deprived	disaster	immediate
remote	restricted	rural	surrounding

1. The new scheme will provide special help to poor people living in . . . . areas.

2. The all-day tour takes in Naples and the . . . . area.

3. There are no leisure facilities in the . . . . area, so we have to travel across town to the nearest swimming pool.

4. The village is in a . . . . area of the island, accessible only by helicopter or boat.

5. I received a £100 fine for speeding in a . . . . area.

6. I'm sorry, I must ask you to leave. This is a . . . . area – you need a pass to enter.

7. Following the earthquake, aid is being rushed to the . . . . area.

8. Bus services in urban areas are excellent, but in . . . . areas they are not so good.

4 Special areas

Use these words to complete the sentences:

baggage reclaim	picnic	play
no-smoking	reception	special

1. There's a . . . . area at most airports where you can watch aircraft taking off and landing.

2. Visitors should wait in the . . . . area until met by an attendant.

3. All restaurants should have a . . . . area.

4. Animals are not allowed in the children's . . . . area.

5. Please remove all litter from the . . . . area when you leave.

6. We had to wait a long time in the . . . . area for our luggage to arrive.

Note

Note the following:

After the party the room was a disaster area with dirty plates and glasses lying all over the place.

---

argument

1 Verb + argument (reasons behind ideas)

Use the correct form of these verbs:

accept   follow   hear   put forward   support

1. His lecture just didn't seem to make any sense. I couldn't . . . . his argument at all. Could you?

2. I've spent the last week doing my research. Now I've got lots of facts and figures to . . . . my argument.

3. In his speech, the Chancellor . . . . a very persuasive argument for raising taxes.

4. I don't . . . . the argument that adults should always be obeyed just because they are adults!

5. Now that we have . . . . all the arguments for and against the proposal, I think we should vote on it.

2 Good and bad arguments

First underline the adjectives which collocate with *argument* in the sentences below. Then decide which adjectives describe a good argument and which describe a poor one.

1. The animal rights people have a compelling argument for banning fox hunting. I'm certainly persuaded.

2. The unemployment issue is a pretty feeble argument against asylum seekers, I'm afraid.

3. The most telling argument for wearing seat belts is the number of lives they save each year.

4. There are strong arguments for and against euthanasia.

5. I find your argument a bit woolly. I'm not really convinced by it.

3 Verb + argument (meaning disagreement)

Use the correct form of these verbs:

get into   listen to   lose   settle   start

1. Jane's very argumentative, so if she tries to . . . . an argument with you, it's best to just ignore her and walk away.

2. We . . . . a terrible argument over who was responsible for the accident and I'm afraid we're not on speaking terms any more.

3. I'm fed up arguing about money day after day. Let's . . . . this argument once and for all.
   > I agree, let's put an end to it right now.

4. Nobody likes to . . . . an argument. We all want to win. But you know the old saying – win the argument and lose a friend!

5. I think it's important to . . . . both sides of an argument before deciding what you think yourself.

4 Common adjective collocations

Complete the sentences below with the following:

endless   friendly   heated
massive   pointless

1. We had a relaxed and . . . . argument about whether people should be allowed to smoke at meetings or not. Nobody got upset.

2. A decision was finally made after quite a bit of . . . . argument had taken place. A number of people were upset by the angry words which were exchanged.

3. At work I had a . . . . argument with my boss, but it has cleared the air. There's no longer any bad feeling between us now.

4. I had an absolutely . . . . argument with my parents over money. It was stupid and served no purpose at all.

5. They have . . . . arguments. They're always at each other's throats. I'm surprised they're still talking.

If you have time, go back and underline all the important collocations in all the exercises in this unit.

Notes

1. In 3-2 you can 'get into an argument' or 'get involved in an argument'. For example:
   Sorry I'm late. I got involved in an argument with the taxi driver over politics!

2. Do you know the following idiom?
   People who always try to see both sides of an argument often end up sitting on the fence.

3. If your argument is not quite right, we say 'there's a flaw in your argument'.

4. To appear reasonable when discussing, you can say either of the following:
   I can see your argument.
   I can see where you're coming from.

attempt

1 Verb + attempt

Use the correct form of these verbs:

abandon   fail   foil   make

1. Acting on information from the French, customs officials have . . . . an attempt to smuggle a large quantity of heroin into the country.

2. Because of bad weather conditions, we were forced to . . . . our attempt to reach the summit of Mt Everest.

3. I wonder what's wrong with Andy. Last night he . . . . a few half-hearted attempts to join in our conversation, and then he left early.

4. All my attempts to start the car . . . . , so we ended up getting a taxi.

Go back and underline all the other interesting collocations in this exercise.

2 Common adjective collocations

Complete the sentences below with the following:

half-hearted   repeated
brave   unsuccessful
desperate   deliberate
final   first

1. I was pleased when I passed my driving test at the . . . . attempt.

2. The driver of the train died at the scene of the accident despite . . . . attempts by the paramedics to revive him.

3. Despite falling and injuring his leg, Jim made a . . . . attempt to finish the marathon.

4. I made a rather . . . . attempt to apologise for my behaviour, but it was obvious that I didn't really mean it.

5. I've made several . . . . attempts to speak to the manager, but he is always 'out of his office at the moment'.

6. For two weeks the army made . . . . attempts to break through enemy lines, all of which ended in failure.

7. If the weather holds, the Chinese team are going to make a . . . . attempt to reach the summit tomorrow.

8. The Foreign Secretary's speech on the Gulf War was a . . . . attempt to embarrass the government.

3 In an attempt to + verb

Match the two halves of these sentences:

1. Two factories were closed
2. Talks are taking place at this very moment
3. Politicians on both sides have called for a ceasefire
4. Anne's very upset. I'm afraid I failed
5. He has succeeded

a. in a last-ditch attempt to avert a strike.
b. in my attempt to persuade her to come to the party.
c. in a desperate attempt to cut costs.
d. in his latest attempt to break the world land speed record.
e. in an attempt to prevent further bloodshed.

Go back and underline all the expressions with *attempt* in this exercise.

"He made a very brave attempt to finish the race."

Notes

1. In 1-2 you can also say *give up*.

2. In 2-4 you can also say a *pathetic* or *feeble* attempt.

3. Note the following passive structure:
   Several attempts have been made on the President's life. (Somebody tried to kill him.)

4. Note this example:
   She made no attempt to conceal / disguise / hide her anger.

5. Note these noun + noun collocations:
   The rescue attempt was hampered by fog.
   He received psychiatric help after his botched suicide attempt.

attention

1 Verb collocations

Use the correct form of these verbs:

need   pay   get   have   hold

1. Children often misbehave in order to . . . . attention.

2. The play was disappointing. It didn't . . . . my attention for very long.

3. Can I . . . . your attention, please? I have an important announcement to make.

4. Babies . . . . a lot of care and attention.

5. As a caring society I think we need to . . . . more attention to the elderly.

First underline the verb collocations in the following. Then divide them into two groups: those meaning 'give attention to something' and those meaning 'something gets your attention'.

1. Don't pay any attention to what Lyn is saying. She doesn't know what she's talking about.

2. There's no point trying to attract the waiter's attention. He's not interested!

3. There are a number of important issues that we need to direct our attention to.

4. Something bright caught the baby's attention and she reached out and tried to touch it.

5. When I've finished studying the European market, I intend turning my attention to South East Asia.

2 Common adjective collocations

Complete the sentences below with the following:

close   immediate
insufficient   meticulous
undivided   unwelcome

1. If you just wait till I've finished writing this letter, I'll give you my full and . . . . attention.

2. Pay . . . . attention to everything I say. It's important that you follow the instructions.

3. 80 people drowned when the ferry sank. The owners had paid . . . . attention to safety.

4. Let's sit in that corner – away from everyone else. We don't want to attract . . . . attention.

5. His paintings are so realistic. He pays . . . . attention to detail.

6. Sorry, I've got to rush. I've just had a telephone call which requires my . . . . attention.

3 Verb phrases with prepositions

Complete the expression in colour with a suitable preposition:

1. The fire inspector called our attention . . . . the fact that some members of staff were not following the correct procedures.

2. If we don't bring this . . . . the attention of the police, nothing will be done.

3. The war diverted people's attention away . . . . the country's economic problems.

4. We're organising a campaign to draw people's attention . . . . the harmful effects of food additives.

5. The election is in four months. This tax cut is obviously designed to distract public attention . . . . from the government's failures.

6. Last night's documentary helped to focus world attention . . . . the plight of the Somali refugees.

"Some people think I pay too much attention to detail!"

Notes

1. In 2-5 we can also say *painstaking* attention.

2. Someone is the 'centre of attention' when everybody wants to see or talk to them.
   For example:
   He's a rock star so he's the centre of attention everywhere he goes.

3. Note the preposition in the following phrase:
   My attention wasn't on my work. My mind was elsewhere.

4. If something *escapes your attention*, you do not notice it:
   The fact that the company was operating without a licence had not escaped the attention of the authorities.

attitude

1 Verb + attitude

Use the correct form of these verbs:

change   harden   shape   understand
show   take   typify

1. I'm afraid our nephew has turned out to be a greedy, self-centred young man. His attitude ...... a complete disregard for his family and others.

2. I've always .... a fairly easy-going attitude towards bringing up my children. Children need freedom to develop and make their own mistakes.

3. John's total lack of interest in the general election .... the attitude of many young people today.

4. What do you think influences our attitudes to marriage?
   > I think our experiences in childhood .... our attitudes to marriage and family life.

5. This book examines how attitudes to sex in Britain have .... since the end of the Second World War.

6. Attitudes towards the US have .... as a result of the recent accidental bombing of civilians.

7. I don't .... your attitude. Why don't you like Ken? Everyone else thinks he's a great guy.

2 Common adjective collocations

Use these adjectives in the sentences:

aggressive   insular   negative
patronising   relaxed   right

1. A meal with Greg can be really depressing. He's got such a .... attitude to everything.

2. The teachers in this school seem to have a very .... attitude to discipline. I thought they'd be much stricter.

3. You can make a career in sales and marketing, but only if you have the .... attitude.

4. Why do football fans cause so much trouble? They've got such an .... attitude to everything.

5. Many US newspapers contain very little international news. This is just one sign of the .... attitudes of Americans.

6. He obviously thinks he's so much better than me, but his .... attitude is beginning to irritate me immensely.

Go back and underline the adjective collocations.

3 Hyphenated adjectives

Use these two- and three-part adjectives:

slap-dash   happy-go-lucky   laid-back
holier-than-thou   devil-may-care

1. My boss is so relaxed, but so efficient. I've never seen her get worried by anything. She's got such a .... attitude towards work.

2. He's the most exciting tennis player of the decade. His .... attitude means he takes the kind of risks nobody else would.

3. Our son's a bit too .... in his attitude to schoolwork. He usually does it while he watches television. It's no surprise that his examination results are so poor.

4. My mother-in-law is always disapproving and saying that she would never do this or that. She thinks she's so morally superior. I can't stand people with such .... attitudes.

5. My brother just accepts whatever happens to him and says he never thinks about the future. He's got such a .... attitude to everything.

Notes

1. Note that *attitude* is followed by *to* or *towards*:
   I find his attitude towards women hard to take.
   I find his whole attitude to his work unacceptable.

2. Note these noun phrases with 'attitude':
   There's been a noticeable change in attitude towards head office in recent months.
   Some people believe that how old you feel is just an attitude of mind.

3. A *complacent attitude* is when you stop trying to improve or change things:
   Lack of competition led to a complacent attitude in both management and the workforce.

4. *Entrenched attitudes* are ones that people have had for a long time and are unlikely to change:
   It will be difficult to change the deeply entrenched attitudes of some of the older union members.

5. *Gung-ho attitudes* are usually over-enthusiastic and politically inappropriate:
   The Prime Minister's gung-ho attitude was not appropriate for such delicate negotiations.

ban

1 Verb + ban

Use the correct form of these verbs:

announce	*defy*	*impose*
introduce	*lift*	*support*

1. The Football Association .... a three-match ban on the player for unprofessional behaviour.

2. Thousands of students .... the ban on political meetings. They held a mass demonstration in the main square demanding freedom of speech and free elections.

3. After the failure of the pay negotiations, the union .... a ban on overtime.

4. The government will .... the ban on fishing for scallops when scientists assure them that the shellfish are safe to eat.

5. Do you remember which airline was the first to .... a smoking ban on all its flights?

6. All delegates except the Japanese .... the worldwide ban on whaling.

2 A complete ban on something

Complete the sentences below with these ideas:

land mines	*tobacco advertising*
the trade in ivory	*sale of handguns*
using e-mail	*human cloning*

1. From Monday there is to be a total ban on .... for personal purposes in office time. Anyone caught booking flights, for example, will be dismissed on the spot.

2. Thousands of children lost limbs in the aftermath of the war. All political parties are calling for a ban on the production and use of ....

3. In the aftermath of Dunblane and the American high school shootings, there were calls for a complete ban on the ....

4. In order to discourage young people from smoking, many western governments have imposed a blanket ban on ....

5. Many famous biologists believe that there should be an outright ban on ....

6. The African elephant is only surviving today because of the worldwide ban on ....

Go back and underline all the expressions meaning *a complete ban*.

3 Put + a ban on

Notice the difference between these sentences:

a. They've banned the advertising of alcohol.
b. They've put a ban on the advertising of alcohol.

Change the following sentences so that they follow the pattern of sentence b:

1. They've banned the sale of alcohol at the match.
....

2. They've banned the importing of UK lamb.
....

3. They've banned all flights into North Korea.
....

4. They've banned the sale of pornography.
....

"The ban is total, complete, 100%! Which word don't you understand?"

Notes

1. In 1-2 'ignored' is also possible.

2. Note the use of 'banned' as an adjective:
   His gold medal was taken away from him when his tests proved that he had been using a banned substance.
   He was arrested for belonging to a banned political party.

3. A 'test ban treaty' is an agreement between countries to stop testing nuclear weapons.

4. Here is a common use of 'ban' as a verb:
   He was banned from driving for three years.

behaviour

1 Verb + behaviour

Use the correct form of these verbs:

affect   change   criticise   explain
tolerate   improve   apologise for

1. Go and report to the head teacher immediately. I'm not standing for this sort of behaviour in my classroom any longer. I simply will not . . . . your appalling behaviour.

2. An insecure family environment can only . . . . a child's behaviour in a negative way.

3. I don't know why you're . . . . my behaviour! You're not exactly perfect yourself.

4. How do you . . . . her behaviour at the party last night? She was rude to almost everybody she talked to, which isn't like her. I'm certainly baffled by her behaviour.

5. The President has . . . . his behaviour, but many people are unwilling to accept that and feel that he should resign.

6. Terry can be a real nuisance in class, but I must say his behaviour has . . . . a lot recently.

7. You can . . . . your behaviour, but you can't . . . . your personality!

2 Common adjective collocations

Use the following adjectives in these sentences:

eccentric   disgraceful   good
anti-social   obsessive   violent

1. The crowd booed when the national anthem was played at the beginning of the football match.
   > I find that sort of behaviour . . . .
   It's completely unacceptable.

2. My mother's problem is she washes her hands over and over again. As you can imagine, this kind of . . . . behaviour can be difficult to live with.

3. The latest studies seem to show that computer games encourage . . . . and aggressive behaviour in young children.

4. Our chemistry teacher is everyone's idea of the mad scientist. His behaviour is somewhat . . . . It's hard to predict what he'll do next.

5. It is important that teachers reward . . . . behaviour.

6. There's no question that playing loud music after midnight in a flat is . . . . behaviour.

3 Noun + preposition + behaviour

Complete the sentences below with these nouns:

model   bounds   standards
excuse   improvement   explanation

1. Our school demands the highest . . . . of behaviour from its students.

2. I don't understand why Maria just got up and walked out. Did she offer any . . . . for her strange behaviour?

3. Nobody should behave like that in public. There's no . . . . for that kind of behaviour.

4. Leaving her to walk home alone so late at night was outside the . . . . of acceptable behaviour. I think you should apologise to her.

5. Since our daughter started her treatment, there's been a definite . . . . in her behaviour. She's much less aggressive at school.

6. The boy next door is always in trouble with the police. However, when he was at school, he was a . . . . of good behaviour.

Go back and underline the complete expressions including the prepositions.

Notes

1. Note the following ways of expressing your disapproval of someone's behaviour:
   There's really no need for that sort of behaviour.
   This kind of behaviour just won't do.
   Your behaviour leaves a lot to be desired.
   His behaviour at the meeting was inappropriate.

2. Good behaviour can be *excellent* or *exemplary*. Bad behaviour can be *unacceptable, strange, violent* and *undesirable*.

3. Note the expression 'be on your best behaviour':
   Now, you're meeting my parents tomorrow. Please be on your best behaviour!

4. Note these types of behaviour:
   We need to understand the causes of criminal behaviour.
   We've learned a lot from animal behaviour.

5. Behaviour is often followed by *to* or *towards*:
   I can understand Geoff's behaviour towards Steve.
   Steve never paid back the money he borrowed.

belief

1 Verb + belief

Use the correct form of these verbs:

cling to	hold
shake	share
strengthen	stand up for

1. My boss . . . . strong political beliefs and expresses them on every possible occasion!

2. Although I don't . . . . your beliefs, I do respect them. I think this is important in a democratic society.

3. We should all have the courage to . . . . our beliefs.

4. He was only fined £100 for killing somebody in a road accident! This case has . . . . my belief in our justice system.

5. My mother's long battle against stomach cancer has only . . . . her belief in God.

6. A week after her husband disappeared in a boating accident, she's still . . . . the belief that he's alive. She refuses to accept that he might have drowned.

2 Common adjective collocations

Use these adjectives to complete the sentences:

firm	genuine
growing	mistaken
popular	unshakeable

1. For years at school I was under the . . . . belief that Anne was Chris's mother. It was only years later I found out she was his step-sister!

2. Contrary to . . . . belief, eating carrots does not improve your eyesight.

3. My brother has an . . . . belief in his own abilities. I've never known anybody with such self-belief and self-confidence.

4. It is my . . . . belief that abortion is immoral. Nobody will ever convince me that we have the right to end life in that way.

5. Fighting has again broken out along the border. There is now a . . . . belief among politicians that war is inevitable.

6. If you want to be a successful salesman, you have to have a . . . . belief in the product you are selling. It's no good just pretending to like something.

3 Expressions with prepositions

Complete the sentences below with on, to or of:

1. Throughout her persecution, Joan of Arc remained faithful . . . . . . her beliefs. She refused to give them up.

2. The fact that millions of people are dying of famine has shaken the foundations . . . . . . my belief in God.

3. Sarah's parents hadn't realised the depth . . . . . . her religious beliefs until she told them she had decided to become a nun.

4. I've never really trusted that woman. I've always had doubts about the sincerity . . . . . . her beliefs.

5. Capitalism is partly based . . . . . . the belief that people work more productively if they are working for themselves.

6. Every religion has its own set . . . . . . beliefs.

"Contrary to popular belief, eating carrots does not improve your eyesight!"

Notes

1. Note the following expressions:
   She may have made the situation worse, but she acted in the belief that she was doing the right thing.
   That's impossible to believe! It's beyond belief!
   It's my belief that a vaccine for AIDS will be found.

2. If you really find something impossible to explain or understand you can say that it 'beggars belief'.
   It beggars belief how one man could have destroyed a bank.

3. Note that we talk of *having* political and religious beliefs.

benefit

1 Verb + benefit

Use the correct form of these verbs:

bring	*derive*
feel	*reap*
include	*outline*
outweigh	

1. Tourism has . . . . many benefits to the area.

2. I want to say that I'm against the building of this new centre. I think the risks of the scheme far . . . . any potential benefits.

3. Book your holiday with us. The benefits . . . . full medical cover while you're abroad.

4. Too many children from poor social backgrounds don't . . . . much benefit from school.
   > No, I know what you mean. I didn't get much benefit from my days at school either.

5. The doctor said that I would start to . . . . the benefits of the new treatment in a few months' time.

6. There's an article in this morning's paper . . . . the benefits of eating fresh fruit and vegetables every day.

7. Joanne is now a millionaire. She's finally . . . . the benefits of all those years of writing.

2 Benefit + of + noun

Complete the sentences with these nouns:

education	*exercise*	*hard work*
helmet	*scheme*	*organic food*

1. He's just beginning to see the benefits of all his . . . . and dedication.

2. Most cyclists are fully aware of the safety benefits of wearing a . . . .

3. Getting a good job was easy as I had the benefit of a university . . . .

4. The report of the town planners emphasised the likely benefits of the new traffic . . . ., but said little about the costs.

5. My two unmarried aunts have been keen swimmers ever since they read about the benefits of regular . . . .

6. I'm a great believer in the benefits of . . . . Most of the things we eat today are full of preservatives and chemicals.

Go back and underline the full expressions.

3 Benefit (payment)

Complete the sentences below with the following:

welfare	*housing*	*unemployment*
fringe	*child*	*means-tested*

1. In the UK all families with children under 18 years of age are entitled to . . . . benefit.

2. Our neighbour lost his job ten years ago and he's been claiming . . . . benefit ever since.

3. A company car and first-class air travel are the main . . . . benefits I get in my job.

4. Everyone used to get child benefit – irrespective of income. Now we're changing to a system of . . . . benefits. Some people think it's fairer.

5. I'm afraid you'll have to pay the full rent for the flat. You're not eligible for . . . . benefit.

6. All employees have to pay into a fund for . . . . benefits such as unemployment and sickness pay.

Notes

1. Note how we describe a lot of benefit:
   You need to take these pills for three or more weeks to get the full benefit.
   The new reward scheme will be of great benefit to our customers.
   We want you to get maximum benefit from your course.
   These new laws will have far-reaching benefits for single-parent families.
   The benefit to the local economy will be incalculable.

2. If you 'give somebody the benefit of the doubt', it means you accept what they say even though you think they may be wrong or lying.

3. Notice these ways of speaking enthusiastically about benefits:
   His book extols the benefits of vegetarianism.
   He's always waxing lyrical about the benefits of bathing in icy cold water – even in winter!

4. Notice the prepositions in these expressions:
   Look, this plan will make us thousands! You can't say no. It's to our mutual benefit.
   She repeated the instructions again for my benefit.
   (just for me)

cause

1 Verb + cause

Underline the verbs which mean 'find':

1. The cause of the fire may never be discovered.
2. The police never actually determined the cause of death.
3. Investigators have been called in to establish the cause of the plane crash.
4. Engineers are trying to isolate the cause of the problem.

2 Common adjective collocations

Complete the sentences below with the following:

common	exact	likely
real	main	underlying

1. Although they can't be certain, the investigators think that the most .... cause of the crash was that the driver of the train had a heart attack.
2. The most .... cause of air accidents is pilot error – not mechanical failure.
3. Although the link is not clear, many politicians believe that unemployment is the .... cause of a lot of urban crime.
4. We don't know why my aunt died. The post mortem will determine the .... cause.
5. Speeding is the .... cause of road accidents.
6. We all know what the inquiry said, but do you think that was the .... cause of John's death?

3 Cause + for

Use these words in the sentences below:

alarm	celebration	complaint
concern	optimism	

1. My grandmother's failing health is giving us cause for .... She might have to go into hospital.
2. We have run into some severe turbulence, but there is no cause for .... Please fasten your seatbelts and remain seated till the 'fasten seatbelts' sign has been switched off.
3. I have no cause for .... The flights, the hotel, the food have all been excellent.
4. Following the breakdown of talks, the present political climate gives little cause for ....
5. Arsenal's victory in the competition was cause for .... and the fans partied till about 3am.

4 Common expressions

Match the two halves to make common expressions with *cause*:

1. What do you think is
2. It's all a matter of
3. I've never had any
4. She's never had a day off
5. We don't yet know

a. without good cause.
b. cause to complain.
c. the cause of death.
e. the cause of the pain?
d. cause and effect.

5 Cause (something people believe in)

A common meaning of *cause* is 'reason', but it can also mean something important that people believe in. For example:

A lot of people leave money in their will to good causes such as the NSPCC (the National Society for the prevention of cruelty to children).

Use a suitable preposition in these sentences:

1. Most people want independence and many young men are willing to fight ...... the cause.
2. These violent demonstrations will do little to further the cause ...... animal rights.
3. Anti-smoking campaigners hope the public will be sympathetic ...... their cause.
4. I don't mind giving money if it is ..... a good cause.

Notes

1. Note the following:
   I've tried everything to get my money back from the company. I'm beginning to think it's a lost cause.

2. In 2-3 you can also say 'root cause' – the basic, underlying cause.

3. In 5-4 *deserving* is also possible.
   Both in a good cause and for a good cause are equally correct.

4. We use the French phrase – a cause célèbre – to talk about a very controversial issue.

5. If you die 'of natural causes', you die of old age – not illness or accident.

6. Notice in exercise 4 you say 'without good cause' and not 'without a good cause'.

7. You can 'champion' a cause. For example:
   Germaine Greer has championed the cause of feminism.

challenge

1 Verb + challenge

Use the correct form of these verbs:

accept   *face*   *issue*
meet   *pose*   *provide*

1. Persuading staff to accept new patterns of work is a challenge . . . . by many companies that want to develop.

2. Have you heard the news? Lewis has just . . . . Tyson's challenge to fight for the world title.

3. The trouble with my current job is that it doesn't . . . . me with enough of a challenge.

4. We need to modernise this business in order to . . . . the challenges of the next decade.

5. In the near future Frankfurt could . . . . a real challenge to London as the financial centre of Europe.

6. The Conservative candidate . . . . a challenge to the rest of the candidates to take part in a public debate. I think they were wise to say no.

2 Common adjective collocations

Complete the sentences with these adjectives:

biggest   *direct*
legal   *enormous*
physical   *real*
new   *unsuccessful*

1. The Scottish football league is a two-horse race. Celtic is the only team that can offer a . . . . challenge to Rangers, the current champions.

2. Climbing is both a . . . . and a mental challenge.

3. I gave up my job as a doctor after twenty years and became a teacher. I felt I wanted a . . . . challenge.

4. One of the . . . . challenges we face today is how to feed the world's growing population.

5. After his . . . . challenge for the leadership of the party, the Minister announced his retirement from politics.

6. The firemen's strike was seen as a . . . . challenge to the authority of the government.

7. After discussions with a lawyer, we have decided to mount a . . . . challenge to the decision to close down the school.

8. Raising the money to build this new hospital has been an . . . . challenge.

3 Big challenges

Match the halves of these sentences:

1. The British athlete, Mark Wilson, put up a strong challenge
2. The strike by transport workers represents a serious challenge
3. Leyton Hewitt is expected to make a major challenge
4. Designing a computer to beat the world chess champion
5. The court will face a tough challenge
6. Real Madrid face a stiff challenge

a. in the next round of the competition.
b. conducting a fair trial in such an emotional case.
c. posed a formidable challenge.
d. in the early part of the race but gradually fell away.
e. to the government's pay policy.
f. for the men's title at Wimbledon this year.

Go back and underline all the expressions which mean *big challenge*.

"A physical and mental challenge!"

Notes

1. In 1-2 'taken up' is also possible. In 1-4 'rise to' is also possible. In 1-5 'represent' is also possible.

2. Note these ways of saying you like a challenge:
   The new manager says he relishes the challenge of rebuilding the club and winning titles again.
   I like the challenge of learning new languages.
   He always chooses the most difficult hills to climb because he loves a challenge.

3. If you 'throw down' a challenge you invite somebody to take part in a game, a fight, or a competition.
   They threw down the challenge that he couldn't eat fifty doughnuts in five minutes.

---

chance

1 Verb + chance (opportunity)

Use the correct form of these verbs:

give   have   improve   take
miss   jump at   need   wait for

1. I can do much better. Please . . . . me one more chance and I'll show you what I can really do.

2. I can't believe how rude Pete was. He snatched the newspaper out of my hand before I . . . . a chance to read it.

3. Don't . . . . this chance to buy three of your favourite videos for the price of one.

4. You should . . . . the chance to travel abroad while you're still young.

5. I had no hesitation in accepting the job in the New York office. It was the chance I had been . . . .

6. I feel that learning English will . . . . my chances of working abroad.

7. It's an important matter so I . . . . a chance to think it over before I make a decision.

8. Do you think I should take the job in Milan?
   > Well, if it was me, I'd . . . . the chance!

2 Common adjective collocations

Complete the sentences with these adjectives:

better   equal   last   second   rare

1. If you don't finish this task within the time limit, you will be eliminated from the contest. Nobody gets a . . . . chance.

2. Many parents today make sacrifices to send their children to good schools and to university. They want their children to have a . . . . chance in life than they had themselves.

3. This weekend, visitors will get a . . . . chance to see inside the rooms of the Royal Palace. This is only the second time the King has allowed the public into his private apartments.

4. Handicaps in sports such as golf give people with different abilities an . . . . chance of winning competitions.

5. This is my . . . . chance to pass the entrance examination. It's my third attempt and I won't be allowed another chance.

3 Verb + chance (possibility)

Use the correct form of these verbs:

fancy   increase   rate   ruin   stand

1. Smoking when you are pregnant may . . . . the chances of damage to your baby.

2. One careless mistake at work . . . . my chances of promotion.

3. At this rate we don't . . . . a chance of getting to the airport on time.

4. I don't . . . . our chances of beating them. They are a very strong team. They haven't lost a home game for two years!

5. How do you . . . . your chances of getting the job?

4 Common adjective collocations

Write the expressions from the sentence with the following meanings:

a. no chance at all   . . . .
b. no chance, but maybe!   . . . .
c. a very very small chance . . . .
d. a good chance   . . . .
e. a very good chance   . . . .

1. We only have an outside chance of making the airport on time. The plane leaves in twenty minutes!

2. Nowadays we have the expertise to ensure that premature babies have an excellent chance of survival.

3. It's only a thunderstorm! The chances of being struck by lightning are a million to one.

4. Fat chance of him coming to give us a hand. He won't lift a hand to help anybody but himself.

5. The team has a fair chance of success this year.

Notes

1. Note the following:
   Is there any chance of a lift to the airport?
   Is there any chance of borrowing the car, Dad?

2. Chance can also mean 'risk':
   If I were you, I'd take a chance and ring her.
   It can also mean 'luck':
   It was pure chance we were on the same plane.

change

1 Verb + change

Use the correct form of these verbs:

accept   *bring about*   *make*
resist   *plan*   *undergo*

1. I've . . . . a few minor changes to your speech. I hope you think I've improved it!

2. A lot of people find it hard to . . . . change.
   >Yes, it's surprising how many of us tend to . . . . any kind of change to the way we live.

3. The government's latest advertising campaign is an attempt to . . . . a change in the way we think about the environment.

4. Medicine has . . . . huge changes in the past 50 years due to the discovery of DNA.

5. The government are . . . . some fairly major changes to the education system over the next couple of years.

2 Common adjective collocations

Complete the sentences below with the following:

last-minute   *minor*   *noticeable*
proposed   *sweeping*   *welcome*

1. Yes, let's eat out tonight. It'll be a . . . . change from cooking!

2. My father's condition still remains critical. There's been no . . . . change in his condition for several days now.

3. I don't mind it if you change things if you give us plenty of notice, but I really object to these . . . . changes.

4. Have you seen the revised plans? The . . . . changes to the building will cost us millions!

5. The problems of the health service won't be solved by making . . . . changes.
   It needs . . . . changes throughout the whole system.

3 Expressions with prepositions

Use a suitable preposition in these sentences:

1. Life is so hectic these days. It's so difficult to keep up with the rapid pace . . . . . . change.

2. It's clear that the present system is no longer working and there is a definite need . . . . . . change.

3. Television is one of the main instruments . . . . . . political change in the world today.

4. It's not true that elderly people are always resistant . . . . change.

5. Public opinion is shifting in favour . . . . . . change.

6. There could never be a better time to act than now. The organisation is ripe . . . . . . change.

4 Change + preposition + noun

Now complete these sentences with a noun:

address   *attitude*   *the law*
plan   *venue*   *weather*

1. There's been a change of . . . . We're leaving on Monday instead of Tuesday.

2. If buses are to replace cars, there'll need to be a complete change in our . . . . to public transport.

3. I've notified the post office of our change of . . . . – so we should get our mail all right.

4. The hall has been double-booked, so please note the change of . . . . for the party.

5. A lot of us were caught out by the sudden change in the . . . . I wish I'd taken an umbrella!

6. The proposed change in . . . . would make abortion illegal again.

"No, I wouldn't say there's been any noticeable change in his condition."

Notes

1. Note the common expression:
   Let's go out tonight – for a change.

2. Note that we use *great, major, sweeping* and *drastic* to talk about big changes.

3. If you have a 'change of heart', it means you change your attitude to something.
   I've had a change of heart. I'm not resigning!

4. If you go away for the night, you need a 'change of clothes'.

choice

1 Verb + choice

Use the correct form of these verbs:

leave	*give*
have	*influence*
make	*restrict*

1. I'm not up here in Alaska because I want to be! Head office never . . . . me a choice!
2. Young people don't realise that the choices they . . . . at school and university can affect them for the rest of their lives.
3. We used to live in London, so we could fly anywhere really easily. Living up here in the north does . . . . your choice of where you can go, but we prefer the quieter life.
4. I wouldn't drive without a seat belt, but I still think people should . . . . the choice.
5. The council denied that financial considerations had . . . . their choice of consultant.
6. I'm afraid you've . . . . us no choice. You've taken so many days off for no reason, we've got no alternative but to ask you to leave.

Go back and underline the verb collocations.

2 Common adjective collocations

Use these adjectives in the sentences:

difficult	*first*
free	*obvious*
deliberate	*straight*

1. Blue wasn't my . . . . choice. I would have preferred red, but they were sold out.
2. Look, there's nothing more to discuss. It's a . . . . choice – either you stop drinking, or you die of liver failure in a month – maybe two!
3. Jean Moore is the only one with the necessary work experience, so she's the . . . . choice.
4. Luke is only 12. Gill and David are getting divorced, so the poor boy has to decide which one he wants to live with. What a . . . . choice for any child to make!
5. First-year students make up their own programmes. They have a completely . . . . choice within a group of subjects.
6. I'm a single mother. It was a . . . . choice to bring up my children on my own.

3 Choice + of + noun

Match the halves of the following:

1. I think you've made the right choice of career.
2. Mrs Burgess obviously doesn't like
3. The main course comes
4. New York is a city of culture.
5. She made an unfortunate choice of words in her speech

a. It has a huge choice of cinemas and theatres.
b. with a choice of vegetables or salad.
c. You'll make a wonderful teacher.
d. her son's choice of friends.
e. and upset a lot of people in the room.

Go back and underline all the expressions with *choice*.

"Choice? They didn't give me a choice either!"

Notes

1. Note the following useful expressions with prepositions:
   I'm afraid it's not my kind of party. I wouldn't have come here by choice.
   There were so many different things to eat. We were spoilt for choice.
   Some children in this area are not able to go to the school of their choice.

2. Note the following useful phrases:
   I had no choice what to study at university. My parents had already decided for me.
   The choice of career lies with you. It's your decision and your decision only.

3. Note the common phrase 'freedom of choice':
   Satellite TV offers viewers greater freedom of choice.

circumstances

1 Verb collocations

Use the correct form of these verbs:

adapt to	*change*	*depend on*
die in	*investigate*	*know*

1. The police are . . . . the circumstances surrounding the disappearance of a substantial amount of money from the company accounts.

2. If you saw somebody drowning, would you try to save them?
   > It would . . . . the circumstances. If the sea was really rough, then no, but if it was in a lake, then I probably would.

3. If we . . . . more of the circumstances around the child's death, the police would have a much better idea of where to start.

4. In the world of medicine everything develops so quickly that you need to be able to . . . . new and continually changing circumstances.

5. I am sorry to say that at present you are not entitled to any benefit. Please contact this department if your circumstances . . . .

6. The little girl . . . . very tragic circumstances when she ran out into the road.

2 Common adjective collocations

Complete the sentences with these adjectives:

exceptional	*exact*	*happier*
present	*suspicious*	*unforeseen*

1. All essays must be handed in by the 12th of April. This deadline will only be extended in . . . . circumstances.

2. Police said that there were no . . . . circumstances surrounding the woman's death. They think she died of natural causes.

3. She's unlikely to accept the job – given her . . . . circumstances. She has a young family and an ageing parent to look after.

4. The concert had to be cancelled due to . . . . circumstances. The main singer became ill and had to be taken to hospital.

5. The press are anxious to know how the pop star died. The police have yet to reveal the . . . . circumstances of his death.

6. I wish we'd met again in . . . . circumstances. Why do we only meet at funerals!

3 Common expressions

Use the following words to complete the following sentences:

any	*certain*	*no*

1. I think abortion is justifiable in . . . . . . circumstances. For example, if the mother might die, then I think it is right to go ahead.

2. Under . . . . . . circumstances must you leave the children on their own.

3. It's never right to take a life, so we oppose capital punishment in . . . . . . circumstances.

We often use 'in / under / considering the circumstances' to say that we understand and accept why or how somebody did something. Match the halves in the following:

4. Under the circumstances, my parents coped very well when I told them I was leaving my wife.

5. Considering the circumstances of the company at the time of the fire,

6. After the bride didn't turn up,

7. In the circumstances, nobody could complain that the picnic was cancelled.

8. Considering the circumstances of the takeover,

a. it just rained and rained all day long.

b. cancelling the wedding was the only thing to do in the circumstances.

c. It's no wonder people were suspicious.

d. the union's refusal to co-operate with the new management was perfectly understandable.

e. I thought they would have been very upset.

Now go back and underline all the expressions with *circumstances* in this exercise.

Notes

1. In 3-2 'under no circumstances' or 'not under any circumstances' is a common expression meaning 'never'.

2. Note the following:
   The fees charged for the course will vary according to individual circumstances.
   They have been forced by circumstances to sell their house.

3. A common excuse for delayed flights or trains is 'circumstances beyond our control'.

comment

1 Verb + comment

Use the correct form of these verbs:

appreciate	apologise for	have
invite	made	pass

1. Do you . . . . any comment on the situation, Mr President?

2. I entirely agree with the comments you . . . . about the state of the underground system.

3. The council has . . . . comments from residents about the plans for the new shopping centre.

4. The interviewer made some rather rude remarks to the Prime Minister's wife. He later publicly . . . . his comments.

5. I would . . . . any comments you might have on my work. All comments and suggestions will be gratefully received.

6. No one in the office has dared . . . . comment on my new hair colour. I think they're all afraid to upset me!

2 Common adjective collocations

Complete the sentences below with the following:

nasty	fair	further	helpful
last	sad	passing	sarcastic

1. OK, you're right. That's . . . . comment. I could have played better. I just wasn't on top form.

2. Everything my client has to say on this matter is contained in the press release. She has no . . . . comment to make at this stage.

3. Your husband passed some very . . . . comments about my wife's appearance at the party. I hope he will apologise.

4. I think Pete's ideas are important and they deserve more than a . . . . comment.

5. My boss isn't nasty or unpleasant, but he has a habit of making slightly . . . . comments about my accent. Why does he do this, I wonder?

6. My tutor made some very . . . . comments on my essay – they were apt and to the point.

7. Ignore my . . . . comment. I wasn't thinking properly!

8. Last night's programme about homeless people in our cities was a . . . . comment on the current state of our society.

"No one dares comment on her new hair-do!"

Notes

1. You can also use 'welcome' in 1-5.

2. In 1-6 notice that you can 'pass comment', but in 1-2 you 'make a comment'.

3. In 2-3 you can also say 'derogatory comments'.

4. In 2-8 'comment' is used to mean a bad picture of something. You can also use 'telling':
   It's a telling comment on our society that some children still don't get enough to eat.

5. Note these *comment + verb* collocations:
   Her comments provoked an uncharacteristic outburst of anger from the Prime Minister.
   The manager's comments do not represent the views of many of us. I, for one, disagree strongly.

6. Note the following prepositional phrases:
   The minister at the centre of the scandal was unavailable for comment last night.
   I was surprised when she accepted his decision without comment.

7. Note how we tell people that we do not wish to talk about something:
   When asked if he was about to resign, the chairman replied 'No comment'.

8. Note the verbs we use to describe our reactions to comments:
   Her comments offended me deeply.
   I was secretly pleased by his comments.

complaint

1 Verb + complaint

Use the correct form of these verbs:

have   investigate   make
receive   refer   uphold

1. I'm not happy with the service and, to be honest, the food was not very warm. I'm not going to . . . . an official complaint, but I think you should know that we were not happy.

2. I'm afraid I . . . . a complaint. Can I speak to the person in charge, please?

3. A senior police officer has been suspended from duty while complaints against him are being . . . .

4. The court refused to . . . . the complaint against the newspaper. The footballer, John Inset, had claimed that the story run by the paper had seriously damaged his reputation.

5. Due to the seriousness of your complaint, it will have to be . . . . to the board.

6. The cinema has . . . . complaints from customers about the lack of parking facilities.

2 Common adjective collocations

Complete the sentences below with the following:

common   constant   justified   preposterous
official   isolated   serious   single

1. This is the fourth time this week! Your . . . . complaints are beginning to annoy me.

2. The most . . . . complaint tourists have about London is the high price of everything.

3. If you are not happy with the treatment you've received, you should lodge an . . . . complaint.

4. I think our complaints are totally . . . . We didn't receive the quality of service we paid for.

5. The new timetable has been successful. We've only received one or two . . . . complaints.

6. I'm very happy with the new members of staff. I haven't heard a . . . . complaint about them.

7. Inspectors visited the school after receiving a string of . . . . complaints from parents about poor standards of teaching.

8. I've never heard such a . . . . complaint in my life! Tony is the most competent person I've ever met.

3 Noun + preposition + complaint

Complete the sentences below with a suitable preposition:

1. If you are unhappy with the work done on your house, get a lawyer to draft a letter . . . . . . complaint.

2. If you feel you have any cause . . . . . . complaint, please contact the manager.

3. This year there has been a record number . . . . . . complaints about the standard of service on Britain's railways. In fact, rail offices around the country have been flooded . . . . . . complaints.

4. If you have good grounds . . . . . . complaint, then it is company policy to offer you compensation.

5. The council has received a constant stream . . . . . . complaints about the noise coming from the Voodoo nightclub in Surrey Street.

6. Having to wait over 24 hours at the airport comes high on my list . . . . . . complaints about our holiday.

Go back and underline the complete expressions using a noun + preposition + *complaint*.

Notes

1. Note the following:
   I really had no cause for complaint. I was treated very well.

2. Note the following verbs used to describe making a complaint:
   She has brought a complaint against her manager for unfair dismissal.
   They have filed a complaint with the local authority about the lack of leisure facilities in the area.
   You can also 'lodge' a formal complaint.

3. Complaints are 'dealt with':
   I'm sorry we are unable to deal with your complaint immediately, but we'll get back to you next week.

4. Notice the expression:
   The manager was dismissed after complaints about the quality of his work.

5. Notice the way to refer to lots of complaints:
   a stream of complaints
   a string of complaints

---

concern

1 Concern (a worry about something)

Use the correct form of these verbs:

appreciate	*express*
cause	*grow*
override	*share*

1. Many doctors have . . . . deep concern about the safety of this new drug.
2. The build-up of enemy troops on the country's southern border is . . . . great concern.
3. I . . . . your concern, but don't worry – I'm all right. I know what I'm doing.
4. Public concern is . . . . over the number of children who leave school without any kind of formal qualification.
5. The headmaster and the staff . . . . your concern about what happened on the trip to the zoo. We must make sure something like this never happens again.
6. Our concern for the safety of the children must . . . . all other concerns.

"His only concern was that he couldn't get into his new Gucci trainers!"

2 Focus on prepositions

Complete the sentences with these prepositions:

over	*for*	*of*	*with*

1. We view the situation developing in the Middle East . . . . . . grave concern.
2. The little girl hasn't been seen for two days and there is now growing concern . . . . . . her safety.
3. The availability of drugs in schools is . . . . . . great concern to parents.
4. There is widespread concern . . . . . . rising crime rates in our cities.

3 Concern (an important thing)

Match the halves below:

1. As CEO my major concern is
2. As aid workers, our overriding concern is
3. The Chancellor's primary concern is
4. This hospital's main concern is

a. to improve the quality of care to our patients.
b. to reduce inflation and improve the economy.
c. to make this company more efficient.
d. to care for the hungry and the homeless.

Now underline the adjectives which mean 'most important'.

Notes

1. In 1-1 you can also use *raise* or *voice*. Other verbs used with *concern* are *brush aside* and *reject*:
   The airline brushed aside concerns about the safety of its ageing fleet of planes.

2. Notice these expressions:
   My private life is no concern of yours.
   Your private life is of no concern to me.
   I'd keep out of this argument if I were you. It's a family matter and it's none of your concern.

3. Note the following:
   I was surprised and angered by his lack of concern for his sick mother.
   You've been given the all-clear. The test results were negative, so there's no cause for concern.
   In his speech, he said that global pollution should be a matter of concern to us all.

4. Note how we express doubt about something:
   My only concern about Beckham is whether he'll be fit to play on Saturday.

5. If we want to talk about our main concern, we can use *sole* or *only*:
   The safety of the hostages is our sole concern.
   Our only concern is for the safety of the hostages.

condition

1 Adjective + condition (state)

Complete the sentences with these adjectives:

> excellent   original
>
> present   showroom
>
> poor   reasonable

1. In my spare time I buy old motorcycles and restore them to their .... condition.
2. You can't use that bike in its .... condition. The brakes need fixing and the back tyre is punctured.
3. Although the lift has been operating non-stop for twenty years, it's still in .... working condition. It's serviced regularly.
4. Nothing's been spent on the house for years. It's really in very .... condition.
5. Although my car is 25 years old, it's still in .... condition. It really does look brand new.
6. I'd buy that car. I know it's 8 years old and it's got some rust, but it's in .... condition for its age. I mean, what else can you get for £1,000 these days?

2 Verb + condition (state of health)

Use the correct form of these verbs:

> aggravate   suffer from
>
> deteriorate   improve
>
> require   treat

1. I'm pleased to say that your mother's condition is ...., but we'll be keeping a close eye on her for a few days just to be on the safe side.
2. My brother .... a rare heart condition. He could drop dead at any moment.
3. This man's condition is critical and .... urgent treatment. If we can't get him to a hospital quickly, he won't survive.
4. Nowadays steroids are used to .... some types of skin condition.
5. I was given tablets to help clear up the rash on my arms, but they only .... the condition. The rash became redder and more itchy and now it's spread to my face and neck.
6. Our neighbour was rushed to hospital last week after her condition suddenly .... She was doing so well, then she just collapsed.

3 Adjective + conditions (circumstances)

Complete the sentences below with the following:

> adverse weather   difficult
>
> ideal   living
>
> cramped   driving

1. The work on the bridge was completed under very .... conditions. At one stage we almost gave up completely.
2. Doctors and nurses are having to work in seriously overcrowded and .... conditions. This town badly needs a new hospital.
3. The match has been cancelled due to .... conditions. Heavy rain has flooded the pitch, making it unplayable.
4. We took the car to Norway, but the .... conditions on the way back were dreadful. We didn't have winter tyres on the car, so we just had to take it slowly.
5. Living or studying in an English-speaking country provides the .... conditions for learning the language.
6. .... conditions in the old folks' home were atrocious. Inspectors said they were the worst they had ever seen.

Notes

1. In 1-5 the expression 'showroom condition' means *perfect condition*. Here is another expression which means that something has never been used:
   These stamps will fetch hundreds of pounds. They're in mint condition.

2. Note the following adjectives to say that living conditions are very bad:
   The prisoners were kept under the most appalling conditions. They had no toilets or running water.
   How can anyone live in such dreadful conditions?

3. Note the following uses:
   You are in no condition to go to work, so just stay in bed and rest.
   I'm not fit. I really am out of condition.

4. Note this common expression:
   We went on strike for better pay and conditions.

consequence

1 Verb + consequence

Use the correct form of these verbs:

consider   *fear*   *ignore*
realise   *suffer*   *understand*

1. I've had too many late nights over the past few weeks. I'm now . . . . the consequences!

2. My friend Neil can be very irresponsible. He's always making snap decisions and never . . . . the consequences.

3. The lawyer said that her client fully . . . . the consequences of her actions and was prepared to go to jail for them.

4. You . . . . the consequences of smoking at your peril. I'd give it up now if I were you.

5. The peace process has broken down again. I think the whole world . . . . the consequences of another war.

6. I can see now that it was a mistake to let people just turn up without letting us know in advance. I didn't . . . . what the consequences would be.

Go back and underline the verb collocations.

2 Common adjective collocations

Complete the sentences with these adjectives:

disastrous   *indirect*   *far-reaching*
inevitable   *tragic*

1. Europeans introduced the rabbit to Australia with . . . . consequences. Their numbers grew very quickly and they became a huge problem to farmers.

2. Following the death of 5-year-old Michael Richards last weekend, the police have reminded parents of the potentially . . . . consequences of allowing children to light fireworks without adult supervision.

3. The government's investment in road building will have some . . . . consequences. For example, fewer goods will be moved by rail.

4. The sharp rise in oil prices in the 1970's had . . . . consequences. The whole world was affected by it in one way or another.

5. Huge traffic jams in the city centre were the . . . . consequence of the rail strike. Everyone took their cars to work and jammed up the roads.

Now choose the best answer in the following:

6. Unfortunately, there were a number of . . . . consequences which nobody could have predicted. *(unforeseen / invisible)*

7. Historians say that it is too early to assess the . . . . consequences of the collapse of the Soviet Union. *(long-term / short-term)*

8. The most . . . . consequences of raising income tax is that the government will lose the next election! *(likely / unlikely)*

"Suffering the consequences!"

Notes

1. In 2-1 *dire* is also possible and in 2-2 *fatal* can also be used.

2. Note the following expression:
   Scientists report that most of the fish population was killed as a consequence of the oil spill.
   We need to compensate those people who are suffering and dying as a consequence of working with asbestos.

3. Note the use of the verbs *face, take,* and *accept*:
   These pilots must now face the consequences of their actions and be brought to trial.
   As a manager, you have to be prepared to accept the consequences of your decisions.
   My boss was responsible for the mess, but I had to take the consequences!

4. Note this useful expression:
   Global warming will have disastrous consequences for millions of people living near the coast.

5. If something is 'of little consequence', it is of no importance.

control

1 Verb + control

Use the correct form of these verbs:

exercise	*go out of*	*have*
keep	*lose*	*take*

1. The rebels have . . . . control of the city. They seized control early this morning when they stormed the presidential palace and assassinated the President.

2. I don't know what happened. I just . . . . control of the car and went into the ditch. I think it must have been a patch of ice.

3. When he was giving his speech at the wedding, you could tell he was very emotional by the way he struggled to . . . . control of his voice.

4. A lot of parents . . . . absolutely no control over their own children — so how do they expect the school to get them to behave?

5. I like a few beers; but you have to . . . . some self-control if you have the car. I always stick to orange juice.

6. As it entered the tunnel, the car she was in . . . . control and crashed. She only lived for a few hours after being rushed to hospital.

2 Adjective collocations

Match the halves to make full sentences:

1. In order to stop young people drinking, the government ought to impose stricter controls
2. The government's economic policy involves keeping tight control
3. After the shooting, a government official said that there would have to be more stringent controls
4. One quality of an effective teacher is the ability to exercise firm control
5. In certain countries the state has total control
6. Some people are afraid that the Chancellor is not in complete control

a. on the ownership of guns.
b. over the press, radio and TV.
c. over difficult students.
d. of the economy.
e. on the sale of alcohol.
f. on inflation.

Notice that the expressions in colour all mean 'very strong' control.

3 Types of control

Complete the sentences with these words:

birth	*crowd*	*passport*	*quality*
remote	*traffic*	*overall*	*air-traffic*

1. The man was arrested as he was collecting his luggage just after he had gone through . . . . control.

2. If you don't want to start a family immediately, your family doctor will give you advice on suitable methods of . . . . control.

3. I hope this new scheme for . . . . control in the city centre will ease congestion.

4. Our strict system of . . . . control ensures that no faulty goods leave our factory.

5. What's on the other channels? I've no idea. Where's the . . . . control?

6. One of the few effective methods of . . . . control involves the use of water cannon.

7. Managers can make most decisions, but the CEO has . . . . control within the company.

8. The reason we were delayed coming back was that . . . . control were on strike!

Notes

1. In 1-1 'gained' is also possible.

2. If you 'lose control', it can also mean to say or do things that you would not usually do:
   He had a terrible temper, and quite often he would completely lose control.

3. Notice the following expressions:
   What I don't like about being on horseback is that I don't feel as if I'm in control.
   There was nothing the company could do about their financial situation. It was totally out of / beyond / outside their control.
   More than 50 firefighters fought to bring the blaze under control.
   The concert has been cancelled due to circumstances beyond our control.

4. 'Self-control' is our ability to control our emotions and behaviour:
   If I had more self-control, I wouldn't eat as many sweets! And then I'd be a lot thinner.

cost

1 Verb + cost

Use the correct form of these verbs:

calculate	claim back	cover
depend on	cut	spread

1. When we had the idea of making a video, we thought we would make a lot of money, but, in the end, we didn't even . . . . our costs.

2. Cheap labour from abroad is being used to keep costs down. A number of factories have also been closed in an attempt to . . . . costs.

3. The cost of repairing the damage caused by the storms has been . . . . at over £20 million.

4. Whether or not we go on holiday to New Zealand will . . . . the cost of the flights.

5 I paid for my hotel with my own credit card, but I'm able to . . . . the cost of it . . . . . . on expenses.

6. Why not pay monthly and . . . . the cost of your house insurance over the year?

2 Common adjective collocations

Complete the sentences with these expressions:

average cost	full cost
at no extra cost	estimated cost
high cost	increased costs
running costs	the cost is negligible

1. When you buy a new computer, you usually get a bundle of software included . . . .

2. The final cost of the new opera house is likely to be in the region of £50 million. This means that the . . . . has more than doubled!

3. Higher tax on fuel means . . . . for the ordinary motorist.

4. The main drawback of the flat in the town centre is its . . . . We simply can't afford it.

5. I'm afraid that the owners of the flats will have to bear the . . . . of the roof repairs. No subsidies or grants are available.

6. I think our next car'll be a diesel. The . . . . are far lower than a petrol car.

7. The . . . . of a new house in the UK last year was £80,000.

8. Don't worry about ringing abroad at this time of the evening. It really isn't very much. . . . .

3 Noun + of + cost

Complete the sentences with these nouns:

breakdown	details	grounds	idea

1. Can you give me an . . . . of the cost of the repairs?

2. The bill will be £400. Here's a detailed . . . . of the costs.

3. The plan to build a new national stadium had to be abandoned on . . . . of cost.

4. The government has cleverly avoided disclosing any . . . . of the financial cost of the war.

4 Expressions with cost + of

Complete the sentences below with the following:

borrowing	damage	health care
living	postage	

1. It will be £30.45 if you add in the cost of . . . . and packaging.

2. The government has reduced the cost of . . . . in an attempt to get the economy moving again.

3. The high cost of . . . . in New York means I'm going to have to come back to the UK.

4. I believe that everyone should pay something towards the cost of their own . . . .

5. People are still clearing away the debris in the streets and trying to assess the cost of the . . . . caused by the tornado.

Go back and underline the expressions with cost of.

Notes

1. In 1-3 'estimated' is also possible.

2. If the cost of something is 'immaterial', you don't care how much it is.

3. Notice these two expressions with similar meanings:
   He's determined to win at all costs / whatever the cost.

4. Notice the following expressions:
   He drank heavily for most of his adult life at considerable cost to his health.
   The trip to the theatre works out at a cost of £25 per head.

5. Cost also means 'effort' or 'loss':
   We won the war, but the cost in human life was huge.
   She's not a very nice person – as I know to my cost!

criticism

1 Verb + criticism

Use the correct form of these verbs:

> *aim*   *resent*
> *take*   *single out for*

1. I'm very angry at the report on my teaching.
   I deeply . . . . the inspector's criticism.

2. The manager is very sensitive. He just can't . . . .
   criticism. I don't know how he got the job.

3. The whole team were responsible for our poor
   performance. I don't understand why I was . . . .
   . . . . criticism by the manager.

4. Criticism has been levelled at the government for
   the increase in hospital waiting lists. Most of the
   criticism has been . . . . at the Minister.

Go back and underline the verb collocations.

2 Preposition + criticism

Use these expressions in the sentences:

> *barrage of criticism*   *open to criticism*
> *note of criticism*   *in response to criticism*
> *sensitive to criticism*   *target for criticism*

1. If you stick to your extreme political views, don't
   complain if you become a . . . .

2. The company has changed its working practices
   . . . . by government
   inspectors.

3. Choose your words carefully. She is very . . . .
   . . . .

4. People in public life must be . . . .
   If they're not, they simply won't survive.

5. Do I detect a . . . . ? I would have
   thought you were the last person to dare to
   criticise me!

6. After the singer's appalling behaviour at the
   awards ceremony, she faced a . . . .
   in the national press.

3 Getting a lot of criticism

**Underline the verbs and phrasal verbs in the
sentences below:**

1. The French government has received strong
   criticism for continuing to test nuclear weapons in
   the Pacific.

2. The police chief has come in for harsh criticism
   over his handling of the riots.

3. The government's economic policies have
   attracted a lot of criticism recently.

4. The controversial film 'Hooligans' has run into
   severe criticism for its use of strong language.

5. The new regulations on immigration have come
   under considerable criticism in the press.

6. The government is currently facing fierce
   criticism over its failure to reduce taxes.

**In the 6 sentences above, which five adjectives
are used to mean 'a lot of criticism'?**

4 Common adjective collocations

Complete the sentences below with the following:

> *constructive*   *growing*
> *mild*   *unjustified*

1. I'm willing to accept your criticism of the way you
   were treated by Reception, but I think your
   criticism of 'the whole staff of the hotel' is wholly
   . . . .

2. My tutor didn't offer any . . . . criticism of my
   poem. He just said he didn't like it. I thought he
   would at least have given me some advice on how
   to improve it.

3. The government is coming under . . . .
   criticism for its failure to send food to the
   starving people of West Africa. More and more
   people are demanding action.

4. Make sure you only say positive things about her
   work. She can't accept even . . . . criticism of
   her paintings. She thinks she's the new Van Gogh!

Notes

1. In 1-4 you can also use *direct*; in 2-6 *a storm of
   criticism*; in 4-3 *increasing criticism* is possible.

2. Here are five main areas of adjectives:
   strong: *severe, harsh, heavy, bitter, fierce, serious*
   growing: *increasing, mounting*
   wide: *widespread, general, fundamental, constant*
   positive: *fair, constructive, legitimate, valid*
   negative: *adverse, hostile, scathing, damaging*

3. Note the expression in 3-2 – come in for criticism.
   This means that someone is criticising you. It is a
   fairly formal usage:
   *Our policies have come in for a lot of criticism from the
   press recently.*

---

crowd

1 Verb + crowd

Use the correct form of these verbs:

attract   avoid   control
disappear into   disperse   mingle with

1. Soldiers fired rubber bullets in order to . . . . the crowd of protesters who were threatening to storm the embassy.

2. Every week Manchester United draw huge crowds. Their last match . . . . a record crowd of over 60,000.

3. One minute Lily was by our side. The next minute she was gone. We searched and searched, but she had just . . . . the crowd. She was nowhere to be seen.

4. I want to get into town early on Saturday to . . . . the crowds. Shall we meet at 9?

5. During the match, plain-clothes police . . . . the crowd to try to identify the main trouble-makers.

6. The police had brought horses and water cannon to . . . . the crowd, but they weren't needed as everyone was very well-behaved.

2 Verb expressions

Underline the verbs that collocate with *crowd* in the sentences below.

1. A large crowd had gathered around the scene of the accident, making it difficult for the ambulance to get through.

2. When the army opened fire, the crowd of protesters scattered. People ran in all directions.

3. Soon after the announcement of the King's death, a crowd began to collect outside the palace.

4. Ten minutes before full-time, the crowd had thinned and the stadium was half-empty.

5. The crowd started to lose interest in the speeches and began to drift away.

6 An excited crowd had congregated around the entrance to the cinema, hoping to catch a glimpse of Tom Cruise and Nicole Kidman.

Which verbs describe the appearance and which describe the disappearance of a crowd?

appear: . . . .
disappear: . . . .

3 Adjective + crowd

Use the following adjectives in these sentences:

angry   assembled   cheering
panic-stricken   capacity   well-behaved

1. The President was welcomed enthusiastically by . . . . crowds, chanting 'Long live the President'.

2. The accused man was jostled and shoved by an . . . . crowd as he left the court. His victims had all been young children.

3. The bishop mounted the platform and began to speak to the . . . . crowd. Many had been waiting for hours to hear him.

4. Police said that the crowd at yesterday's match were very good-humoured and . . . . This was in sharp contrast to the unruly crowd that had caused so much trouble at the previous match.

5. Ten people lost their lives in a fire in a night-club last night. They were trampled to death as the . . . . crowd tried to escape.

6. The Cup Final was watched by a . . . . crowd. There wasn't an empty seat in the stadium.

Go back and underline the complete expression in each sentence.

> ## Notes
>
> 1. If you 'stand out from the crowd', you are different in some way.
> *With her bright pink coat and hat, the Queen stood out from the crowd around her.*
>
> 2. If you are 'one of the crowd', you are just like everyone else.
> *Now that I've left the band, I just want to lead a quiet life and be one of the crowd.*
>
> 3. Note the following example:
> *When Robbie Williams appeared on stage, the crowd went wild.*
>
> 4. Note the verbs which can follow 'crowd':
> *The crowd just melted into the side streets.*
> *The crowd poured out of the football ground.*
> *The crowd roared its approval.*
> *The crowd cheered / booed / hissed / jeered.*
> *The crowd lined the streets, waving flags.*

danger

1 Verb + danger

Use the correct form of these verbs:

expose to	*flirt with*	*pass*
face	*realise*	*reduce*

1. Unfortunately, the swimmers didn't . . . . the danger they were in until it was too late.
2. During the first Gulf War, it was thought soldiers would be . . . . considerable danger through the use of chemical weapons.
3. Make sure you use plenty of sun cream to . . . . the danger of skin cancer.
4. My brother is a real dare-devil. He loves to . . . . danger. He's always taking risks.
5. The minute I saw the snake, I stood perfectly still until the danger had . . . .
6. Children crossing this road . . . . constant danger from lorries and other heavy traffic.

2 Common adjective collocations

Match the two halves below:

1. As lots of people are unaware of the hidden dangers in their homes,
2. Leave immediately. You are in great danger.
3. Fire is an ever-present danger in this region.
4. Some kind of sixth sense seemed to warn me of impending danger.
5. The doctors say that she is out of immediate danger, but

a. If I hadn't looked up, I would have been hit and probably killed by a falling stone.
b. So, don't light camp fires in the forest.
c. she's still critically ill. She's still on the danger list.
d. I think someone is about to try to kill you.
e. the government has issued a leaflet, explaining how to safeguard against these unseen dangers.

3 Danger + of / to

Complete the following with 'of' or 'to':

1. The judge described him as a danger . . . . society and sent him to prison for life.
2. Children need to be educated about the dangers . . . . drug-taking.
3. A police spokesman said that there was no danger . . . . the public at any time.
4. Many people continue to ignore warnings about the dangers . . . . driving too fast.

4 Expressions with of

Complete the sentences below with the following, then underline the complete chunk in each sentence.

aware	*element*	*face*
possibility	*reminder*	*whiff*

1. The couple fell to their deaths on Mont Blanc. The accident was a salutary . . . . of the dangers of mountain-climbing.
2. As the tanks arrived, there was a . . . . of danger in the air. The crowd sensed it and became very tense.
3. Hang-gliding is not a sport to be taken lightly. You have to understand that there is an . . . . of danger involved in it.
4. My grandfather was awarded a medal in the First World War for showing great courage in the . . . . of great danger.
5. First, can I make sure that you are all fully . . . . of the dangers of sailing in this part of the world.
6. Afghanistan is still a dangerous place. You must be alert to the . . . . of danger when travelling alone in remote areas.

5 In danger of

Look at this example:

Some animals are in danger of becoming extinct.

Make sentences of your own on the topics below.

1. The world's rainforests – cut down
   . . . .
2. The Leaning Tower of Pisa – fall down
   . . . .
3. The Polar Ice Cap – melt
   . . . .
4. Venice – flood
   . . . .

Notes

1. If a someone who has been very ill is now getting better, you can say that 'they are now out of danger'.
2. Notice this expression:
   His reckless driving put the lives of the passengers in danger.

---

date

1 Verb + date

Use the correct form of these verbs:

> bring forward   confirm   delay
> fix   change   make

1. We don't have a date for our next meeting. We need to . . . . one before we all leave today.
2. Can we . . . . the date of our AGM? We said May 16th. Is that still all right with everyone?
3. The date of the wedding had to be . . . . six months when Di discovered she was pregnant.
4. A series of strikes by construction workers has . . . . the opening date of the new airport by six weeks.
5. Sorry we had to . . . . the date of the meeting. So many of us couldn't make the 14th that we really had no choice.
6. We both like opera so why don't we . . . . a date to go and see *La Traviata* one day next week?

2 Common adjective collocations

Complete the sentences below with the following:

> completion   earliest possible
> expiry   later
> particular   sell-by
> closing   firm

1. I'm afraid I'm tied up all next week. The . . . . date I can make is the second of July.
2. It's important that you keep an eye on the . . . . date of your credit cards.
3. Retain this receipt, since you may need it at a . . . . date if you need to return the goods.
4. The building company will have to pay compensation if the work continues beyond the agreed . . . . date.
5. You'd better hurry up! The . . . . date for entries to the competition is the 4th of August.
6. Never eat food which has passed its . . . . date.
7. We're still not able to give you a . . . . date for the meeting. We've still got to contact half the committee.
8. I bought an open ticket because I didn't want to tie myself down to coming back on a . . . . date.

Go back and underline the adjective collocations.

3 Date + preposition + noun

Complete the sentences with these nouns:

> applications   birth   general election
> manufacture   meeting   wedding

1. Make sure you fill in your name, address and date of . . . .
2. In Britain, the party in power has the right to choose the date of the next . . . .
3. We're thinking of the end of June, but we haven't set a specific date for the . . . . yet.
4. The closing date for . . . . is May 31st.
5. The date of our next . . . . has been changed, hasn't it?
6. What's the exact date of . . . . of your car?

"Of course I know the exact date of manufacture! The real question is why do YOU want to know!"

Notes

1. In 1-1 *arrange, decide on* and *set* are also possible. In 2-3 *future* is also possible.

2. Note the expressions *up-to-date* and *out-of-date*:
   Our monthly newsletter will keep you up-to-date with all the latest developments.
   The information in the brochure is hopelessly out-of-date.

3. Note these common expressions:
   This is the best machine we have produced to date.
   What's today's date?
   There's been a mix-up over the dates of the conference.

4. A 'date' can also mean a romantic meeting:
   Can I speak to Marie, please?
   > I'm afraid she's out on a date with her new boyfriend.

5. If you go out on 'a blind date', it is with somebody you have not met before:
   I can't believe you went on a blind date!
   > Neither can I, but he turned out to be really nice!

---

day

1 Determiner + day

Use these determiners in the sentences:

a	*all*	*any*
every	*some / one*	*one*
other	*these*	*very*

1. I passed by your house the . . . . day, but I didn't have time to call in.

2. I've enjoyed your company. I hope we meet again . . . . day soon.

3. Organic food is very popular . . . . days.

4. Take the tablets three times . . . . day, but don't take more than ten in any . . . . day.

5. Carol's expecting her first child. The baby is due . . . . day now.

6. Due to staff training this office will be closed . . . . day Monday and will re-open at 9am on Tuesday.

7. The accident happened on the . . . . day that we were leaving for Greece so we had to cancel the holiday.

8. I read a national newspaper . . . . day – 365 days a year. I like to keep in touch with what is happening in the world.

2 Common adjective collocations

Complete the sentences with these adjectives:

big	*dying*	*hard*	*lazy*
long	*lucky*	*8-hour*	*nice*

1. My dad came home exhausted after a . . . . . . day at the office.

2. In Scotland the days are very . . . . . . in summer. It's light until about 11 at night in the middle of June.

3. Tomorrow is my sister's . . . . . . day. She's getting married.

4. It was the Americans who started saying, 'Have a . . . . . . day!' Now we're all saying it!

5. I'll remember your generosity until my . . . . . . day. I'll never forget it.

6. We spent a . . . . . . day at the seaside. We just lay on the beach all day long.

7. Today is your . . . . . . day! We have exactly one copy of the new Harry Potter left in the shop!

8. I work a full . . . . . . day from 9 till 5.

Go back and underline the adjective collocations.

3 Preposition + day

Complete the sentences below with *for* or *during*:

1. Because of the extreme heat, we travelled at night and rested . . . . the day.

2. This Saturday we're going up into the hills . . . . the day to have a picnic.

3. I'm afraid the restaurant is only open . . . . the day. We close at six.

Complete the following with *by, to, or after*:

4. The job is pretty monotonous. You have to do the same boring things day . . . . day.

5. My dad's recovering slowly. He's growing stronger day . . . . day.

6. Your day-. . . . .-day duties will include answering the mail and making appointments.

Notes

1. In 1-1 *the other day* means a few days ago.
   In 1-3 *these days* means now or nowadays.
   In 1-5 *any day now* means very soon.
   In 1-7 *the very day* means the same day.

2. Note how we express disbelief:
   Bill says he's going to stop smoking.
   >That'll be the day!

3. If something 'makes your day', it makes you very happy:
   Being told I was doing a great job by the boss really made my day.

4. Here are more common expressions with *day*:
   You're going to have an accident one of these days if you keep on driving like that.
   We've been really busy today!
   > Yes, it's been a long day.
   I'm going to bed. I've got a full day's work ahead of me tomorrow.
   There are only five shopping days left until Christmas. I'd better start looking for presents.
   Do you remember the good old days when you didn't need to lock your door at night?
   > Yes, those were the days!

5. Note this example:
   Peter isn't in the office today. He's having a day off.

6. In the following expression, 'days' means 'life':
   After a long and distinguished career, the professor ended his days in poverty.

decision

1 Verb + decision

Use the correct form of these verbs:

influence	*justify*
abide by	*reverse*

1. Nobody knows how the headmaster can . . . . his decision to spend £3,000 on computers when there is an acute shortage of books in the school.

2. Our boss is a very honest and fair man. No matter what you say or what you offer him, you will not . . . . his decision in any way.

3. All competitors must . . . . the judges' decision. No appeals will be allowed.

4. I'm sorry, but we can't . . . . our decision without having another board meeting. The next one isn't for four months.

face	*regret*
question	*put off*

5. I don't . . . . my decision to leave school at 16. I think it was the right choice for me at the time.

6. They've decided to wait a few years before having children. I hope they realise that they can't . . . . the decision indefinitely!

7. Newchester United have lost their last four games and lots of us are beginning to . . . . the manager's decision to leave the team's star player out of the team.

8. Now that you've been promoted, you'll . . . . difficult decisions on a daily basis. Good luck!

2 Useful expressions

Match the two halves to make sentences:

1. Don't try to force me to choose. I refuse to be hurried
2. Mike's so annoying. He always leaves important decisions to
3. I hope I've made
4. There may come a time when you'll regret
5. I'm not altogether happy about the decision, but

a. *I think I can live with it.*
b. *into a decision.*
c. *the last possible moment.*
d. *that decision.*
e. *the right decision.*

Go back and underline all the collocations with decision.

3 Common adjective collocations

Complete the sentences with these adjectives:

informed	*joint*
tough	*wise*

1. In order to make an . . . . decision about which course to take, you should read the college prospectus. It contains facts and details for every course that the college runs.

2. Both candidates are ideal for the job. There's so little to choose between them that it's going to be a . . . . decision to reach.

3. Just look at that rain! I think our decision not to go to the beach today was a . . . . one.

4. I heard your wife wasn't keen on moving house. > That's just not true! It was a . . . . decision.

final	*courageous*
rash	*controversial*

5. My father warned me against making . . . . decisions. He advised me to take plenty of time to think things over.

6. After many hours of heated discussion the government arrived at the . . . . decision to bring back the death penalty for murder.

7. Beatrice Wzylo, the famous actress, took the . . . . decision to tell the world about her addiction to sleeping pills.

8. As yet, no . . . . decision has been taken about the future of the company, but we're all afraid it may have to close.

Which three verbs in the sentences above can replace *make* in 'make a decision'?

Notes

1. In 1-3 'abide by a decision' is a very formal expression. In speech you might use 'stick to': *So, are you sticking to your decision not to come?*

2. In 3-5 you can also say a 'snap decision'.

3. There a number of adjectives used to talk about important decisions: *This is a crucial decision. I hope you realise this decision is irreversible. There's no going back now! This is a momentous decision in the history of our nation.*

demand

1 Verb + demand (firm request)

Use the correct form of these verbs:

> give in to   justify
> renew   make
> meet   receive

1. Starting at 12 noon, the hijackers are threatening to kill one passenger an hour if their demands are not . . . .

2. We've just . . . . a final demand for the gas bill. If we don't pay it within seven days, the gas company are threatening to cut off the gas.

3. Children need to learn that they can't have everything they want. You shouldn't . . . . their demands all the time.

4. The unions presented a long list of reasons to . . . . their demands for a shorter working week.

5. The animal rights people have . . . . their demands for the abolition of all forms of hunting.

6. Demands have been . . . . for the immediate release of all political prisoners.

2 Verb + demand (need or desire for goods)

Use the correct form of these verbs:

> be   cope with
> create   fall
> outstrip   rise

1. Due to fears of more terrorist attacks, the demand for transatlantic flights has . . . . in recent months.

2. There . . . . so little demand for tickets for the concert that it had to be cancelled.

3. The workforce is working round the clock, but we are finding it difficult to . . . . the recent surge in demand for our products.

4. When demand for a product . . . . supply, the price of that product usually rises. That's why property prices have gone through the roof.

5. Demand for mobile phones has . . . . sharply. This increase is partly due to lower prices.

6. The main role of advertising is to . . . . a demand for a particular product.

Go back and underline other interesting collocations in this exercise.

3 Noun expressions

Complete the sentences with these nouns:

> parent   pilots   police
> job   time   work

1. I don't want a job which makes heavy demands on my . . . . I want a social life as well!

2. Enforcing this new law on dropping litter will make impossible demands on the . . . . I don't think it'll work in practice.

3. The emotional demands of looking after an elderly . . . . can be overwhelming.

4. I don't know how working women cope with the conflicting demands of . . . . and family life.

5. I've decided to hand in my resignation. The salary is good, but the demands of the . . . . . are excessive.

6. Flying into crowded airports like Heathrow makes enormous demands on . . . .

4 Expressions with prepositions

Use these expressions in the sentences below:

> in demand   on demand
> demand for   demands on

1. Good secretaries are always . . . .

2. Some people believe that abortion should be available . . . .

3. I'm far too busy. There are just too many . . . . my time at the moment.

4. In recent years we've seen the . . . . good quality one-bedroom flats grow and grow.

Notes

1. If someone is 'unequal to the demands of the job', they can't do it.

2. Note the following way of saying that people want something:
   By popular demand, the show will run for another week.

3. In business you often need to talk about 'the law of supply and demand'.

4. Common adjective expressions are:
   emotional demands   financial demands
   conflicting demands   huge demands

---

description

1 Verb + description

Use the correct form of these verbs:

contain	*defy*	*fit*
give	*issue*	*write*

1. It had been a clear night. The girl saw her attacker clearly, so she was able to . . . . the police an pretty accurate description of him.

2. No words could describe the beauty of the scenery. It . . . . description.

3. Police have . . . . a description of a man they wish to question in connection with a fatal accident in the city centre.

4. A boy, ... the description of the missing child, was seen walking along the riverbank just before midnight last night.

5. . . . . a short description of your home town.

6. Tonight's documentary on new medicines is not suitable for children as it . . . . a shocking description of animals being used to test drugs.

2 Common adjective collocations

Complete the sentences with these adjectives:

apt	*brief*	*detailed*
vague	*vivid*	*accurate*

1. A member of the public has come forward with a full and . . . . description of the men who robbed the post office. The police are now confident that they will catch the robbers.

2. Her description of the scenery was so . . . . that when I closed my eyes I could see snow-covered mountains clearly in my mind.

3. 'Like a fish out of water' is an . . . . description of how I felt at the party. I felt so awkward and uncomfortable.

4. What can you say in 50 words? The . . . . description on the back cover of the book is only intended to give you a quick idea of what the book is about.

5. If the police asked you to give a description of someone you met 2 months ago, how . . . . would it be?

6. We only had a very . . . . description of Thupten, but we had no trouble recognising him as soon as he appeared through customs.

Go back and underline the adjective collocations.

"Yes, 'like a fish out of water' is a very apt description of how I'm feeling!"

Notes

1. In 1-4 'matching' is also possible.

2. When you apply for a job, it is normal to be given a 'job description'.
   I refused to work on Sunday as there was no mention of working at weekends in my job description.

3. Note the following expressions:
   There were planes of every description at the air show. (of all kinds)
   When the dentist hit the nerve in my tooth, the pain was beyond description.
   He's a great writer with remarkable powers of description.

4. Three adjectives used to describe something in a very special and memorable way are: graphic, lurid, and vivid. For example:
   There's a lurid description in chapter 4 of the affair between the young girl and the priest.
   Jo gave us a vivid description of her experiences travelling round India.
   The description of what the murderer did to his victims was graphic in the extreme!

5. A 'general description' provides the main ideas or facts. For example:
   The internet guide only gives a general description of Bangkok. If you want more details, you're better buying a proper guidebook.

detail

1 Verb + details

Use the correct form of these verbs:

absorb   check   disclose   go into
send   finalise   take   uncover

1. Please .... that these details are correct before you sign the form.
2. Please write, enclosing a stamped addressed envelope, and we will .... you details of the health plan.
3. The city council have refused to .... details of its plan to close the city centre to traffic.
4. I don't understand why some newspapers dig into the past of politicians in an attempt to .... details of their previous love affairs. It's sick!
5. There's too much information in this leaflet. I'm having difficulty .... all the details.
6. I can't .... details at the moment; it would take too long. I'll just give you the gist of what he said and I'll fill you in later with all the details.
7. The police .... all the details and said they would get back to me within the week.
8. We can't .... the details of our holiday yet. I won't know when I can get time off till Friday.

2 Giving details

Match the two halves of these sentences.
Underline the verbs which mean 'giving details'.

1. Can you give us ...
2. Police have so far released ...
3. The jurors were given strict instructions from the judge not to reveal ...
4. A company spokesman refused to disclose ...
5. The government recently announced ...
6. He talked to the press and divulged ...
7. The travel company has provided us with ...

a. *full details of our journey across Australia.*
b. *details of its plan to improve the health service.*
c. *a few more details. For example, does the price include travel insurance?*
d. *no details of the missing children.*
e. *details of its revolutionary new product until the official launch.*
f. *any details of the case to the press.*
g. *details of our private conversation. You can't trust anybody these days!*

3 Common adjective collocations

Use the following adjectives in these sentences:

final   further   gory
minor   personal   precise

1. If you need more information about the holiday accommodation, ... details can be found on our website.
2. All we know is that Di's had an accident, but we don't know the .... details.
3. Fill out one of these application forms with all your .... details.
4. The report contains a lot of unimportant issues. We must be careful not to let these .... details distract us from the big issues.
5. Richard's description of the blood and everything almost made me sick. He wasn't happy till he'd told us all the .... details of the accident.
6. We've agreed the general outline of the agreement, but the .... details have still to be worked out.

4 Expressions with prepositions

Use *in, into, about* and *on* in the following:

1. We'll need to examine the plan ...... greater detail before we can give it our approval.
2. They are still arguing ...... the details of the arrangements.
3. I won't go ...... detail. All I'm prepared to say is she was fairly critical.
4. Contact the number at the bottom of the page for more details ...... how to obtain a passport.

Notes

1. In 3-2 you could also use 'exact'.
2. Note these expressions:
   Artists need to have an eye for detail.
   Proof-reading needs great attention to detail.
   They had planned the trip down to the smallest detail.
3. Note this noun phrase:
   The guidebook contains a wealth of detail on the history of revolutionary France.
4. If someone notices everything, eg spotting spelling mistakes, you can say that they 'have an excellent eye for detail'.

---

difference

1 Noticing differences

Match the two halves of these sentences:

1. I used margarine instead of butter, so
2. This coffee is half the price of that one and yet
3. As humans we can
4. It looks and feels exactly like a genuine five-pound note, but I'm sure anybody with a trained eye will
5. The medical treatment he's receiving seems to be working and

a. you can certainly see a difference. He doesn't look so tired and he has some colour in his cheeks.
b. spot the difference immediately.
c. I hope nobody notices the difference.
d. you really can't tell the difference. They taste almost the same.
e. detect small differences in smell but a dog's nose is much more sensitive.

Go back and underline all the verb + *difference* collocations.

2 Common adjective collocations

Use the following adjectives in these sentences:

fundamental	irreconcilable	no
real	striking	subtle

1. I couldn't tell the two paintings apart until an expert pointed out the very . . . . differences between them.
2. I don't think Charles and Edward will ever see eye-to-eye on anything again. Over the years . . . . differences of opinion have developed between them.
3. Please give generously to our charity. A donation of just £1 can make a . . . . difference to the quality of life of children in some of the poorest countries in the world.
4. There are . . . . differences between the capital and the rest of the country. The rich lifestyle of the area around the city is in sharp contrast to the poverty of the rural areas.
5. It makes . . . . difference to me whether she goes or stays. It doesn't really affect me.
6. The . . . . difference between you and me is that you like spending money and I like saving it!

When you have finished this exercise and the next, go back and underline all the expressions with *difference*.

3 Big differences

Match the two halves of these sentences:

1. Putting in central heating made
2. There's a substantial difference
3. Although there were marked differences on how to spend the money
4. There's a big difference between
5. When my brother said sorry for what he had said about me,

a. between the opinions of men and women on the issue of abortion.
b. a world of difference to my parents' house.
c. the service on the two airlines.
d. it made all the difference.
e. the finance group made a decision in a surprisingly short time.

Go back and underline the adjective + *difference* collocations.

4 Difference + preposition

Complete the sentences below with a suitable preposition:

1. There are significant differences . . . . the legal systems of England and Scotland.
2. The difference . . . . price is so small it's not worth arguing about.
3. He doesn't earn much so the extra money will make a big difference . . . . him.
4. If you're thinking of a holiday . . . . a difference, why not try Finland?

Notes

1. In 3-5 the expression 'all the difference' means that there was a complete change:
   I've decided to stay on the committee.
   > Great! That'll make all the difference! We didn't want to lose your experience.

2. 'Differences' can mean 'arguments':
   Let's forget our differences and be friends again.
   My mother asked us to settle our differences.
   We've had our differences in the past, but we're friends again.

3. Note this common question:
   He's speaking Dutch, not German! Don't you know the difference?

difficulty

1 Verb collocations

Use the correct form of these verbs:

be in   cause   foresee
get into   overcome   present

1. Credit cards make it extremely easy for young people to . . . . difficulty with debt.

2. We're confident that these difficulties will be . . . . before the play starts.

3. It was in the six o'clock news that a large oil tanker . . . . difficulties off the coast of France. It's in danger of breaking in two.

4. My father's had a mild stroke and it has . . . . difficulties with his speech.

5. The task should . . . . no difficulty for someone of his ability.

6. I don't . . . . any difficulties so long as we keep to our planned route.

2 Common adjective collocations

Complete the sentences with these adjectives:

current   financial   learning   main
marital   technical   unforeseen

1. The President's live broadcast was delayed because of . . . . difficulties.

2. We offer a free counselling service to couples with . . . . difficulties.

3. The . . . . difficulty with this new approach is that it takes twice as long as the old one.

4. He says he's having . . . . difficulties and that he can't pay the rent.

5. My sister works in a special school for children with severe . . . . difficulties.

6. I think I've got a plan for getting us out of our . . . . difficulties.

7. An . . . . difficulty has arisen, so I'm afraid we'll have to postpone the meeting.

Now match the two halves of the following:

8. The town was very busy.
9. Arsenal won easily.
10. The burglars found the door unlocked.

a. *They never seemed to be in any difficulty.*
b. *We had great difficulty finding somewhere to park.*
c. *They had no difficulty getting in.*

Now underline the expressions with difficulty.

"It's three months now and I'm still having difficulty walking."

Notes

1. In 1-3 'run into' is also possible.
   In 1-6 'expect' is also possible.
   In 2-6 'present' is also possible.

2. Note the common structure *have difficulty (in) doing something.*
   It's three months since he broke his leg, but he still has difficulty walking.
   He's a loving person, but he has difficulty showing affection.

3. We use a number of verbs to describe having difficulties:
   Some parents experienced difficulty getting their children into the school of their choice.
   Officials have encountered difficulties in getting the aid through to the refugees.
   If you meet any difficulties, let me know and I'll help you out.

4. Note how we talk about lots of difficulties:
   Her path to becoming the first woman president was beset with difficulties.
   The situation is fraught with difficulties.

5. An insurmountable difficulty is one which cannot be overcome.
   The government faces insurmountable difficulties in getting its new tax bill passed.

6. Note the common expressions *with / without difficulty:*
   The boxer got to his feet with difficulty.
   You should be able to find the hotel without much difficulty.

direction

1 Verb + direction

Use the correct form of these verbs:

ask for   *change*   *give*
head in   *look in*   *take*

1. She waved at him across the street to draw his attention but he wasn't .... her direction.

2. I think we're lost. Let's stop and .... directions.

3. Which direction do you think the government will ....?

4. He .... me directions to his house, but I got lost and had to call him on my mobile.

5. The wind .... direction suddenly. Our dinghy capsized and we all ended up in the water.

6. The missing child was last seen .... the direction of the park.

2 Common adjective collocations

Complete the sentences with these adjectives:

clear	*clockwise*
general	*opposite*
right	*same*
wrong	*westerly*

1. Excuse me. I wonder if you could point me in the .... direction for the railway station? I'm a stranger here.

2. The hotel's website provides .... and precise directions on how to get there. It's not marked on most maps. It's so isolated.

3. When the youths saw the police coming they ran off in the .... direction.

4. In the northern hemisphere water escapes down the plughole in a .... direction.

5. Continue in a .... direction for about 2 miles, until you reach a small farm, then turn right.

6. We seem to be going in the .... direction. Can I join you?

7. He disappeared off in the .... direction of the pub, but I'm not really sure if that's where he was heading to.

8. If you're trying to get to Faversham, I'm afraid you're going in the .... direction. You must have missed the turn-off a few miles back.

Go back and underline the adjective collocations.

3 Quantifier + direction

Use these quantifiers in the sentences:

all   *both*   *each*   *every*   *one*

1. From the top of the mountain we could see for miles and miles in .... direction.

2. British motorways usually have three lanes in .... direction. Some have four.

3. When the police arrived, the crowd scattered in .... directions.

4. He doesn't know what to do. He's being pulled in .... direction by his heart and in the other by his head.

5. Due to an accident, traffic is moving very slowly in .... directions.

"The wind changed direction suddenly!"

Notes

1. Note the following:
   I'm bad at finding places. I've got no sense of direction.
   Like many teenagers, I had no sense of direction in life. I just didn't know what to do with myself.

2. Note the following expressions:
   Many believe that the decision to cut interest rates is a step in the right direction to economic recovery.
   I clearly need a change of direction at work. I'm bored doing the same thing every day.

3. 'Directions' can mean 'written instructions':
   Don't forget to read the directions on the packet before taking the pills.
   Just follow the directions on the packet and you will end up with a perfect sponge cake!

4. Note this more formal expression:
   This is a step in the right / wrong direction.

disaster

1 Verb + disaster

Use the correct form of these verbs:

avert	*court*	*head for*
spell	*end in*	*strike*

1. Disaster . . . . when the plane's engine failed shortly after take-off.

2. An airliner came close to disaster while approaching Kennedy Airport yesterday. Fortunately, the disaster was narrowly . . . . by the quick reactions of the pilot.

3. The business was . . . . financial disaster until a new manager arrived to save the situation.

4. The discovery of foot and mouth disease in British cattle . . . . disaster for many British farmers. Many went out of business as a result.

5. Drinking and driving is stupid and irresponsible. If you do it, you are simply . . . . disaster.

6. The trip to the island . . . . disaster when the small boat we were in hit a rock and sank in a matter of minutes.

Go back and underline the verb collocations.

2 Common adjective collocations

Complete the sentences with these adjectives:

ecological	*impending*	*major*
nuclear	*natural*	*utter*

1. There's not much you can do about . . . . disasters like floods and earthquakes.

2. I'm not going to bore you with all the details. It's enough to say that the whole event was a total and . . . . disaster.

3. Many scientists believe that the destruction of the rain forests is an . . . . disaster that threatens the future of life on Earth.

4. When the emergency services arrived at the scene of the accident, they soon realised that they had a . . . . disaster on their hands.

5. On the morning of the final climb to the summit of Mt Everest, I woke with an overwhelming feeling of . . . . disaster. I was right. Two of our party of seven died that day.

6. Everyone knew before it happened that Chernobyl was a . . . . disaster waiting to happen.

3 Noun + preposition + disaster

Complete the sentences below with a suitable preposition:

1. It was impossible to comprehend <u>the full scale . . . . the disaster</u>.

2. Following the rail crash, the government has promised a full investigation . . . . the disaster.

3. The reason . . . . the disaster was engine failure, not human error.

4. Hospitals up to fifty miles from the site . . . . the disaster were inundated with casualties.

5. The recent wave of strikes has brought the country to the brink . . . . economic disaster.

6. Letting Fernando organise the trip is a recipe . . . . disaster. Everything is likely to go wrong.

7. The earthquake is just the latest in a long line . . . . . . disasters that have hit the country recently.

8. The director accepted full responsibility . . . . the disaster and resigned on the spot.

Now go back and underline the complete expressions. The first is done for you.

Notes

1. In 2-4 you could also say a 'full-scale disaster'.

2. Note the following ways of saying something is a complete disaster:
   The trip was an unmitigated disaster from start to finish.
   The whole project was an out-and-out disaster.

3. If you say somebody is 'a walking disaster', you mean they are always having accidents:
   He's broken his leg again! That boy is a walking disaster! Everything happens to him.

4. Note the expression in 2-6 – *a disaster waiting to happen*. It is similar in meaning to the expression in 3-6 – *a recipe for disaster*:
   This plan to open offices in every major European city is a recipe for financial disaster.

5. 'A disaster area' or 'disaster zone' is one where something awful has happened:
   The government officially declared the town a disaster area after the typhoon destroyed most of the buildings.

doubt

1 Verb + doubt

Use the correct form of these verbs:

cast   *confirm*   *have (x2)*
raise   *remove*

1. The latest accident on the London to Norwich line has . . . . serious doubts about the safety of the braking system on the new trains.

2. An order for two new ships for the navy has . . . . any doubts about the shipyard's future.

3. New evidence has emerged since the trial that . . . . doubt on the guilty verdict.

4. I'm . . . . doubts about taking the job in Paris – maybe I'll just stay here where I'm comfortable.

5. The painting didn't look authentic. An examination by an expert has . . . . our doubts.

6. I . . . . no doubt whatsoever that William will be a great leader and an asset to the company.

2 Determiner + doubt

Use these words to complete the sentences:

any   *my*   *no (x2)*   *some*

1. . . . . doubt cod liver oil is very good for you, but I just don't like the taste of it!

2. Our son, Alan, is still in . . . . doubt about whether to go to university or not.

3. Give me a ring if you're in . . . . doubt about how to use the new software.

4. They say they'll be here by eight, but I have . . . . doubts!

5. There was . . . . doubt in my mind that he was lying. I could tell by his shifty eyes.

3 Common expressions

Use these expressions to complete the sentences:

in doubt   *no doubt about it*
open to doubt   *without doubt*
beyond all reasonable doubt

1. David Beckham is . . . . one of the most famous football players in the world today.

2. If . . . . , consult your doctor before continuing with this medication.

3. Whether they can finish the bridge on time is still . . . .

4. The prosecution's task in a court case is to establish a person's guilt . . . .

5. Crolla's makes the best ice cream in town. . . . . !

4 Adjective collocations

Complete the sentences with these adjectives:

slightest   *serious*   *niggling*

1. After watching Bob's disastrous lesson, I have . . . . doubts that he'll qualify as a teacher.

2. I haven't the . . . . doubt that James will pass. He's one of the best in the class.

3. I've had . . . . doubts about Michael. I can't put my finger on it. I just feel something isn't right.

grave   *lingering*   *growing*

4. Although he was found not guilty of murder, there are still . . . . doubts about his innocence.

5. I've been having . . . . doubts about taking that job in Singapore. I think I'm too old to be going abroad again.

6. What do you think about this plan to open up in Scandinavia?
> I've got . . . . doubts about it myself. It's a notoriously difficult market for outsiders.

Go back and underline all the collocations in the exercises in this unit.

Notes

1. In 3-5 'little' is also possible.

2. Note that we can *raise, voice,* or *express* our doubts about something:
   The meeting will give you an opportunity to voice any doubts you may have about the project.

3. Note the following expressions:
   I knew without a shadow of a doubt that he was guilty.
   He may not have been telling the truth, but I felt I had to give him the benefit of the doubt.
   He says the building will be ready on time, but I have my doubts.

4. Note the following common expression:
   Doubts have arisen over the reliability of the new air-traffic control system.

effect

1 Positive and negative effects

Which of the adjectives in colour are positive and which are negative?

1. There is abundant evidence that smoking has a harmful effect on your health.

2. Many chemicals have a damaging effect on the environment.

3. People today are aware of the beneficial effects of exercise. That's why so many join leisure clubs.

4. Watching too much television is having an adverse effect on John's progress at school.

5. The girl was kept locked up in a darkened room, but she seems to have suffered no ill effects.

6. The Victorians swore by the therapeutic effects of sea-bathing.

7. The bad behaviour of our neighbour's children is having a detrimental effect on our own children.

2 Adjective expressions

Use the following adjectives in these sentences:

calming	combined	deadening	noticeable
overall	opposite	desired	profound

1. His mother put her arm around her to help her relax, but it had exactly the . . . . effect. She just froze! I don't think they'll ever get on.

2. I didn't realise it at the time, but my father's death had a . . . . effect on me. It's taken me a long time to get over it.

3. The music they play in planes is designed to have a . . . . effect on the passengers.

4. Alcohol has a . . . . effect on the senses. That's why it's dangerous to drink and drive.

5. The doctor gave me some drugs to relieve the pain, but they had no . . . . effect. Two hours later I felt exactly the same.

6. There have been a number of criticisms of the government in the press in recent weeks. However, the . . . . effect of these has not damaged the Prime Minister's popularity.

7. Most of the victims of the fire died from the . . . . effects of smoke and heat.

8. Unfortunately, my apology to Jackie has not had the . . . . effect. She still ignores me! Some people just don't know how to forgive!

Go back and underline the adjective collocations.

3 Useful expressions

Match the two halves to make complete sentences:

1. The outbreak of war in the Middle East had <u>a dramatic effect</u>

2. These tablets will help with the pain, but unfortunately they don't have a long-lasting effect

3. The recent advertising campaign has had a marked effect on sales. In fact,

4. In tonight's programme we'll be looking at the long-term effects

5. I'm afraid that the new drug has had no significant effect

a. of unemployment.

b. we'll have to take on new staff to keep up with the increased demand.

c. on stopping the spread of the disease.

d. – you'll need to take two every couple of hours.

e. on petrol prices. They almost doubled overnight.

Go back and underline the complete expressions. The first is underlined for you.

Notes

1. In 2-3 you can also say 'soothing effect'.

2. Two common verbs are 'take' and 'come into':
   The new regulations take effect at midnight tonight.
   We don't expect the new law on inheritance to come into effect till late in the autumn.

3. If something has a 'knock-on effect', it causes something else to happen:
   Today's strike will have a knock-on effect on all flights for the next few days.

4. Drugs can have unpleasant 'side-effects':
   The possible side effects of the drug include headaches and nausea.

5. 'After-effects' can come some time after you have taken medicine.

6. Global warming and 'the greenhouse effect' are two major issues of today.

7. 'Special effects' are the techniques used by film-makers to make their films look spectacular:
   The special effects in the three Lord of the Rings films were amazing!
   I'd go to see it just for the special effects!

---

effort

1 Verb + effort

Use the correct form of these verbs:

expend	*go into*
make	*require*
reward	*save*

1. If you want to get good grades, you'd better start . . . . more of an effort. As it is, you'll be lucky to scrape a pass.

2. Learning a language as a child seems to involve no effort at all, but learning it as an adult . . . . a lot of time and effort.

3. Following record sales over the Christmas period, the staff were . . . . for their efforts with a New Year bonus of £300.

4. I'd tackle the problem now if I were you. It'll only take a couple of hours and it'll . . . . you a lot of time and effort in the long run.

5. A lot of effort has . . . . making this event a success. I'd like to thank all of those who were involved.

6. After . . . . all that effort on training to be a doctor, she decided that she wanted to do something else. What a terrible waste of time!

2 Adjective + effort

Use these adjectives to complete the sentences:

concerted	*extra*
feeble	*supreme*
determined	

1. My father is making a huge effort to stop smoking. > Good for him! Tell him I'm also making a . . . . effort to kick the habit! I haven't had a cigarette for a week!

2. It's not an easy book to read but it's extremely interesting. It's well worth putting in the . . . . effort to understand it.

3. Jon can be so irritating. He made a . . . . effort to help me with the dishes. I think he dried one plate and then went round telling people he had done the dishes!

4. Some people can lose weight virtually overnight, but for most people, dieting requires a . . . . effort of will.

5. Now, for many of our guests this will be their first time abroad, so let's all make a . . . . effort to make our Russian colleagues welcome.

3 Common expressions

Match the two halves of the sentences below:

1. If we fail, it won't be for
2. This company has invested a great deal of
3. He passed his exams with
4. I know it's a long climb to the top of the hill, but the view from the top is
5. Everybody on our social committee has put in
6. We've started a massive advertising campaign

a. *time and effort* in setting up training schemes.
b. *well worth the effort.*
c. *in an effort to* recruit more blood donors.
d. *the minimum of effort.* He's obviously very bright.
e. *want of effort.*
f. *a great deal of effort* to make the weekend a success.

4 Noun + effort

Use these nouns to complete the sentences:

waste	*prize*	*relief*	*war*	*fund-raising*

1. The . . . . efforts of local people have resulted in over £10,000 being raised for cancer research in the past year.

2. . . . . efforts in the Congo are being hampered by the on-going civil war.

3. People started to wear yellow badges to show their support for the . . . . effort.

4. The only . . . . I won at school was one for effort. At least I tried! And that's more important than coming first!

5. A lot of grammar study is a . . . . of time and effort. Collocation is much more useful.

Notes

1. Note the use of the quantifiers *every* and *no* in the following common expressions:
   Every effort is being made to rectify the problem.
   We will spare no effort to find out who did this.

2. 'In an effort to' means 'in order to':
   We've reduced our workforce in an effort to cut costs.

3. If something is a 'real effort', it is very difficult:
   Dad's very weak now. It's a real effort just to talk.

event

1 Verb + event

Use the correct form of these verbs:

> cancel   mark
> witness   shake
> sponsor   take part in

1. When Nelson Mandela visited the city, hundreds of doves were released to . . . . the event.

2. I'd like to thank everyone who . . . . today's marvellous fund-raising event. I think you'll all agree we've had a wonderful day and we have also managed to raise over £20,000!

3. Nobody who . . . . the events of September 11th – either live on TV or first hand – will ever forget them.

4. Most big sporting events are . . . . by large multinational companies like Nike or Pepsi.

5. The explosion of the atom bomb over Hiroshima was an event that . . . . the world.
   >It was also an event that changed history.

6. Will the event be . . . . if it rains or will it be held indoors instead?

2 Common adjective collocations

Match the two halves of these sentences:

1. We'll be staging a number of
2. Everything went exactly as planned.
3. Three people died when the building collapsed. Unfortunately, I was a witness to
4. Early this morning the President suffered a heart attack. We have the latest report on today's
5. The resignation of the Prime Minister was
6. If you are into films and film stars,
7. Getting a place at university
8. When my sister lost her second child,
9. The folk festival has now become

a. *dramatic events* at the White House in a few minutes.
b. *the main political event* of the year.
c. *is a major event* in the lives of many young people.
d. *then the Oscars is the biggest social event* of the year.
e. *The whole event* went like clockwork.
f. *an annual event,* held every June.
g. *it was a traumatic event* for the whole family.
h. *special events* to celebrate 25 years of independence.
i. *the tragic event* and it's something I'm going to have trouble living with.

3 Noun expressions

Fill in the gaps in the sentences below with the following nouns:

> chain   course   summary   version

1. We were suspicious of Bill's . . . . of events. That's why we started a full-scale investigation and discovered he had been stealing money from the company for over ten years! I mean, he had a yacht and house in St Tropez!

2. It's difficult to believe that the decisions we are about to take will influence the future . . . . of events. It's a strange feeling knowing that you can affect history!

3. The air accident report has outlined the . . . . of events that caused the accident which resulted in the deaths of hundreds of people.

4. I haven't got time to go into detail so this is just a brief . . . . of events from the Festival.

"The whole event should have gone like clockwork!"

Notes

1. In 1-1 'celebrate' is also possible.

2. Note the following common expressions:
   In the event of a collision, the airbag will inflate instantly.
   In the unlikely event of a breakdown, call 189 4320 for roadside assistance.

3. In 1-4 'a sporting event' can mean the whole competition or an individual competition. For example:
   The 100 metres is not his best event.

4. Large events are 'staged':
   Our organisation has a lot of experience of staging international sporting events.

excuse

1 Verb + excuse

Use the correct form of these verbs:

> have   look for
> make up   provide with
> run out of   use as

1. I think I've . . . . excuses for not doing my homework, so I'd better get started!

2. So, why was Ted late again this morning?
   > Who knows? As usual he . . . . some excuse about his car breaking down, but nobody believes a word he says any more.

3. Football teams always blame the referee when they lose a game, but everyone knows they only . . . . him . . . . . an excuse for their poor playing.

4. I'm sorry I . . . . no excuse for being late. It was my own stupid fault. I slept in.

5. Our son, Josh, is really lazy. He's always . . . . an excuse to avoid doing any work around the house.

6. My father's illness . . . . me . . . . an excuse not to have to go to Mary's leaving party. I was glad to see her go!

2 Common adjective collocations

Use these adjectives to complete the sentences:

> convenient   good
> old   poor

1. No, he didn't come and help us after promising to. He gave some . . . . excuse about falling asleep in front of the TV and expected us to believe it.

2. Dad will be absolutely furious! We'll have to think up a pretty . . . . excuse for staying out so late.

3. He's always making the same . . . . excuse for not finishing his work on time. I'm becoming sick and tired of listening to them. Can't we just fire him?

4. Fortunately, I have a . . . . excuse for missing the meeting. My son's been taken ill at school and I've got to take him home.

We use a number of verbs for providing excuses. Find the four in the sentences above:

> . . . .
> . . . .

3 Poor excuses

We use a number of words to describe poor excuses. Underline them in the sentences below:

1. You missed the bus! That's a lame excuse – you should have left the house a bit earlier.

2. I'm afraid I can't come – I've got to go home and feed my dog.
   > Oh, come on, that's a pathetic excuse!

3. He said he couldn't play because he had hurt his finger. What a feeble excuse!

4. You won't come out with me because you're planning to wash your hair! That's not much of an excuse!

"He's always making up excuses to get out of doing any housework!"

Notes

1. Note the following expressions:
   There's no excuse for that kind of behaviour. The guilty players should be thrown out of the team.
   She only needs the slightest excuse to go shopping. Don't encourage her!
   I'm tired of listening to your excuses.

2. Notice the structures that can follow *excuse*:
   It's just an excuse to do nothing.
   It was just an excuse for doing nothing.

3. Note this common question:
   So what's your excuse?

4. Note this common structure:
   There's no excuse for what he did.
   There's no excuse for such rudeness.
   There's no excuse for arriving late.

---

expectation

1 Common expressions

Divide the sentences below into three groups:

   A = better than expected
   B = as expected
   C = worse than expected

1. The concert was fantastic – it lived up to all our expectations.
2. The film has been a surprise success. Box-office receipts have exceeded all expectations.
3. It is a fact that the reality of a holiday often falls short of expectations.
4. The increase in interest rates is broadly in line with expectations.
5. Unfortunately sales of the new product have failed to meet expectations.
6. The English course fulfilled all our expectations.
7. The restaurant was quiet and relaxing, but the food didn't come up to our expectations.
8. The book's success has surpassed everyone's expectations.
9. The standard of service on the cruise liner was well below expectation.
10. The apartment they were thinking of buying didn't measure up to their expectations.
11. The campaign has produced results way beyond expectations.
12. Profits are way below expectations.

2 Collocation check

Complete these sentences using words from exercise 1 above:

1. The firework display was far better than we had expected. It really . . . . all our expectations.
2. When Rod told us he had booked a table at the Manor Restaurant, we were so excited, but it really didn't live . . . . our expectations. Everybody was so disappointed.
3. My parents' world cruise was meant to be the trip of a lifetime, but it . . . . far short of their expectations. Nearly everyone got food poisoning at some point in the trip!
4. All the indications so far are that this year's figures are going to be a huge improvement and . . . . with the finance director's expectations and predictions.

3 Common adjective collocations

Complete the sentences with these adjectives:

   clear   *different*   *general*
   high   *unrealistic*   *wildest*

1. Our daughter passed all her exams with flying colours so we have . . . . expectations for her future.
2. The amazing success of our team this year has exceeded our . . . . expectations.
3. Although society is changing, there is still a . . . . expectation that couples will have children soon after they marry.
4. The article was obviously written before the election results in the . . . . expectation of a Nixon victory.
5. Some parents have . . . . expectations of their children and put too much pressure on them.
6. Sue and Steve went into marriage with very . . . . expectations, so their divorce comes as no surprise to me.

4 Prepositional expressions

Complete each expression with one preposition:

1. She went . . . . . . the expectation of meeting him.
2. Contrary . . . . . . expectation, they got on well.
3. It didn't live . . . . . . to our expectations.
4. It fell well . . . . . . our expectations.
5. It was in line . . . . . . our expectations.
6. It fell short . . . . . . our expectations.
7. It didn't measure . . . . . . to our expectations.
8. We all had great expectations . . . . . . her future.

Notes

1. Note the following:
   I knew I didn't have the necessary experience, so I applied for the job more in hope than expectation of actually getting it.
   Against all expectations, the building of the new school was completed on time.

2. Note the verb collocation 'raise expectations':
   Meetings between the two countries have raised expectations that a peace agreement is likely.

---

experience

1 Verb + experience

Use the correct form of these verbs:

bring	have
gain	base on
learn	share

1. She didn't . . . . much experience of marketing, but they gave her the job anyway.

2. My father believes that it is better to . . . . from experience rather than from books. Personally, I think that you need to do both.

3. I've . . . . a lot of valuable experience in the classroom this year. I now feel I'm a much better teacher than I was when I qualified a year ago.

4. The new CEO is like a breath of fresh air. He . . . . years of experience to the company.

5. Margaret, perhaps you'd like to . . . . your experience with the rest of the class?

6. The novel is about growing up in China in the 60's. It's . . . . the author's own experience.

2 Adjective + experience

Match the two halves of these sentences:

1. Training is provided, so
2. Studying at a university can be
3. John'll be late. I know from
4. How can you talk about poverty when you've had
5. The reason I didn't make it to the second stage of the interviews is that I lacked
6. The diving course involves a one-hour lecture and

a. the *necessary experience* **for the job.**
b. *past experience* **that you can't rely on him.**
c. *two hours' practical experience* **in the swimming pool.**
d. *a rich and rewarding experience.*
e. *no previous experience* **is required for the job.**
f. *no direct experience* **of it?**

3 Noun expressions

Match the two halves of these sentences:

1. They won't consider him for the job because of
2. He's worked in a number of different areas so
3. We'll meet to review the proposed plans
4. Dealing with problems in the classroom is all

a. *in the light of past experience.*
b. *a matter of experience.*
c. *his lack of experience.*
d. *his breadth of experience makes him ideal for the job.*

4 Common adjective collocations

We also use the word *experience* to describe the effect something has on us. Fill the gaps below with the following adjectives:

bitter	satisfying	traumatic

1. The death of a close relative is a . . . . experience, often leaving people emotionally drained.

2. We learned through . . . . experience that you can't trust Brian. He's let us down too many times.

3. McEnroe had the . . . . experience of finally beating his old rival, Borg, in the final.

exhilarating	fascinating
memorable	formative

4. Nobody in the family will ever forget the trip to our grandfather's birthplace. It was a . . . . experience.

5. Living in Central Africa was a . . . . experience. There was always something new and interesting to see or do.

6. Going abroad on a school trip can be a very . . . . experience for some children.

7. For most people a parachute jump is an . . . . and unforgettable experience.

Notes

1. In 2-3 'first-hand' is also possible.
   In 2-4 'personal' is also possible.

2. Note the prepositions that follow *experience*:
   have experience of teaching
   have experience with children
   have experience as a teacher

3. We use the expression 'in my experience' very often at the beginning of what we want to say:
   In my experience, this kind of skin rash will disappear in a day or two.

4. If we do something very exciting – for example, going up in a hot air balloon – we can say:
   That was quite an experience!

5. If you have a bad experience – for example, you lend money to a friend and they don't re-pay you, you can say:
   I suppose I should just put it down to experience!

explanation

1 Verb + explanation

Use the correct form of these verbs:

defy	demand	give
hear	owe	think of

1. I heard you coming in at five o'clock this morning. You said you would be home by midnight. I'm waiting to . . . . your explanation.

2. The instructor . . . . us a very clear explanation of how the machine worked. It was very easy to follow.

3. This is the second time you've failed to attend the meeting. I think you . . . . us all an explanation.

4. No wonder you're angry! If Gwen was paid to produce the report by last Friday, I think you can . . . . an explanation from her as to why nothing has appeared.

5. Nobody can understand why the Prime Minister has given the job to one of his best friends. It's a strange decision that . . . . explanation.

6. I can't . . . . an explanation for Pete's bad behaviour. He's usually so well-behaved.

2 Common adjective collocations

Complete the sentences with these adjectives:

no apparent	convincing
a very detailed	an immediate
the most likely	logical
any other possible	

1. I'm sorry I'm late. The manager insisted on going into . . . . explanation of every aspect of the job and I just couldn't get away.

2. . . . . explanation for Steve's absence is that his plane has been delayed.
   > Yes, I can't think of . . . . explanation.

3. When I caught my oldest son trying on my best dress, I demanded . . . . explanation! He said he was going to a fancy-dress party!

4. There seems to be . . . . explanation for the attack. It's beginning to look like an act of mindless violence.

5. That's not a very . . . . explanation. I'll believe you, but thousands wouldn't!

6. Our dog has been acting strangely lately, but there's probably some perfectly . . . . explanation for its odd behaviour.

3 Noun + of + explanation

Use these words to complete the sentences:

some sort of	by way of	a word of

1. His first wife just left without . . . . explanation. One day she was there; the next she had gone!

2. I told the policeman – . . . . explanation – that I hadn't seen the speed limit sign. He just laughed and booked me!

3. There must be . . . . explanation for John's sudden resignation. It's just come out of the blue!

4 More common expressions

Match the two halves of these sentences:

1. Can you just give us a quick explanation of
2. There are lots of possible explanations
3. The official explanation for the crash blames
4. The only explanation I can think of is
5. The generally accepted explanation of the disaster

a. that he's lost his memory.
b. is human error.
c. how the system works?
d. the driver of the London-bound train.
e. why girls do better at school than boys.

"There's probably some perfectly logical explanation!"

Notes

1. Note the different verbs:
   He didn't offer any explanation for his late arrival.
   The director went into a long explanation.
   Nobody could come up with an explanation.

2. Note this expression:
   He gave no explanation as to why he wasn't there.

3. If an explanation is 'far-fetched' or 'not very plausible', it is difficult to believe.

---

facts

1 Verb + facts

Use the correct form of these verbs:

be based on	*check*
distort	*give*
retain	*stick to*

1. My brother has a good memory and finds it easy to . . . . facts. I'm the opposite. I forget things easily.

2. You'll find everything you need to know about us in this booklet. It . . . . you all the basic facts and figures about the company.

3. Professional journalists should always take the trouble to . . . . their facts before writing a story. Mistakes can be costly.

4. Don't give us your opinion or tell us who you think is responsible. Just . . . . the facts. That's all we need to know at the moment.

5. Newspapers are often accused of . . . . the facts. No wonder many people don't believe what they read these days.

6. Many of Shakespeare's plays such as *Macbeth* and *Julius Caesar* are . . . . historical facts.

2 Common adjective collocations

Complete the sentences with these adjectives:

disturbing	*hard*
interesting	*necessary*
useless	*well-known*

1. Don't fill your head with . . . . facts. Make sure you learn things that can help you get on in life and get a decent job.

2. The book is full of . . . . facts about the British Royal Family. For example, did you know they had to change their name?

3. Our sales manager, Mr Thompson, will be able to help you. He has all the . . . . facts and figures at his fingertips.

4. It's a . . . . fact that boys develop later than girls.

5. The police will have to support their case with . . . . facts if they are to prove that Manson was the killer.

6. The newspaper claims to have unearthed some . . . . facts about the way the government is wasting taxpayers' money.

3 Expressions with prepositions

Use a suitable preposition to complete the sentences:

1. The fact . . . . the matter is we can't afford a new car at the moment.

2. I thought the course would be difficult, but . . . . actual fact, it was quite easy.

3. I know . . . . a fact that she hasn't paid the bill.

4. No, I'm not leaving. As a matter . . . . fact, I'll be here for another three weeks.

5. Lucy was delighted she'd got the job in Singapore – apart . . . . the fact she'd have to leave her dog behind in the UK.

6. It took me two years to get a decent job, ... the fact I got a first-class degree!

4 Common expressions

Complete the sentences with these expressions:

the facts of life	*get your facts right*
a statement of fact	*face the facts*

1. Before you start blaming us, you should . . . .

2. Come on, Sue! . . . . ! You're not as young as you used to be.

3. My parents made sure I knew . . . . before I was ten.

4. The government is totally corrupt! Is this . . . . or just another one of your crazy ideas?

Notes

1. Note the following expressions:
   How do you account for the fact that crime is actually falling for the first time for years?
   I resent the fact that some people get better medical care because they have money.
   She's finding it hard to accept the fact that her husband has left her.
   The book contained some interesting facts and figures about the Space Shuttle.

2. 'A fact of life' is a negative situation that must be accepted:
   Unemployment seems to be a fact of life nowadays.

3. 'The facts of life' explain where babies come from!

failure

1 Verb + failure

Use the correct form of these verbs:

> admit   put (...) down to
> blame   criticise
> end in   feel

1. I . . . . such a failure! That's the third time I've tried to pass my driving test.

2. The government has been widely . . . . for its failure to cut hospital waiting lists.

3. The attempt to climb K2 without oxygen . . . . failure. The climbers had to turn back when they were only three hundred metres from the summit.

4. The easy way out is to . . . . others for our failures. We should all face up to our own shortcomings.

5. Men are often too proud to . . . . failure and ask for help.

6. He . . . . the failure of his business . . . . bad luck, not bad management.

2 Adjective collocations

We use a number of adjectives to emphasise failure. Match the two halves of these situations:

1. The office block had cost millions, but nobody was interested in renting offices so far from the city centre.

2. My older brother always did brilliantly at school and university,

3. The hospital simply wouldn't listen to what we had to say about the treatment of our baby.

4. After three hours of heated discussion, we had got nowhere, so we all went home.

5. It used to be that if you hadn't got married by the age of twenty-five,

6. The scheme to recruit more business people into teaching never got off the ground.

a. *you were considered* a total failure *as a woman.*

b. *It was* a complete failure. *The pay simply wasn't high enough to attract them.*

c. *The meeting had been* a dismal failure.

d. *We were frustrated by* their total failure *to understand the nature of our complaint.*

e. *The whole enterprise was* a costly failure.

f. *so, although I did quite well, I always felt a* comparative failure.

3 Noun + of + failure

Use these nouns in the following sentences:

> risk   sense   catalogue   history   fear

1. The health service in this country has a long . . . . of failure.

2. . . . . of failure is one of the main reasons many students don't perform in examinations to the best of their ability.

3. I have to admit there is a slight . . . . of failure with this type of operation. It's only about 5%, but it's still a risk.

4. Sir Michael's time as Minister has just been one long . . . . of failures.

5. It's very important not to give children a . . . . of failure.

4 Noun + failure

Complete the sentences below with these nouns:

> business   heart   power   crop

1. A series of . . . . failures has led to widespread famine.

2. It was a . . . . failure which plunged the town into darkness last night.

3. She died of . . . . failure.

4. The decline in the economy led to an increase in . . . . failures of over 50% last year.

Notes

1. In 1-3 'resulted in' is also possible.

2. Note the underlined expressions:
   The attempt to save the men trapped on board the submarine was doomed to failure right from the start. Frank is still coming to terms with the failure of his marriage.

3. Accidents are often caused by 'mechanical failure' of some kind:
   The official report on the rail crash blamed mechanical failure as the main cause of the accident.

4. Note the preposition in this expression:
   My father was a complete failure as a salesman.

fight

1 Verb + fight

Use the correct form of these verbs:

be engaged in   carry on   give up
lose   put up   step up

1. Workers at Ford's lorry plant are determined to . . . . a fight to save their jobs.

2. More money has been promised to help scientists to . . . . the fight to find a cure for AIDS.

3. In response to public pressure, the government has promised to . . . . the fight against drugs.

4. My company . . . . a bitter fight with the local council, who are refusing us planning permission for a new factory.

5. Although jailed for twenty years by the military government, he refuses to . . . . his fight for freedom of speech.

6. If you ask me, the police seem to be . . . . the fight against crime.

2 Common adjective collocations

Use these adjectives to complete the sentences:

brave   easy   fair   good   tough

1. I'm not surprised we lost. Fairford United were a much better side, but we managed to put up a . . . . fight.

2. It won't be an . . . . fight. The government will have to work hard to convince people that this change to the law is in their interests.

3. The new director has got a . . . . fight on his hands. I'm not sure it was a good idea to take on the union. I can't see them accepting the new working conditions that he wants.

4. Sue died after a . . . . fight against breast cancer.

5. I don't know what he's complaining about. It was a . . . . fight. The referee couldn't have been fairer.

3 Expressions with prepositions

Use these prepositions in the sentences:

for   over   against   with   to

1. It'll be a fight . . . . . . the bitter end.
2. Hurry up! We're in a fight . . . . . . time.
3. They had a fight . . . . . . who should drive.
4. He was in a fight . . . . . . an older boy.
5. The fight . . . . . . the gold medal will be interesting!

4 Focus on word grammar

Match the two halves of these sentences:

1. This new drug could be a major breakthrough in the fight
2. As citizens we all have a part to play in the fight
3. He believes he's innocent and he's continuing the fight
4. Union president, Harry Muldon, is leading the fight
5. The church has played a big part in the fight

a. *to clear his name.*
b. *for the rights of the unborn child.*
c. *to stop compulsory redundancies.*
d. *against MS.*
f. *against crime.*

Note the patterns: fight for/against + noun
**   fight to + verb**

"It looks like a fight to the bitter end!"

Notes

1. Note the expressions with 'fight':

   A motorcyclist lost his fight for life after being critically injured in a collision with a bus.
   Only one company can succeed. It will be a real fight to the death.

2. A fight can also be a physical struggle:

   A fight broke out between rival groups of football fans. Police were on the scene in minutes and broke up the fight before it escalated into a riot.
   He put up a real fight when the police arrested him.
   My son is always getting into fights.

3. Note how we say that something is going to be difficult:
   You'll have a fight on your hands to get your ideas past the board.

freedom

1 Verb + freedom

Use the correct form of these verbs:

allow	enjoy
fight for	give up
restrict	value

1. We don't believe in . . . . our son's freedom in any way. We think he should be allowed to do exactly what he wants to do.
2. On the one hand, many young couples would love to have kids, but on the other hand, they don't want to . . . . their freedom.
3. If teachers don't . . . . their students the freedom to express themselves, they will never learn to think for themselves.
4. Freedom of speech is a freedom worth . . . . Why governments want to curb people's freedom of speech is beyond me.
5. I . . . . my freedom above everything else. It's far more important to me than money or success.
6. There is little censorship in the UK so the newspapers . . . . considerable freedom to publish what they want.

2 Common adjective collocations

Complete the sentences with these adjectives:

complete	fundamental
greater	hard-won
new-found	artistic

1. We now take for granted that we can say what we think. It's a . . . . freedom in all modern societies.
2. My parents gave me . . . . freedom to do whatever I liked when I was a teenager.
3. The new regulations will at last give hospitals and schools . . . . freedom to decide how to spend their own money.
4. Her two children have gone off to university and she says she's enjoying her . . . . freedom.
5. We will not let this government take away the . . . . freedoms that our grandparents fought and died for.
6. A lot of writers and painters feel they have to go abroad to find the kind of . . . . freedom they need to express themselves fully.

3 Noun + preposition + freedom

Complete the sentences below with the following nouns:

bid	land	sense
struggle	symbol	taste

1. After 25 years in prison, it was his first . . . . of freedom.
2. Over the centuries, many refugees considered America to be a . . . . of freedom and opportunity.
3. I feel such a . . . . of freedom when I leave the crowded city and climb alone in the hills.
4. The aid workers were killed when they made a desperate . . . . for freedom from their captors.
5. The car is often seen as the . . . . of personal freedom.
6. It's difficult to believe, but the . . . . for freedom is still going on in many countries today.

4 Freedom + of + noun

Complete the sentences below with these nouns:

choice	individual	movement
press	speech	

1. Our students are allowed freedom of . . . . over what to wear to school. There's no official school uniform.
2. This law will restrict the freedom of the . . . . to publish details about people's private lives.
3. It's a good idea to wear loose clothing to the yoga class. It gives you greater freedom of . . . .
4. Freedom of . . . . is guaranteed by our constitution. People can say what they think.
5. The freedom of the . . . . must always be balanced against the rights of the community. People can't always do what they would like to do.

Notes

1. In 2-1 'basic' is also possible.
2. As well as talking about the freedom 'to do' something, we also talk about freedom 'from' something, for example, 'freedom from oppression'.

---

help

1 Verb + help

Use the correct form of these verbs:

ask for	appreciate
offer	get
seek	use
need	provide

1. Thanks for everything you've done for my parents. They really . . . . all your help.

2. My car broke down in the city centre and I tried to push it to the side of the road. There were lots of people standing watching, and not one of them . . . . any help whatsoever.

3. Do you need any help with the cooking?
   > No, but I could . . . . some help with the washing up if you're not too busy.

4. I wouldn't normally . . . . your help, but the fact is I'm desperate. Could I use your phone? Ours is out of order and I don't have a mobile.

5. Look! That old lady has collapsed. Go and . . . . help. There's a policeman over there.

6. Initially he turned to his family for help in dealing with his depression, but he was eventually forced to . . . . psychiatric help.

7. In the current emergency, we . . . . all the help we can get.

8. The Samaritans are an organisation which . . . . telephone help to people who are suicidal.

2 Common adjective collocations

Use the following adjectives in these sentences:

extra	great	invaluable
financial	professional	individual

1. My mother was a . . . . help to me while my wife was in hospital having our third child.

2. We received . . . . help from many people while writing this book. We couldn't have completed it without their contributions.

3. If you suffer from depression, it's best to get . . . . help. First, talk to your doctor.

4. I passed my mathematics exam, thanks to the . . . . help my dad gave me in the evenings.

5. Most teachers simply don't have the time to give some students the . . . . help they need.

6. A lot of older people do without things rather than ask for . . . . help.

3 Ways of asking for help

Match the two halves of these sentences:

1. It is a well-known fact that
2. We were surprised by the number of volunteers who responded to
3. We are grateful to all those parents who answered
4. A five-year-old girl has gone missing. Her parents have made

a. *our appeal for help* with disabled children.
b. *a desperate plea to the public for help* in finding her.
c. *a suicide attempt is often* a cry for help.
d. *our call for help* in raising funds for the school.

4 Expressions with prepositions

Match the two halves of the sentences:

1. The survivors of the earthquake are
2. Our confidential telephone lines are
3. These flowers are
4. It's now three days since the disaster struck and

a. *a token of my appreciation for all your help.*
b. *in dire need of help.* The government must get food and medicine to them quickly.
c. *offers of help* are flowing in from all over the world.
d. *a tremendous source of help* to those people who are depressed and lonely.

Notes

1. Note the expression 'to manage something with the help of':
   I managed to make myself understood with the help of my Spanish phrase book.

2. Note this common expression:
   The map he drew wasn't much help. I still got lost!
   Come on! You're not much help!

3. Note how we offer to help:
   Let me know if I can be of any help to you.
   Would you like some help with the washing up?

4. Note the more formal collocation:
   The CID enlisted the help of a graphologist, an expert on handwriting.

5. In the UK a 'home help' is somebody who helps the elderly or disabled with their housework.

6. A 'helpline' is a telephone number you can ring for advice or information.

hope

1 Verb + hope

Use the correct form of these verbs:

abandon	*cling to*
give	*raise*
hold out	*offer*
pin (hope) on	*have*

1. My strong belief in God . . . . me hope during those difficult times and helped me to remain positive.

2. Rescuers have given up hope of finding any survivors. They have . . . . all hope of finding anybody alive inside the collapsed building.

3. You shouldn't . . . . all your hopes . . . . . . getting this job. Apply for other positions as well.

4. With so many people wanting to see the concert, I don't . . . . much hope of getting a ticket at this late stage.

5. Without work, most of these young people . . . . . . no hope for the future.

6. The new information which has come in from tribesmen in the north of the country . . . . hope that the hostages are still alive.

7. This new treatment for cancer . . . . hope to thousands of patients worldwide. It's not a wonder-cure, but it is a step in the right direction.

8. My sister still . . . . the hope that one day her long-lost son will walk through the door – even though she hasn't heard from him for over 20 years.

2 Destroying hopes

Match the two halves of these sentences:

1. Hopes of an economic recovery
2. I failed a vital exam so all my hopes of
3. A knee injury
4. Hopes of finding the missing child
5. Our hopes of holding the birthday party outside
6. Last night's defeat by Liverpool

a. *becoming* a doctor were *quashed.*
b. *are fading* fast.
c. *have been dashed* by the sharp rise in the price of oil.
d. *ended* Arsenal's hopes of *playing* in Europe next season.
e. *ruined* my hopes of success in the tournament.
f. *were defeated* by the weather.

Notice the verbs in colour.

3 Common adjective collocations

Use these adjectives to complete the sentences:

faint	*false*	*high*
new	*only*	*best*

1. She has . . . . hopes for her children – one is planning to be a lawyer and the other a doctor.

2. All our hopes rest with you. Nobody else can help us. You're our . . . . hope.

3. Scientists have developed a revolutionary drug which may give . . . . hope to the millions of people who suffer from hay-fever.

4. Power-sharing between the two warring factions offers the country its . . . . hope for a peaceful outcome.

5. Don't lose hope. There is still a . . . . hope that he may recover from his injuries.

6. I don't want to raise any . . . . hopes, but I do still believe your son is alive and well.

"This injury has ruined my hopes of playing in the final."

Notes

1. 'In the hope of' is a useful expression:
   I moved to London in the hope of finding work.

2. Note how we tell somebody to be realistic:
   Don't get your hopes up. There are 50 people after the same job!

3. 'Live in hope' means we are optimistic:
   Pete's 37 and not married yet, but we live in hope!

4. Note these expressions:
   There is little hope of any improvement.
   Our only hope was to get Lee to a hospital fast.

5. 'A glimmer of hope' is a small amount of hope:
   A liver transplant offers him a new glimmer of hope.

6. If something is 'beyond all hope', it won't improve:
   The political situation is now beyond all hope.

idea

1 Verb + idea

Use the correct form of these verbs:

consider   *come up with*   *get across*
reject   *go along with*   *sell*

1. He's a really good speaker. He has that rare ability to . . . . complex ideas in the kind of language everybody can understand.

2. We've been . . . . the idea of moving to a smaller flat now that the children have left home. We've actually been toying with the idea for a year or so.

3. The committee needs to . . . . some ideas for raising funds for the new church. Does anybody have any good ideas?

4. She's always . . . . the idea of getting married. She says she prefers the freedom of being single.

5. I think my proposal would help improve the company, but I'm having a lot of trouble . . . . the idea to my boss. He's not convinced that it would work.

6. She'll never . . . . the idea, so it's not worth mentioning it to her.

2 Liking and disliking ideas

Study the seven expressions in colour:

1. I want to become a racing driver but my father is dead against the idea.

2. She has an open mind and she is always receptive to new ideas.

3. In the UK there is a lot of resistance to the idea of a common currency. Many people remain bitterly opposed to this idea.

4. I'm not wild about the idea of going to boarding school, but I have no choice in the matter.

5. On the whole, I'm in favour of the idea. >Yes. We're also sold on the idea. We think it can only improve the quality of the service.

6. Some politicians were extremely hostile to the idea of giving free needles to drug addicts.

Now fill in the prepositions. Then mark them: (L) = like or (D) = dislike:

a. dead . . . . . .
b. receptive . . . . . .
c. a lot of resistance . . . . . .
d. bitterly opposed . . . . . .
e. not wild . . . . . .
f. in favour . . . . . .
g. sold . . . . . .
h. hostile . . . . . .

3 Common adjective collocations

Use these adjectives in the sentences below:

brilliant   *faintest*
half-baked   *fixed*
funny   *original*
vague   *fair*

1. The company is looking for a creative person with fresh and . . . . ideas.

2. You'll never get my mother to change her mind on anything! She has very . . . . ideas on almost every subject.

3. What a . . . . idea! Why didn't I think of that! How do you always manage to come up with the bright ideas?

4. He's got some strange ideas on bringing up kids. >Yes, Frank does have some . . . . ideas at times, doesn't he?

5. I think I've got a . . . . idea of what to do, but I'll get back to you if I have any problems.

6. I haven't the . . . . idea what you're talking about. I don't know anything about your missing bag!

7. I wish they would tell me what I'm meant to be doing in more detail. At the moment I only have a very . . . . idea what my job is.

8. I wish Terry would work out his ideas properly. He keeps coming up with . . . . ideas – which nobody takes seriously.

Notes

1. In 3-6 'foggiest' is also possible.

2. 'A rough idea' is not precise.
   Can you give me a rough idea of the cost involved?

3. Note the verbs in the following expressions:
   Don't worry. You'll soon get the idea how this program works. It's very user-friendly.
   Fiona is very enthusiastic and is always bursting with ideas.
   I got the idea from an article in a magazine.

4. Note these collocations using 'have':
   You must have some idea of who did this!
   I have no idea where Lucan has gone.

5. Note the following expression:
   Sitting in the rain watching two men hit a ball for hours is not my idea of fun.

image

1 Verb + image (how others see us)

Use the correct form of these verbs:

change	create	improve
shed	tarnish	project

1. Millions have been spent on advertising in an effort to . . . . a sexy image for the new perfume from Chanel.

2. Since winning the gold medal at the Olympic Games, his image has been . . . . by accusations of drug use which he hotly denies.

3. Many businesses hire public relations consultants to help them . . . . their image in the market place.

4. Getting a totally new hair-do is the way most women try to . . . . their image.

5. Eastbourne on the south coast of England is trying hard to . . . . the dull image the public have of it and promote itself as an attractive seaside resort.

6. Sometimes it's difficult to find out what pop idols and filmstars are really like – all you ever see is the image they . . . . on the screen.

2 Common adjective collocations

Use these adjectives to complete the sentences:

clean	new	right
public	stereotyped	staid and stuffy

1. The police in the UK are often accused of having a . . . . image of black people and other ethnic minorities.

2. I changed my hairstyle and replaced my entire wardrobe in order to create a . . . . and younger image.

3. Like most politicians, the prime minister's . . . . image is very different from the person underneath.

4. Museums are trying hard to shed their . . . . image and become more interesting and attractive to young people.

5. There is no doubt that recent events have damaged the . . . . image that the President has successfully cultivated over the years.

6. Today all political parties have to project the . . . . image if they are going to attract the female vote.

3 Verb + image (picture)

Use the correct form of these verbs:

appear	blot out	capture
conjure up	produce	project

1. Some horrific images of war were . . . . by TV crews filming on the battlefield.

2. Slowly, a blurred image began to . . . . on the screen. Man had landed on Mars.

3. I've tried to . . . . the image of my mother's sad face, but it just keeps coming back to me.

4. The Hubble telescope . . . . sharper images of stars than those of any telescope on earth.

5. For many people, the word 'tropical' . . . . images of palm trees and deserted beaches.

6. A giant image of Madonna was . . . . onto a huge screen above the stage. Her fans went wild.

"Yes, Mum, it IS a new image, but is it younger?"

Notes

1. In 1-3 'promote' is also possible.
   In 1-5 'shake off' is also possible.

2. This expression means 'identical':
   William is the spitting image of his father.

3. Things can be 'bad for your image':
   Daly's advisers said it would be bad for his image to be photographed with the protesters.

4. Note the expression 'fit (somebody's) image of something':
   Wearing jeans and no tie, Mr Jones hardly fits most people's image of a headmaster!

5. Note the expression 'part of somebody's image':
   I don't need glasses – they're just part of my image.

impact

1 Verb + impact (effect)

Use the correct form of these verbs:

assess	feel	have
lose	make	minimise

1. Internet shopping is beginning to . . . . a serious impact on the traditional bookshops.
2. Henman was one of the first British tennis players for years to . . . . a real impact on the world of tennis.
3. The authorities are doing everything within their power to . . . . the environmental impact of the oil spill.
4. It will be very difficult to . . . . the likely impact of allowing twice as many students to have access to a university education.
5. During the 1980s, the industrial north of the country . . . . the full impact of the economic recession.
6. When the Berlin Wall came down and the former Eastern Bloc countries opened up, the campaign for nuclear disarmament . . . . much of its impact.

2 Common adjective collocations

Choose the more natural collocation from the pair in brackets:

1. *Lady Chatterley's Lover* is an important book because it has had a . . . . impact on public opinion in Britain since it was published. *(major / large)*
2. Some politicians are worried that tougher environmental laws could have a . . . . impact on the economy. *(poor / detrimental)*
3. Has the experience of being in prison had a . . . . impact on you or have you just put it behind you? *(long-term / lasting)*
4. The recent ban on cigarette advertising has had a(n) . . . . impact on the number of teenagers smoking. *(recent / immediate)*
5. Management aren't worried about the strike. They are convinced that it will only have a . . . . impact on business. *(tiny / negligible)*
6. Scientists are discussing ways of reducing the . . . . impact of wind farms on the landscape.
(visual / visible)

7. Going to the theatre for the first time as a small boy made a . . . . impact on me. *(huge / severe)*
8. We didn't know the . . . . impact of the disaster at Chernobyl until years after it happened. *(complete / full)*

3 Impact (collision)

Use the correct form of these verbs:

absorb	survive	take	withstand

1. The crew . . . . the initial impact of the crash, but died in the fire which followed.
2. Good running-shoes prevent injury by . . . . the impact of the foot striking the ground.
3. Containers carrying nuclear waste are designed to . . . . an impact with a speeding train without breaking open.
4. Many of the dead were in the first coach of the train which . . . . the full impact of the crash.

"I like it! I like it! This is definitely going to reduce the impact on the environment!"

Notes

1. In 2-1 'significant, huge and profound' are also possible.
   In 1-3 'cushion' is also possible.

2. Note the following prepositional phrase:
   The bomb exploded on impact – nobody stood a chance.

3. Note the expression 'the force of the impact':
   The force of the impact knocked me to the ground.

---

impression

1 Verb + impression

Choose the correct verb in each sentence:

1. When I was introduced to Jill, I did my best to be friendly, but I . . . . the impression that she just wanted to be left alone. *(got / gave)*

2. It's important to . . . . a good impression when you meet a new customer. *(get / create)*

3. During the interview, I watched and listened to the candidate and I . . . . the impression that she didn't really want the job. *(formed / faced)*

4. Don't get me wrong, but I . . . . the impression that you're finding the class a bit easy. *(have / feel)*

5. Remember that it . . . . a bad impression if you're late for an interview. *(makes / gets)*

6. We had a lovely meal with the Blairs, but we both . . . . the impression that all was not well with their relationship. *(gave away / came away with)*

7. You're . . . . the impression that you don't really like being here. *(getting / giving)*

8. I really want to . . . . the right impression when I meet your aunt. What shall I wear? *(get / convey)*

Go back and underline the verb collocations.

2 Common adjective expressions

Use the correct adjective in these sentences:

distinct	favourable
general	initial
lasting	strong
wrong	right

1. My first impression of Istanbul was very . . . . I took an instant liking to it.

2. The best schoolteachers usually make a . . . . impression on their students, who remember them all their lives.

3. Look, you really must get your hair cut. You don't want to give the . . . . impression on your first day in the new job, do you?

4. What were your first impressions of the school? > My . . . . impressions were very positive.

5. In job interviews, successful candidates tend to be the people who know exactly how to make the . . . . impression very quickly.

6. Travelling through the Amazon rainforests made a deep impression on me. It also made a . . . . impression on my wife.

7. As I walked along the dark lane, I couldn't see anybody, but I had the . . . . impression I was being watched.

8. The . . . . or overall impression she gave was one of kindness and generosity.

3 Positive and negative impressions

Match the two halves of the sentences.
Negative impressions:

1. Don't take your visitors anywhere there are beggars. You don't want to give them

2. The way they are always laughing gives

3. If you only visit the university, you'll get

4. So they're only friends! I was under

5. The film gave the very misleading impression

a. the mistaken impression that they were married.

b. a wrong impression. The town isn't really very nice.

c. a misleading impression of their relationship. They're actually a very unhappy couple.

d. that Glasgow is a very violent city.

e. a false impression of the city.

Positive impressions:

6. The kids' performance gave an excellent impression

7. Monet's paintings give a tremendous impression

8. Meeting the President made a great impression

a. of the youth of today.

b. on me.

c. of light and sky.

Notes

1. In 3-4 'be under the impression' means to believe that something is true when it is not:
   I'm sorry, I was under the impression that you were Wendy's father.
   She's under the impression that I have a lot of money. I just don't know where she got that idea!

2. Note how we ask for an opinion:
   What's your impression of Mr Acton as a manager?

3. Note that 'impression' also means to copy somebody's voice or behaviour:
   He does a good impression of George Bush.
   You should hear his impression of Hugh Grant!

4. When they don't have a photograph, the police often issue 'artist's impressions' of criminals, based on descriptions by witnesses.

improvement

1 Verb + improvement

Use the correct form of these verbs:

> be   bring about
>
> make   notice
>
> show   suggest

1. It's about 30 years since I was in the British Museum. I've . . . . a lot of improvements. It's a much more exciting place now.

2. Isn't it great that John's teachers said that his work has . . . . steady improvement throughout the year!

3. I know a lot of improvements have been . . . . to our computer system since it was first installed. If anyone can think of any more, please don't hesitate to let me know.

4. Major spending is required to . . . . much-needed improvements in the health service.

5. Could you read over my essay and . . . . any improvements before I hand it in?

6. There has . . . . a gradual improvement in living standards over the past decade.

2 Common adjective expressions

Match the two halves to make sentences:

1. If we want people to use their cars less,
2. Despite the new sewage treatment plant,
3. The last six months
4. A few months after I stopped smoking
5. If you follow this exercise programme for a month,
6. Teachers' salaries are going up by 20%
7. Since Marco started going to evening classes
8. I'm glad you've re-written this essay –
9. Thanks to the doctors and nurses in the intensive-care department

a. I saw *a huge improvement* in my health.

b. so we can only afford *minor improvements* to school buildings.

c. it's *a vast improvement* on your first attempt.

d. there has been *a marked improvement* in his English.

e. we need *substantial improvements* in public transport.

f. you'll see *an enormous improvement* in your stamina.

g. have seen *a slight improvement* in the economy.

h. there's been *a remarkable improvement* in Bill's condition.

i. there has only been *a marginal improvement* in the quality of water on our beaches.

3 Large and small improvements

Use the nine adjectives in exercise 2 and the following to make a list of adjectives meaning 'large' and 'small', which can be used with *improvement*:

> considerable   massive   modest   minor
>
> significant   sharp   radical   real

1. Small: . . . .

   . . . .

2. Large: . . . .

   . . . .

4 Expressions with prepositions

Use these nouns to complete the sentences:

> areas   cost   number
>
> prospect   signs   room

1. My teacher said my work was satisfactory, but there was still . . . . for improvement.

2. The consultant's report highlights several . . . . for improvement within the company.

3. The economy is continuing to show . . . . of improvement.

4. Sadly, the doctors say there is little . . . . of any improvement in my aunt's condition.

5. Due to unforeseen circumstances the . . . . of the improvements has risen by fifty per cent.

6. The new car incorporates a . . . . of major improvements making it one of the safest to drive.

Look back at all the exercises in this unit and underline all the collocations.

Notes

1. Notice how we can use 'improvement on' to compare two performances:
   Her time today in the 200 metres was a big improvement on her performance in the Olympics.
   The band's performance tonight was a huge improvement on last night's disaster.

2. Notice this common expression:
   It will be some time before we see any improvement in Sheila's condition.

incident

1 Verb + incident

Use the correct form of these verbs:

highlight   *investigate*
occur   *cause*
report   *witness*

1. There was a serious accident in the middle of town last night. The police have appealed for anyone who . . . . the incident to come forward.
2. I saw some older boys bullying one of the first-year students. I felt I had to . . . . the incident to the headmaster.
3. A number of windows in our church were smashed at the weekend. The police are . . . . the incident.
4. Somebody walked out of the building yesterday with two of our computers. This incident . . . . our need to improve our security system.
5. A man was shot dead in the city centre last night. The incident . . . . outside the Crown Hotel around three o'clock in the morning.
6. A French jet flew into Russian airspace and . . . . a major diplomatic incident.

2 Noun + preposition

Use these nouns in the sentences below:

account of   *investigation into*
knowledge of   *reports of*
seriousness of   *wake of*

1. There have been . . . . an incident at the airport. The police are already at the scene.
2. Police said there would be a full and thorough . . . . the incident.
3. Relations between the countries are strained in the . . . . the latest cross-border incident.
4. When she was accused of starting the fire, she denied all . . . . the incident.
5. I gave the police a full and exhaustive . . . . the incident in the underground.
6. Some of the older pupils were found with drugs. The headmaster has tried to play down the . . . . the incident to save the reputation of the school.

Go back and underline the noun + preposition + *incident* expressions.

3 Common adjective collocations

Choose the most natural collocation from the pair in brackets:

1. The yacht sank after it hit the pier. A tourist with a video camera caught the . . . . incident on film. *(full / whole)*
2. What do you remember most about your days in the army?
   >Well, apart from a lot of hard work, one . . . . incident sticks in my mind, but perhaps it is too unpleasant to talk about over dinner. *(single / particular)*
3. There was a very . . . . incident involving a group of youths outside a pub in London late last night in which a number of people were badly injured. *(severe / serious)*
4. We are sorry to hear that your money was stolen while you were a patient at this hospital. We are sure this was a(n) . . . . incident as this is the first complaint of this kind which we have received. I enclose a cheque for £20 to replace the money you lost. *(isolated / remote)*
5. News is coming in of a . . . . incident involving two passenger trains in the south of India. *(main / major)*
6. The army said that the recent shelling of civilians was a . . . . incident and they wish to assure people that it will not happen again.
   (regretted / regrettable)

Notes

1. Note the following expressions:
   Protesters threw eggs and tomatoes at the President, who was visibly shaken by the incident.
   Mugging is becoming a serious problem. There have been countless incidents in recent months.
   The alleged incident was said to have taken place in the office canteen.
   Quick thinking by the police in keeping rival fans apart averted a serious incident.

2. The expression 'without incident' means without any trouble:
   The demonstrators were well-behaved and the protest passed without incident.

---

influence

1 Common adjective collocations

Complete the sentences with these adjectives:

calming	corrupting
disruptive	outside
profound	pervasive
undue	positive

1. Our youngest son, Harry, can get very excited and a little wild at times, but his sister has a very . . . . influence on him.

2. I find it hard to teach when your daughter is in class. She has a . . . . influence on the rest of the students. Perhaps she should see someone about her behaviour.

3. Will's a bit depressed at the moment. I think he needs to mix with people who will have a more . . . . influence on his life.

4. Our mother didn't let us watch television when we were children. She believed it would have a . . . . influence on us.

5. Today you can't escape the . . . . influence of television. It's everywhere.

6. Of all the teachers I had at school, one sticks in my mind. He was amazing! He had a . . . . influence on everyone he taught.

7. International observers accused local politicians of interfering with the election by exerting . . . . influence on voters.

8. I think that decision-making in our hospitals and schools should be free from . . . . influence.

2 Expressions with prepositions

Match the two halves of these sentences:

1. The British were a major influence upon
2. If you have any influence with Joanne,
3. We have no influence over the children:
4. The driver of the bus involved in the accident was found to be under the influence of drugs
5. I have very little influence on

a. who will get the manager's job.
b. when he was tested back at the police station.
c. modern-day India and Pakistan.
d. they do as they please.
e. try to get her to change her mind and withdraw her resignation.

Go back and underline all the prepositions.

3 Verb + influence

Use the correct form of these verbs:

fall under	have	linger on
lose	use	be under

1. My father . . . . no influence whatsoever on my choice of career. He wanted me to go into banking!

2. Millie is no longer the quiet, well-behaved child she used to be. She has . . . . the influence of some older girls at school and now wants to go out clubbing all weekend – and she's only just 13!

3. My uncle's a judge. He hopes to exert his influence to make the planning department change their minds. It won't be the first time he has . . . . his influence in this way.

4. When the teenager was caught driving the stolen car, he was found to . . . . the influence of alcohol.

5. Religion in the West isn't the force it used to be. It's . . . . much of its influence.

6. Although Princess Diana died years ago, her influence still . . . . I think it will continue for many years to come.

"They have no influence over their children!"

Notes

1. In 3-2 'come under' is also possible.
   In 3-3 'exert' and 'exercise' are also possible.

2. Note the following ways of describing big influences:
   The church no longer has a strong political influence.
   The media has a powerful influence on public opinion.
   In your teens, your peer group usually takes over from your parents as the major influence on you.
   Professor Wilkins had a great influence on the shaping of the government's education policy.
   The Royal Family still exerts considerable influence.

information

1 Verb + information

Use the correct form of these verbs:

find   gather   provide
share   take in   withhold

1. Information about safety procedures on this Boeing 737 can be . . . . in the seat pocket in front of you. Please read it carefully.

2. I'm sure the *Rough Guide to Bangkok* will . . . . all the information you'll need.

3. I know this is a lot of information to . . . . all at once. You'll need time to absorb it all.

4. I've been to several libraries to . . . . information for my research project, but I still haven't collected enough.

5. I was arrested and charged with deliberately . . . . information from the police. How can I tell them it was my son who stole the car!

6. Conferences are excellent events for professional people like scientists and doctors to . . . . information and exchange ideas.

2 Common adjective collocations

Use these adjectives to complete the sentences:

confidential   further   misleading
reliable   latest   vital

1. All the details of your medical history will be treated as strictly . . . . information. No other organisation will have access to it.

2. Check that all the information on your form is correct before sending it in. You may be prosecuted if you give false or . . . . information.

3. Police want to trace the driver of a red car seen outside the bank yesterday afternoon around 3pm. They believe the driver might hold . . . . information which could help to catch the bank robbers.

4. We have . . . . information that a hijack attempt will be made on a British plane some time in the next week. As a result, security has been increased at all airports.

5. For . . . . information on any of our products, phone 0181 690 9368. Alternatively, consult our website for the . . . . information.

3 Noun + of + information

Use these nouns to complete the expressions:

access   amount   mine   piece   scrap

a. a tremendous . . . . of information
b. a very interesting . . . . of information
c. every . . . . of information
d. a constant . . . . of information
e. . . . . to the information

Now use these complete expressions below:

1. Here's . . . . ! The paper says that drinking green tea helps you to live longer.

2. The material about the Government's arms sales to Zimbabwe was classified, so we were denied . . . . we needed for our investigation.

3. My Gran knows so much about everything. She is . . . .

4. I'm really interested in keeping stick insects. I've read . . . . I can find on the subject.

5. You can store . . . . on a computer.

Notes

1. In 1-2 'contain' is also possible.

2. Note how we can say something has a lot of information:
   The book is packed with useful information.

3. Note the phrase 'for the information of':
   This announcement is for the information of those passengers who have connecting flights to the UK.

4. An 'information centre' is a place where you can get information or advice.

5. IT or 'information technology' is the use of computers for storing and using information. The internet is sometimes referred to as 'the information superhighway'.

6. Note these more formal ways of gathering information:
   Police have received information that the robbers may already have left the country.
   Weapons inspectors have obtained information on a possible burial site of weapons of mass destruction.

instructions

1 Verb + instructions

Use the correct form of these verbs:

follow   *hold on to*   *provide*
understand   *read through*   *repeat*

1. Always . . . . the instructions on medicines very carefully before taking them.

2. If you . . . . the step-by-step instructions in this leaflet, you will have no trouble assembling this latest innovative product from IKEA.

3. A comprehensive manual . . . . full instructions on how to set up this computer.

4. Always . . . . the instructions in case you have any problems in the future.

5. I can be a bit slow, so you will probably have to . . . . the instructions a few times!

6. If you don't . . . . my instructions, please let me know. We can't afford to have any accidents.

"Just follow the step-by-step instructions! They must be joking!"

2 Common adjective collocations

Match the two halves of these sentences:

1. This model plane kit comes with step-by-step instructions for assembly,

2. Detailed instructions are supplied with this product,

3. I find unnecessarily complicated instructions very irritating –

4. My grandfather left a set of specific instructions in

5. The first aid handbook provides clear and concise instructions

a. on what to do in an emergency.

b. why can't manufacturers write in plain English?

c. which are easy to understand and follow.

d. telling you clearly what to do at each stage of the process.

e. his will, outlining who was to get what after his death.

3 Types of instructions

Complete the sentences below with these words:

cooking   *manufacturer's*   *assembly*
payment   *safety*   *washing*

1. In order to build this table, follow the . . . . instructions in this leaflet.

2. To ensure that you get the best out of your new food processor, it is important to follow the . . . . instructions carefully.

3. Before using these fireworks, read the . . . . instructions contained in the accompanying booklet.

4. I think you'll find the . . . . instructions are on a label inside the jersey.

5. The . . . . instructions say 'bake the pie for 40 minutes at 200 C'.

6. To buy on-line using a credit card, click here and follow the . . . . instructions.

Notes

1. Note that *instruction* can also mean 'orders':
   She left strict instructions that she was not to be disturbed.
   He is acting on direct instructions from the President.
   The spy remained under cover and waited for further instructions from headquarters.
   Following the riots, armed soldiers have instructions to shoot looters on sight.

2. Note the following ways of saying you can't understand instructions:
   I've read the instructions, but I'm still none the wiser.
   I can't make head nor tail of these instructions.

3. Note how to say that you followed instructions very carefully:
   I followed your instructions to the letter, but the video still won't record.

4. 'Instruction' – singular – also means 'training':
   I'm going for some special instruction on driving on snow and ice.
   You are strongly advised to take a course of instruction before attempting to fly this hang-glider.
   The skiing instruction on our holiday was excellent. The instructor was brilliant!

5. Note how 'according to' is used:
   According to the instructions, you put this here, not there.

interest

1 Common adjective collocations

Complete the sentences with these adjectives:

main   *keen*   *passing*
real   *shared*   *unhealthy*

1. We looked at a number of brochures, but I could tell by her lack of enthusiasm that she had no . . . . interest in going on holiday with me.

2. We're more than a little worried by our son's . . . . interest in guns and death.

3. I have a wide range of interests but my . . . . interest is bird-watching.

4. When Jane and I first met, we discovered we had a number of . . . . interests – classical music, modern painting, and skiing.

5. No, my husband no longer collects stamps. It was only a . . . . interest.

6. During his visit, the Prince expressed a . . . . interest in seeing how chocolate was produced.

2 Verb + interest

Choose the correct verb in the following:

1. Half-way through this morning's grammar lesson, my interest began to sag. I began to . . . . interest. I'd heard it all before. *(lose / forget)*

2. Spielberg's latest film has . . . . a lot of interest. Everybody is talking about it. *(shown / aroused)*

3. What kind of father is Edward? He doesn't seem to . . . . much interest in his children. He never takes them out anywhere. *(show / hold)*

4. My wife and I . . . . an interest in gardening. We spend most of our free time either working in the garden or visiting gardens. *(hold / share)*

5. These days it takes a very good lecturer to . . . . the students' interest for an hour. *(hold / take)*

6. Teachers who . . . . a real interest in their students find that they get better results than teachers who just do their jobs and no more. *(take / get)*

Now match the two halves of these sentences:

7. Unlike her brother,
8. The use of child labour is an issue
9. Our youngest son, Jamie, is only 12,
10. I think last night's programme on Channel 4
11. Do you think it's right for parents
12. Why did so many teachers in the past

a. *which has* aroused a great deal of public interest.
b. *to* take an interest in *the children's friends?*
c. kill most students' interest in *their subjects?*
d. *Beth has never* expressed any interest *in sport.*
e. *but he seems to be* developing an interest in *girls.*
f. *has* created quite an interest in *the new electric car.*

3 Noun + of + interest

Complete the sentences below with these nouns:

lack   *site*   *places*
spark   *building*   *source*

1. You certainly won't be bored in Edinburgh. There are many . . . . of interest to visit.

2. My young children continue to fascinate me. They are a constant . . . . of interest.

3. The trip was cancelled due to . . . . .of interest. Only three tickets had been sold.

4. Despite our best efforts to get our children interested in classical music, they didn't show a single . . . . of interest!

5. The Pompidou Centre in Paris is a . . . . of huge architectural interest.

6. Just down the road from here is a . . . . of great historical interest. It was where one of the biggest battles between England and Scotland took place.

Notes

1. In 2-2 'generate' and 'attract' are also possible.
   In 2-3 'take' is also possible.

2. 'Outside interests' are interests not connected to your job.
   He has no outside interests. His work is his life.

3. If something is 'in the public interest', it means it is for the good of the people:
   The government believes it is in the public interest that these facts are made known.

4. Interests can also be advantages or benefits:
   The interests of local fishing communities must be protected.

5. Note these two common adjective expressions:
   I read your article with great interest.
   I took a keen interest in what he had to say.

issue

1 Verb + issue

Use the correct form of these verbs:

address   avoid
raise   resolve
care about

1. My mother has always voted for the Green Party. She . . . . very deeply . . . . environmental issues.

2. Our head of department is always side-stepping difficult issues. His normal tactic is to . . . . a lot of issues by saying they are not his responsibility.

3. I know you would like to bring up the issue of salaries, but I'd prefer it if you . . . . it at the next meeting.

4. If we don't . . . . this issue fairly quickly, we'll need to start paying people off.

5. There was hardly anything in the Prime Minister's reply. He never properly . . . . the issue of unemployment in the North East.

2 Verb + noun + on the issue

Notice these two common patterns:

1. verb   noun   on the issue
   reach   an agreement   on the issue of (jobs)

2. verb   on the issue
   clash   on the issue of (jobs)

Match the two halves of these situations:

1. I can't see us reaching any sort of agreement.
2. We can't give an opinion until we have more information.
3. The union will ballot the whole membership on the issue of job cuts.
4. I'm glad agreement has been reached.
5. The players and the management of the club are in disagreement.
6. We know little of his views at present.

a. *It was time everyone overcame their differences on the issue.*
b. *Opinion is so deeply divided on so many issues.*
c. *They've clashed on the issue of pay and conditions.*
d. *I think it's important that everyone gets a chance to vote on the issue.*
e. *For example, we don't know where he stands on the issue of free care for the elderly.*
f. *We're just going to reserve judgement on this issue until the report is published.*

3 Common adjective collocations

Complete the sentences with these adjectives:

complex   emotive   politically sensitive
pressing   real

1. Using animals to test new drugs is a highly . . . . issue.
   > Yes, it's the kind of controversial issue that arouses a lot of strong feelings and opinions.

2. It's not a question of whether we need a new office or not – we all know the present accommodation is unsatisfactory. The . . . . issue is whether we can afford it.

3. For me euthanasia is a black and white issue. It's wrong to take life and that's that!
   > Well, I disagree. It's a much more . . . . issue than you think.

4. None of the main political parties seems willing to talk about free health care for the elderly. I think it's one of the most . . . . issues facing us today.

5. The fight against drugs is regarded as a . . . . issue. We need to do something about this problem urgently if we are to prevent it getting out of control.

Use these adjectives in the sentences:

broad   good   growing   sound   wide

6. The President declared that his country had a very . . . . record on the issue of human rights.

7. The talks between the two leaders covered a . . . . range of issues.

8. Don't worry. The minister has a . . . . grasp of the issues involved.

9. The negotiators were in . . . . agreement on the main issues.

10. There is a . . . . consensus of opinion on this issue.

Notes

1. In 1-2 'duck' is also possible.
   In 3-1 'controversial' and 'contentious' are possible.
   In 3-2 'key' is also possible.

2. Note these expressions:
   Money is not the issue. (not the main thing)
   I must take issue with you. (object)

3. You 'make an issue of' something when you create an argument about something unimportant.

item

1 Adjective + item

Complete the sentences with these adjectives:

bulky   faulty   essential   important
main   next   missing   valuable

1. The police arrived soon after the break-in and asked us to do our best to make a list of all the . . . . items.

2. During the emergency, people stocked up on . . . . items like food and candles.

3. I think the . . . . item on the agenda for this afternoon's meeting is going to be the resignation of our secretary. I wonder why she's leaving.

4. Most modern hotels provide a safe in your room where you can keep . . . . items. For a small charge they will keep more expensive items in the hotel safe at Reception.

5. Please note that the most . . . . items are listed in bold type in the booklet.

6. Heavy and . . . . items are expensive to transport by air. That's why it's cheaper using surface post.

7. Now, let's move on to the . . . . item on the agenda.

8. Our policy is to replace . . . . items without question.

2 Expressions with nouns

Match the two halves of these sentences:

1. Most people today see their PC just like a television set,

2. All items for the agenda for our next meeting

3. I remember when a fridge was considered a luxury item,

4. Please note that this insurance policy doesn't cover you for loss or damage

5. Old clocks like this one have become collectors' items

6. Several items of clothing

a. to household items such as towels and bedding.
b. because they're becoming increasingly rare.
c. were found at the scene of the crime.
d. a consumer item just like anything else in their home.
e. but for most people today it's a necessity.
f. must be with me at least one week in advance.

Go back and underline the noun collocations.

3 Items as single things

Complete the sentences below with these words:

each   individual   ten
particular   single

1. Can I pay for . . . . item separately?

2. For many people their house is their largest . . . . item of expenditure.

3. That . . . . item is not for sale, I'm afraid.

4. . . . . items of furniture have a price tag on them.

5. This checkout is for customers with . . . . items or less.

"It's now a collector's item!"

Notes

1. Note that item can refer to a report on TV:
   The 9 o'clock news carried an item about an old age pensioner who'd starved to death.
   The programme featured an item on one-parent families.

2. Note the following expression:
   The management cannot accept liability for items stolen from your car while it is in the car park.

3. This is a common expression:
   The customs official checked through the contents of my suitcase, item by item.

4. Note these common expressions using 'of':
   A watch is the main item of jewellery worn by men.
   A maximum of three items of clothing is allowed into the changing rooms.
   The local museum has a number of items of great historical interest.

---

judgement

1 Judgement (making decisions)

Which set of verbs fit best in the sentences?

- a. trust / rely on / depend on
- b. showed / exercised / used
- c. challenged / doubted / questioned
- d. use / rely on / exercise
- e. form / come to

1. I'm afraid whether to marry Sandra or not is not something I can give you advice on. You'll have to .... your own judgement.

2. I think recent events have called into question the director's judgement.
   > Be careful. No one has ever .... his judgement before.

3. What do you think we should do about this money that's missing from the accounts? I'm finding it hard to .... a judgement on what course of action to take.

4. I .... my wife's judgement on financial matters. She's got a degree in economics.

5. The speaker .... good judgement in his choice of words when that guy asked all those difficult questions.

2 Verb + judgement

Complete the sentences below with the more natural collocation:

1. Until I've heard your brother's side of the story, I think I'm going to .... judgement.
   (keep / reserve)

2. What do you think of our new headmaster?
   > It's still too early to .... a judgement but so far he seems OK. (form / make)

3. Mike's appalling behaviour at the meeting just .... my earlier judgement of him. He's the rudest person I've ever met. (confused / confirmed)

4. Who are you to .... judgement on my behaviour? Just remember you're no saint yourself!
   (make / pass)

5. I think I'll .... your judgement when it comes to deciding which wine to order. You know a lot more about it than me. (trust / believe)

6. When it comes to trusting people, ... your own judgement. Don't listen to what other people think. (depend on / rely on)

3 Useful expressions

Complete the sentences with these expressions:

in my judgement
against my better judgement
a distinct lack of judgement
an error of judgement

1. As a very experienced politician, the Minister should never have allowed the Sultan to pay for his hotel accommodation. He showed ....
   ....

2. ...., we should not have accepted Jim's resignation. He was too valuable a person to lose.

3. I went to the party .... I should have stayed at home and tried to get rid of this cold.

4. To say that you were guilty of .... when you spoke to the press about the disagreements at the meeting is the understatement of the year. I think you'll soon be looking for a new job.

Go back and underline other useful collocations in this exercise.

Notes

1. Note how we talk about good judgement:
   His decision was based on sound judgement.

2. Note how we express lack of confidence in someone's judgement:
   Because no WMD have been found, people are calling the PM's judgement into question.
   I've lost thousands in the stock market. It really has destroyed my confidence in the judgement of my financial advisor.

3. Note these expressions which show a negative influence on our judgement:
   A judge must never allow any personal prejudice to colour his judgement.
   Don't let your disappointment cloud your judgement.
   The alcohol had impaired the driver's judgement.
   I mustn't let my feelings interfere with my professional judgement.

4. 'The Day of Judgement' or 'Judgement Day' describes the Christian idea that one day our lives will be judged by God.

knowledge

1 Verb + knowledge

Use the correct form of these verbs:

broaden   *deny*   *live with*
provide   *use*   *have*

1. He claims that he knew nothing about the decision to sell the land cheaply to a private developer. He . . . . all knowledge of the affair.

2. This small booklet . . . . background knowledge to the school.

3. The best way to . . . . your knowledge of world affairs is to read a good newspaper every day.

4. He has a serious heart condition. I don't know how he manages to . . . . the knowledge that he might have a heart attack at any moment.

5. An occasion may arise when you can . . . . your knowledge of French. You never know when it might come in handy.

6. Many of these students do not . . . . much knowledge of the history of their own country.

2 Common adjective collocations

Complete the sentences with these adjectives:

prior   *working*   *common*   *general*

1. You didn't know that Sue and Bill were having an affair? But we've all known about it for months now. It's been . . . . knowledge for ages!

2. We're looking for someone with a good . . . . knowledge of information systems.

3. How good is your . . . . knowledge?

4. Do I need any previous knowledge of computing in order to join the course?
   > No, it's an introductory course and requires no . . . . knowledge whatsoever.

wide   *basic*   *full*   *specialist*

5. With a . . . . knowledge of Italian you should be able to order a meal in a restaurant in Rome.

6. Through years of study he has acquired a . . . . knowledge of painting and music.

7. It needs . . . . knowledge to repair most electronic equipment.

8. The documentary about the Royals was made with the King's . . . . knowledge and approval.

3 Useful expressions

Match each expression with its meaning:

1. To my knowledge, no one knew what Robert was planning.

2. Has he resigned?
   > Not to my knowledge.

3. I was annoyed when he took the car without my knowledge.

4. With our alarms you can go out, secure in the knowledge that your house is safe.

a. confident
b. as far as I know
c. I didn't know
d. not as far as I know

Now use the expressions in these sentences:

5. I don't think Desmond has applied for the job – at least . . . . !

6. I think we can all sleep safely in our beds tonight, ... that the killer is now behind bars.

7. If I find out that someone used my computer . . . . , I won't rest till I find out who it was.

Notes

1. In 1-3 'expand' is also possible.
   In 3-1 we can also say 'to the best of my knowledge'.

2. Enough knowledge to do something is described as 'background or working knowledge':
   You don't need to be an expert, but we do expect you to have a good working knowledge of spreadsheets.

3. Note how we describe having a lot of knowledge of something:
   An in-depth knowledge of databases is not necessary as training will be given.
   As a policeman you should possess detailed knowledge of certain aspects of the law.
   The Prime Minister's personal secretary has an intimate knowledge of the inner workings of the government.

4. Note how we say somebody knows more than anybody else about something:
   His knowledge of Scottish football is unrivalled.

5. A 'general knowledge quiz' is a competition with questions on a very wide range of topics.

limit

1 Verb + limit

Choose the correct verb in the sentences:

1. I think we should . . . . a time limit on applications. Shall we say all applications must be received by Friday 13th? *(set / seek)*

2. At present you have to be 18 in order to vote. A growing number of people want the limit . . . . to 16. *(decreased / lowered)*

3. The police are warning drivers to keep to the speed limit. There will be tough penalties for those drivers who . . . . it. *(top / exceed)*

4. I've had enough. I've . . . . the limit of my patience with this child. See if you can get him to eat his food! *(got / reached)*

5. Parents need to . . . . limits on the amount of time their children spend on the internet. *(take / impose)*

6. The race is over 50 kilometres of rough countryside, so I think it will certainly . . . . the limits of my ability and endurance. *(test / check)*

7. I'm nearly 70 and I . . . . my limits. I don't have the strength to go shopping every day now. *(know / get)*

2 Common noun expressions

Use the following expressions in the sentences:

age limit	speed limit
city limits	time limit
spending limits	credit limit

1. The city council maintain that they will need to cut back on some public services in order to meet the latest . . . . set by the government.

2. There are speed cameras all over the place, so make sure you keep to the . . . . while you're here.

3. When you finish the report, just put it in my in-tray. There's no . . . . – but as long as I have it sometime next week, that'll be fine.

4. Recently, there have been calls to reduce the . . . . for voting from 18 to 16.

5. At the moment I've got a £3,000 . . . . on my Visa card, but I'm thinking of increasing it so that I can buy a second-hand car.

6. We live just outside the . . . .

3 Common adjective collocations

Match the two halves of these situations:

1. The driver had been drinking all day and when the police stopped him,
2. When some pictures come up for auction,
3. The company is willing to fund the event,
4. The level of fluoride in the drinking water was
5. In order to control inflation the government has set
6. Some species of fish are now in real danger of disappearing.
7. I'd pay £5,000 for a Jaguar in that condition,
8. The Russian boats are not allowed to fish

a. but costs must be kept *within reasonable limits.*
b. above the prescribed limit *set by the authorities.*
c. inside a five-mile limit.
d. strict limits *on public spending this year.*
e. but that would be *my absolute limit.*
f. he was well *over the legal limit.*
g. The North Sea has been fished *beyond acceptable limits.*
h. It's obvious that some people are so rich they have *no upper limit* on what they are prepared to pay.

Notes

1. In 1-2 'reduce' is also possible.

2. Note the prepositions in these expressions:
   You can bring in cigarettes up to a limit of 200 per person.
   There's a limit to the amount of pain any human being can bear.

3. Note these expressions using verb + 'to the limit':
   The medical services were stretched to the limit.
   It was a very long race and it pushed me to the limits of my ability.
   The sudden influx of Irish football supporters is straining hotels in the town to the limit.

4. The following expressions mean that there is no limit to what can be done:
   The sky is the limit for what professional footballers can earn these days.
   Zidane's talent knows no limits. He's simply the most brilliant player ever.

5. Note this more formal expression:
   Overseas companies must still operate within the limits of the law.

look

1 Verb + look (appearance)

Use the correct form of these verbs:

give	have	like
see	spoil	tell

1. You should have . . . . the look on her face when I told her I was leaving – it was priceless!
2. Did you see the frosty look old Mr Donaldson . . . . me? He's obviously angry with me for some reason.
3. We could . . . . by the look on her face that something terrible had happened.
4. If you ask me, the pink doors . . . . the look of the house. They look ridiculous.
5. We shouldn't judge people by their appearance, but I don't . . . . the look of that guy one bit.
6. I don't know what Jim does, but he . . . . the look of an accountant or bank manager.

2 Adjective collocations (act of looking)

Match the two halves of these situations:

1. Take a <u>close look</u> at this picture
2. I wonder if I could have a quick look at
3. I think we need to take a completely fresh look at the problem.
4. This morning's programme takes a light-hearted look at the world of acting.
5. He took a long, lingering look at his old home
6. The book takes a critical look at
7. I've only had the chance to have a cursory look over the papers,
8. I think you need to take a long, hard look at yourself.

a. modern politics in South Africa.
b. and see if you recognise anyone.
c. so I can't say I fully understand the problem.
d. your newspaper, please?
e. This discussion is getting us nowhere.
f. It promises to be very amusing.
g. before setting off for the airport and a new life in New Zealand.
h. You're becoming become selfish and self-centred.

Now go back and underline all the adjective + *look* collocations. The first one is done for you.

3 Verb + look (act of looking)

Use the correct form of these verbs:

get	have	sneak	take

1. I've . . . . another look for my watch, but I still can't find it anywhere!
2. Our daughter . . . . one look at the doctor's needle and fainted there and then!
3. We were standing at the back, so we pushed our way to the front of the crowd to . . . . a better look at the carnival as it passed.
4. I have to confess that I . . . . a look at her private diary when she was out of the room. I couldn't believe what I read.

4 Adjective collocations (appearance)

Use these adjectives in the sentences:

curious	distant	filthy
vacant	hurt	wild

1. There was a . . . . look in her eyes – her mind was obviously on something else.
2. Do you remember a boy in our class at primary school? His name was Dave Smithers. He wasn't very bright and always had a . . . . look in his eyes as if nobody was there!
3. The stranger had a . . . . look in her eyes. It was hard to tell if she was frightened or simply crazy.
4. Why did you give me such a . . . . look during the meeting? It wasn't you I was criticising!
5. We just couldn't stop laughing. That's why we were getting such . . . . looks from passers-by!
6. Why have you got such a . . . . look on your face? You look as though someone has just criticised you.

Notes

1. In 2-1 a 'good look' is also possible.
   In 4-4 'dirty' is also possible.
2. Notice these expressions:
   Do you mind if I take a look around?
   He put on weight and started to lose his looks.
   Mary has her father's good looks.

luck

1 Verb + luck

Use the correct form of these verbs:

believe	*bring*
hold	*push*
run out of	*trust*
wish	*have*

1. So far I haven't . . . . any luck finding a job. I haven't had one interview yet.

2. She wears some kind of charm around her neck. She thinks it'll . . . . her luck.

3. I could hardly . . . . my luck when I found my wallet still lying in the middle of the road where I dropped it.

4. The prisoner evaded police for four days, but he eventually . . . . luck when he was caught on video stealing food from a small store.

5. However hard you prepare for an exam, you still have to . . . . to luck to a certain extent. Last year I was in luck when one of the essay titles I had prepared came up in the final examination.

6. At my leaving party my boss shook my hand and . . . . me luck in my new career.

7. The team are playing well and if their luck . . . . they could win the cup and the championship.

8. You didn't get caught last time, but don't . . . . your luck! You might not be so lucky next time.

2 Common adjective collocations

Choose the more natural collocation in the sentences below:

1. Superstitious people believe that if you walk under a ladder, it brings you . . . . luck.
   (bad / poor)

2. . . . . luck with your driving test tomorrow!
   (great / good)

3. You say 'Oh, ... luck' to somebody to express sympathy with them when something unlucky has happened to them.
   (hard / terrible)

4. It was . . . . luck that we met. I wasn't even supposed to be in London that day.
   (complete / sheer)

5. . . . . luck next time! I'm sure with a little extra practice you'll be able to beat him.
   (better / greater)

3 Useful expressions

Use these expressions in the sentences below:

for luck	*in luck*	*out of luck*

1. You're . . . . ! We've got one pair of these shoes left in your size in black.

2. I always wear this cross round my neck . . . .

3. I'm sorry, you seem to be . . . . We don't have this model in stock at the moment.

by a stroke of luck	*a run of luck*
with a bit of luck	*your lucky day*

4. This is . . . . ! We've just had a cancellation. The dentist can see you this morning.

5. . . . . someone was passing, heard my mother shouting for help and called the police.

6. I had . . . . at the casino last night, but in the end I lost more than I won.

7. Come on, this isn't a difficult climb. We'll be back in time for dinner . . . .

"I think I'll risk the bad luck!"

Notes

1. In 2-3 'bad' or 'tough' luck are also possible.
   In 2-4 'pure luck' is also possible.

2. Note how we ask if somebody has been successful:
   Have you had any luck with your job-hunting?
   Any luck with your flat-hunting?

3. If you're 'down on your luck', you are in need of money after a period of bad luck:
   I bought the car from a friend who was down on his luck.

4. We often reassure people that life will get better:
   Perhaps your luck will change. You never know!

5. When we say 'Some people have all the luck!', we wish we had what they had:
   I've just won £10,000 on the lottery!
   > Some people have all the luck!

material

1 Verb + material (thing)

Use the correct form of these verbs:

contain	made from
modify	recycle
treat	use

1. Not many people realise that the Romans were the first to .... concrete as a building material.

2. We can assure our customers that all our products are .... natural materials.

3. I think it would be wrong to allow scientists to .... human genetic material in order to produce the 'perfect' human being.

4. The outer material of the garment has been .... with wax to make it waterproof.

5. One aim of the Green movement is to encourage people to .... more of their waste materials.

6. A lot of older buildings .... harmful materials such as asbestos.

2 Common adjective collocations

Complete the sentences with these adjectives:

hardest	inflammable
raw	recyclable
waste	radioactive
synthetic	hard-wearing

1. My country has few natural resources and has to import most of its .... materials.

2. Highly .... materials like petrol have to be handled with great care.

3. Seat covers on trains and buses take a lot of wear and tear so they need to be made from strong, ... materials.

4. Our products are environmentally-friendly. We package all of them in .... materials.

5. Most .... materials can be put in a washing machine. Unlike many natural fabrics they don't shrink when washed.

6. Diamonds are one of the .... materials known to man.

7. The transport of .... materials is still one of the biggest problems for the power industry.

8. .... materials should be recycled whenever possible.

3 Material (ideas / information)

Complete the sentences below with these words:

reading	indecent	classified	publicity

1. All sorts of .... materials are being used to promote the latest video – TV ads, videos, posters and leaflets.

2. These documents relating to the last war won't be available to the public for 50 years as they contain .... material.

3. I've listed some useful .... material at the end of the handout.

4. Employees caught downloading .... material from the internet will be sacked immediately.

valuable	fresh	copyright	relevant

5. I'm afraid this is .... material. You're not allowed to copy more than 10% of it and only for private use.

6. The band can't go on playing the same old songs year after year. It's time they produced some .... new material.

7. Professor Smith travelled the world gathering .... material for his book.

8. When I was researching my family tree, I found a lot of .... material in the public library.

Notes

1. In 3-4 'obscene' is also possible.

2. Note the following:
   He's a good soldier but I don't think he is officer material. (not good enough to be an officer)

3. We talk about *building, reading, teaching and writing materials:*
   There were bricks, cement and other building materials scattered all over the site.
   There is always a shortage of teaching materials in this school.
   You'll find some paper and writing materials over there on the desk.

4. Notice this expression using *noun + of + material:*
   Samples of the material were sent for analysis.

5. Remember that 'material' can be used as a general term to mean 'things'. It also has a specific meaning when it means 'cloth':
   Her coat was made of very expensive material.

---

matter

1 Verb + matter

Use the correct form of these verbs:

be   discuss   get
look into   bring   settle

1. Have you . . . . this matter with anyone else?

2. This kind of damage to the environment should . . . . a matter of concern to us all.

3. We took the matter up with the manager and he promised to . . . . it.

4. I said I'm sorry, so why can't you let the matter drop?
   > Okay. I promise not to . . . . the matter up again.

5. Let's . . . . this matter once and for all. We've been trying to resolve it for months now.

6. We've no time to deal with that just now, so let's . . . . on with the matter in hand and try to finish what we've started.

2 Common adjective collocations

Complete the sentences with these adjectives:

easy   urgent   delicate   different
serious   trivial   complex   personal

1. Look, this is a rather . . . . matter. Wendy can't afford to go on the trip and I'd like to offer to pay for her, but I'm worried that she might be offended.

2. It might seem funny to you, but setting fire to a wastepaper bin is no laughing matter – it is a very . . . . matter indeed!

3. I don't mind bees, wasps, flies and things like that, but spiders are a . . . . matter entirely!

4. OK, have it your way. The colour of the paper is such a . . . . matter that it's not worth fighting about.

5. Please try to find him. There is an extremely . . . . matter I need to talk to him about. Tell him that it can't wait till tomorrow.

6. Excuse me, Mr Thompson, could I talk to you in private? It's a . . . . matter.

7. It should have been a simple matter, but getting through to the helpline was no . . . . matter!

8. Collocation can be a very . . . . matter!

3 Noun + of + matter

Match the two halves of the following:

1. He denies any knowledge of the matter.
2. A holiday would be wonderful,
3. We need to get to
4. This is by no means the end of the matter –

a. but the fact of the matter is that we can't afford one.
b. I won't give up the fight that easily.
c. He says he wasn't involved.
d. the heart of the matter before we can help.

4 On the matter

Complete the sentences with the following:

advice   discussion   light
nothing   word

1. My bag is missing and I was hoping you might be able to shed some . . . . on the matter.

2. Of course I'll take . . . . on this matter, but I already know what I'm going to do.

3. When asked about his reasons for resigning, he had . . . . to say on the matter.

4. You can't go to the concert. And that's my last . . . . on the matter. Don't bring the subject up again! You're too young.

5. You won't get anywhere, I'm afraid. They refuse to enter into any . . . . on the matter.

Notes

1. Note this common question:
   What's the matter? You look like you've seen a ghost!

2. Note this common expression:
   Well, if there's no choice in the matter, I suppose I'll have to go to the meeting.

3. Note these expressions using *matter + of + noun*:
   Can't we do this tomorrow? It's hardly a matter of life or death, is it?
   Safety standards in the industry have been a matter of concern for many years.
   Which is the best cheese? It's a matter of personal taste.
   It can only be a matter of time before war breaks out.

4. One way of disagreeing with someone is to say:
   Well, I think it's a matter of opinion.

5. Notice this expression:
   Don't get involved, Clare. This is a family matter.

measures

1 Verb + measures

Use the correct form of the verbs in brackets:

1. The government needs to . . . . all necessary measures to stop the influx of asylum seekers.
(adopt / adapt)

2. Immediate measures need to be . . . . to protect the thousands of historic buildings under threat of demolition.
(taken / got)

3. New measures are being . . . . to try and ease traffic congestion in Birmingham city centre.
(started / introduced)

4. The government is . . . . measures to restrict the sale of cigarettes to adults over 21.
(considering / thinking of)

5. In his speech last night the Prime Minister . . . . new measures to combat organised crime.
(announced / declared)

6. Urgent measures are . . . . to contain the outbreak of the disease before it spreads.
(needed / wanted)

7. I voted against because I . . . . these measures on principle. I don't think anybody should be made to work on a Sunday if they don't want to.
(oppose / refuse)

Go back and underline all the verb collocations.

2 Types of measures

Use these words in the sentences below:

temporary	*safety*
security	*unpopular*

1. At times of high inflation, ... measures are sometimes necessary to get the economy back on an even keel. Such measures generally lose the government votes.

2. When the rain started, I had to cover the roof with a plastic sheet as a . . . . measure until we got the roofers to come and fix the leak.

3. One main drawback of improved . . . . measures in cars is that they can encourage some people to think they are safe, so they drive faster.

4. The introduction of identity cards is just one of the new . . . . measures our company has taken this year.

desperate	*half*
preventative	*precautionary*

5. His financial difficulties have forced him to take some really . . . . measures. He's had to sell his house and car to pay off his debts.

6. Floods will become an increasing problem in this area unless . . . . measures are taken now.

7. During yesterday's protest march through the streets of Paris, police in riot gear were present as a . . . . measure.

8. . . . . measures never work. You've got to do things properly or not at all.

Go back and underline the full expressions.

3 Measures to . . .

Complete the following sentences with these verbs and underline the adjective collocation in each sentence which means 'strong':

control	*prevent*	*save*

1. Tougher measures are needed to . . . . drugs being smuggled into prisons.

2. Stringent measures have been introduced in our office to . . . . on electricity and heating costs.

3. The government have taken drastic measures to . . . . public spending.

Notes

1. Note the expressions describing the effects of measures:
Measures to reduce costs are beginning to take effect. The measures will affect the entire population.

2. Note the expressions which describe the purpose of measures:
These new measures are designed to close / are intended to close / are aimed at closing the gap between the rich and the poor.

3. Note the difference between *safety measures* and *security measures*:
These new safety measures mean that more people will survive road traffic accidents.
The latest security measures at Heathrow are due to a new bomb scare.

4. A measure can also be an amount of liquid:
James's measures are on the generous side!

meeting

1 Verb + meeting

Use the correct form of these verbs:

attend   *break up*   *chair*
drag on   *hold*   *postpone*

1. The meeting tonight will be . . . . in the school hall. I thought it was going to be in the community centre.

2. Who is going to . . . . the meeting? Until we have an election for the committee, we need a volunteer.

3. I was told that the meeting would close at 10pm, but it didn't . . . . until after midnight.

4. I couldn't . . . . the meeting due to my busy schedule, so I sent my apologies.

5. Something urgent has come up. Could we . . . . our meeting till tomorrow or will we just have to cancel it?
   > Don't worry. I'll get my secretary to rearrange the meeting for next week.

6. I was so bored at yesterday's meeting. I fell asleep on more than one occasion. The meeting seemed to . . . . and on for hours.

2 Common adjective collocations

Complete the sentences below with the following:

chance   *first*   *well-run*   *public*
emergency   *private*   *staff*   *important*

1. There will be a . . . . meeting at the town hall tomorrow to discuss the controversial plans to build a supermarket on the school playing fields.

2. A . . . . meeting with a publisher on a train led to my career as a writer.

3. The Prime Minister called an . . . . meeting of the Cabinet to discuss the crisis in Iraq.

4. The two Presidents had a . . . . meeting at the airport before they made a statement to the waiting press about the crisis.

5. Missing my flight cost me dear! It meant I missed an extremely . . . . finance meeting.

6. The headmaster announced his retirement at the last . . . . meeting of the academic year.

7. I liked Jean right from our very . . . . meeting.

8. Thanks to our excellent chairman, our meetings are very . . . .

3 Organising meetings

Choose the correct verb in the following and use it in its correct form:

1. Could you telephone me to . . . . a meeting? *(arrange / re-order)*

2. We need to talk to them about this. I'll . . . . a meeting for next week. *(mend / fix)*

3. I've . . . . a meeting with the director for Friday afternoon. Let me know if you can make it. *(pencil in / pencil)*

4. I'll try to . . . . a meeting with the lawyer for Friday to get these documents signed. *(set down / set up)*

5. A few unexpected problems have arisen, so they've . . . . an urgent meeting for this evening. *(call / ring)*

4 During a meeting

Complete the expressions in colour using the correct form of these verbs:

adjourn   *appoint*   *call*
excuse   *start*   *leave*

At 2pm the chairman . . . . the meeting to order. As several of us hadn't met before, we . . . . the meeting by introducing ourselves. Then John Wilson was . . . . to take the minutes of the meeting. We then started to work our way through the agenda for the meeting. At 5.30, Angela Thomas . . . . herself from the meeting and several others said that they had to . . . . the meeting by six o'clock. As a result, the chairman decided to . . . . the meeting until 10 the next morning.

Notes

1. A meeting place is a building or place where people meet regularly:
   The café at the corner of Bread Street is a popular meeting place for young people.

2. Meeting also means a game or competition:
   This will be the fifth meeting this season between the two clubs.

3. A 'meeting of minds' is when people have the same opinions or ideas:
   At the peace conference there was a real meeting of minds between the two leaders – at last!

---

memory

1 Verb + memory

Use the correct form of these verbs:

bring back	blot out
commit	put behind
etch	jog
lose	search

1. I've been . . . . my memory all week for the name of that guy I was at college with, but all I can remember is it starts with 'g' – a name like 'Goodfellow' or 'Goldsmith'.

2. When I was at school we had to . . . . a lot of poems to memory.

3. Elderly people tend to . . . . their memory bit by bit and become increasingly forgetful.

4. Listen to it again. It might . . . . your memory and help you to remember who the singer was.

5. These photographs . . . . lots of great memories of our holiday in Egypt.

6. John can't stop thinking about the accident. He finds it impossible to . . . . the memory. However, I'm sure the memory will fade with the passing of time.

7. My first sight of you will always be . . . . on my memory. You were wearing that light blue dress and your hair was flying in the wind as you got out of your Porsche.

8. Sooner or later you're going to have to . . . . the memory of your first wife . . . . you. How can we live if you keep talking about her?

2 Common adjective collocations

Complete the sentences with these adjectives:

distant	earliest
fond	short-term
hazy	living
painful	terrible

1. I have a great memory for faces, but a . . . . memory for names. What's your name again?

2. I have very . . . . memories of living in the country. It was such a relaxed way of life.

3. Dave's mother died when he was only four years old, so he only has a . . . . memory of what she looked like.

4. My . . . . memory is of being taken to the park and feeding the ducks.

5. The storms we have experienced recently are the worst in . . . . memory – according to the weathermen.

6. My time at university is now a . . . . memory. It seems so long ago.

7. For over thirty years Bernard had suppressed some . . . . memories from his troubled childhood.

8. I can remember things that happened when I was a very young child, but my . . . . memory is awful. Now, where did I leave my glasses!

3 Kinds of memory

Match the first and second parts:

1. I've got a photographic memory.
2. I've got no memory for places.
3. I've got a very retentive memory.
4. I've got a very long memory.

a. I'll never forget what you used to do to me at school.
b. I can't remember whether it was Modena or Turin where we met first.
c. I can see a painting in a gallery and then recall all the details days later.
d. I can remember every word of Hamlet's great speech.

Notes

1. Note these expressions:
   They have erected a statue in memory of those who died in the two world wars.
   It's extremely long but he is able to recite the whole poem from memory.
   He was called Brian, if my memory serves me right.
   He suffered loss of memory after his accident.
   Are you one hundred percent sure? Memory can play tricks on you.
   Che Guevara died years ago but his memory lives on.
   This place holds lots of memories for us.
   I was sure I'd met you before, but my memory must be playing tricks on me!

2. We can also 'refresh' our memories:
   I looked at the map to refresh my memory of the route to the youth hostel.

3. 'A trip down memory lane' is to spend time remembering the past:
   We returned to our old school for a trip down memory lane.

---

method

1 Verb + method

Use the correct form of these verbs:

adopt　　　*devise*　　　*fail*
recommend　　*use*　　　*work*

1. In no way am I going to .... any of these new teaching methods. I'll stick to the tried and tested methods that I've always used.

2. That method doesn't look like it is going to .... We'll need to come up with an alternative method of doing it. Any suggestions?

3. The methods of communication .... in the eighteenth century were primitive by today's standards.

4. Believe me, this method of growing tomatoes never .... I get a bumper crop every year.

5. In the 1930's scientists .... an efficient method of producing rubber from oil.

6. We .... the filter method as the best way to make coffee.

2 Common adjective collocations

Complete the sentences with these adjectives:

infallible　　　*reliable*
popular　　　　*traditional*

1. In the UK more and more people are unhappy with modern food production and are calling for a return to .... methods of farming.

2. The author of this book claims to have discovered an .... method for making money. He says that it never fails.

3. Frying used to be the most .... method of cooking before people became more health conscious.

4. The pill is generally regarded as the most .... method of contraception.

practical　　　*unorthodox*　　　*effective*

5. Despite his .... methods, his students achieved excellent exam results.

6. The French are generally credited with developing the first .... method of producing photographs.

7. Vaccination is the most .... method for preventing some of the worst childhood illnesses – like measles.

3 Method + of

Complete the sentences below with the following:

birth control　　　*crowd control*
pain control　　　*payment*
earthquakes　　　*teaching*
reaching agreement　　*transport*

1. Travelling by plane is still one of the safest methods of ....

2. The methods of .... include lectures, seminars, and tutorials.

3. Scientists are still struggling to devise a reliable method of predicting ....

4. The most commonly used method of .... involves the use of tear gas and mounted police.

5. There are several possible methods of .... – credit card being the most popular.

6. Thank goodness for modern methods of .... I hate to think what it must have been like to be seriously ill a couple of hundred years ago.

7. Condoms are an effective method of .... if used with care.

8. Non-confrontational methods of .... are always the best.

"It's still one of the safest methods of travelling."

Notes

1. Note the following expressions:
   I have no quarrel with his methods. (They are OK.)
   I think his methods stink. (I think they are awful.)

2. We use the expression 'there's method in his madness' when we mean that although someone is doing something in a strange way, there is a good reason behind it.
   I wonder why Malcolm is coming in an hour early every morning? It's not like him.
   > Ah, you obviously don't know he's applied for promotion. There's method in his madness!

mind

1 Verb + mind

Use the correct form of these verbs:

have	broaden
change	cross
clear	make up
spring	train

1. He's quite a stubborn person. Once he's .... his mind, he never budges. He sticks to his decision, no matter what happens.

2. I'm not going on that plane, so don't try to persuade me. Nothing, and I mean nothing, will make me .... my mind.

3. I often find it difficult to .... my mind after a hard day at work. Thoughts about work just keep running through my head. My wife wants me to take up yoga or something like that.

4. Some people go on courses to .... their minds to think positively.

5. I'm trying to encourage my kids to travel more, but they just want to stay at home. I keep telling them that travel .... the mind.

6. Sometimes I think this car .... a mind of its own. Whenever I am in a desperate hurry, it decides not to start!

7. It never .... my mind that James would resign. I mean, he's not the resigning type, is he?

8. Do you know anyone who would be a good person to organise our Christmas party?
   > No, nobody .... to mind – and don't look at me!

2 Common adjective collocations

Complete the sentences with these adjectives:

enquiring	open	suspicious
warped	sharp	one-track

1. He's a typical male. He's got a .... mind! All he ever thinks about is sex!

2. Although my grandad's now 92, his mind is remarkably agile and alert.
   > Yes, he still has a really .... mind for someone of his age.

3. Most young children show an interest in learning new things. They seem to be born with an .... mind. It's a pity that many of us lose this as we grow older.

4. I'm not sure if your solution to the traffic problem will work, but I'm keeping an .... mind till I hear what all the other proposals are.

5. The film is full of violence, murder and bad language. It can only have a negative effect on the innocent minds of young people. In my opinion, it is the work of a sick and .... mind!

6. No, I didn't play with your computer while you were out. What a .... mind you've got! Don't you trust anybody?

3 Expressions with prepositions

Use these words to complete the expressions:

back	clear	doubt	frame	peace

   a. at the ..... of my mind
   b. in the right ...... of mind
   c. complete ...... of mind
   d. not really ...... in my mind
   e. no ..... in my mind

Now use these complete expressions below:

1. Take out a five-year guarantee and have .... If this radio breaks down, we will repair it or replace it free of charge.

2. There is .... that he murdered Caroline Walker in cold blood.

3. Can we talk about this later? I'm not .... to start discussing money.

4. I'm .... about what we're aiming for. Are we trying to find a solution or just spend hours talking and getting nowhere?

5. I just haven't got round to calling my mother. It's been .... to call her for several days now.

Notes

1. Note this way of saying what you don't like:
   It was nice, but it wasn't quite what we had in mind.

2. This expression means someone is mad:
   Marrying Cecil? Are you out of your mind?

3. Note these common expressions:
   The event is still fresh in most people's minds.
   Thanks for your suggestion – I'll keep it in mind.
   Sorry, but I've got a lot on my mind at the moment.
   I just can't seem to get him out of my mind.
   When I met the PM my mind went a complete blank.
   This building is designed with the elderly in mind.

mistake

1 Verb + mistake

Use the correct form of these verbs:

correct	*learn*	*make*
point out	*realise*	*repeat*

1. Making mistakes is an important part of learning a language. If you don't make mistakes, you don't . . . . from them.

2. I think if you can admit that you've . . . . a mistake, it is a sign of strength, not weakness.

3. When I got home, I found out that I had been calling my girlfriend's father by the wrong name. I felt such a fool when I . . . . my mistake.

4. Like many people, I find it difficult to avoid . . . . past mistakes. Why do we make the same mistakes over and over again?

5. Read through your work carefully and . . . . any mistakes that you find.

6. If you . . . . some people's mistakes to them, they get very defensive. I don't know why!

2 Common adjective collocations

Complete the sentences below with the following:

costly	*dreadful*	*fatal*	*occasional*
genuine	*stupid*	*common*	*understandable*

1. The most . . . . mistake people make is to water their plants too much.

2. It was a perfectly . . . . mistake to make. I assumed Jane and Morgan were married, too!

3. The skaters made the . . . . mistake of assuming that the ice was thick enough to take their weight. Unfortunately, there was a thaw on. The ice gave way and they drowned.

4. I should have scored 100% in the examination, but I made one . . . . mistake.

5. I can accept that anybody makes the . . . . mistake. We all do, but if it becomes a habit then you're in trouble.

6. Going to the football match when he should have been at work proved to be a very . . . . mistake for Jeff. He was sacked.

7. When he removed the wrong kidney from the patient, the surgeon made a . . . . mistake.

8. I'm sorry, sir, but a . . . . mistake has been made. We will do our best to find you a double room immediately.

3 Verb + for + mistake

Use these verbs to complete the expressions:

apologise	*check*	*refuse*	*take*

a. . . . . *to accept responsibility for*
b. . . . . *the blame for*
c. . . . . *profusely for*
d. . . . . *over your work for*

Now use these complete expressions below, using the correct form of the verbs:

1. He thought I was the secretary and not the manager because I was a woman, but he . . . . his mistake when I introduced myself. You should have seen his face!

2. Nobody should have to . . . . other people's mistakes.

3. It's always a good idea to . . . . mistakes before you hand it in.

4. Five hundred pounds has gone missing from my bank account, but the bank . . . . the mistake.

"Now Gran, how many times do I have to tell you that the most common mistake people make is to water too much!"

Notes

1. Note these expressions:
   Marrying you was the biggest mistake of my life!
   His work is always full of spelling mistakes.

2. Note the useful expression 'It's a mistake to think that . . . :
   It's a mistake to think that violence will solve this issue.

3. 'By mistake' means *accidentally*:
   Someone must have left the window open by mistake.

4. Note these expressions with 'make a mistake'.
   I made the mistake of inviting him to the party.
   I won't make the same mistake again!
   Don't worry. It's an easy mistake to make.
   If you make a mistake, just cross it out.

moment

1 Verb + moment

Use the correct form of these verbs:

have   dread   last   pause for
spare   take   wait   choose

1. Could you look through my report when you .... a moment or two?

2. As I boarded the plane, I began to panic, but thankfully, the feeling only .... a moment.

3. Don't worry. You won't feel a thing. This won't .... a moment.

4. I'm terribly busy. I can only .... a few moments, I'm afraid. Now, what was it about?

5. Could you .... a moment, please. I'll be with you as soon as I can.

6. It was now my turn to make a speech. This was the moment I had been .... all day.

7. The headmaster is in a terrible mood today. If you want to speak to him, you should .... your moment very carefully!

8. The lecturer .... a moment and asked if there were any questions.

2 Common adjective collocations

Choose the more natural collocation from the pairs below:

1. Sorry, have I caught you at a .... moment? Would it be better if I called back later? *(bad / terrible)*

2. Her finest moment came when she won a gold medal at the Olympics. She said it was the .... moment of her life. *(luckiest / proudest)*

3. My most .... moment was when I was out with my wife shopping and we bumped into one of my ex-girlfriends. *(embarrassing / embarrassed)*

4. For one .... moment, we thought the climber was going to fall. *(dreadful / bad)*

5. The new exhibition in the National Museum covers the .... moments of Sweden's history. *(best / key)*

6. I've been so busy today – I'm still waiting for a .... moment when I can grab a sandwich. *(calm / quiet)*

7. There were a few .... moments as the plane came in to land in last night's storm. *(anxious / worried)*

8. There was a .... moment of calm and we were able to take off. *(short / brief)*

9. Why do you always leave things to the .... moment? *(final / last)*

10. At the .... moment Dave said 'I do', who do you think walked into the church? Celia, his ex-wife! *(precise / crucial)*

3 Word grammar

Match the two halves of these sentences:

1. I'm waiting for the right moment
2. Gaining independence was a great moment
3. A tourist managed to capture
4. There's no news, but I'll call you
5. I spent a few moments
6. The team jumped up and down,

a. the awful moment on film.
b. the moment I hear anything.
c. savouring their moment of victory.
d. to break the bad news that he's failed.
e. in the country's history.
f. thinking about what I was going to say.

4 Preposition + moment

Use a suitable preposition in the sentences:

1. I loved you ...... the very first moment I saw you.

2. I'm just going to the canteen. I'll be back .... a moment.

3. Why do you always leave it .... the last possible moment before packing your bags?

4. Doctor Ferguson is busy .... the moment. Can I take a message?

5. Would you mind looking after my bag .... a moment while I buy a ticket?

6. Peter left the room quietly. We followed him ..... a few moments.

Notes

1. Note the following expressions:
   At this moment in time, we don't know the outcome.
   You have to be ready to leave at a moment's notice.

2. If you do something 'on the spur of the moment', you do it without planning:
   I decided to go with them on the spur of the moment.

---

movement

1 Verb + movement (act of moving)

Use the correct form of these verbs:

allow	co-ordinate
detect	monitor
restrict	retrace

1. Long skirts tend to . . . . movement, so I usually wear trousers to work. They give you greater freedom of movement.

2. As the disease progresses, the patient loses the ability to . . . . his movements and needs help with the simplest of tasks.

3. The alarm goes off the second these infra-red sensors . . . . the slightest movement.

4. Detectives are trying to . . . . the young girl's movements on the night she disappeared.

5. An important job of the security forces is to . . . . the movements of suspected terrorists.

6. The law will be changed to . . . . free movement of goods within Europe.

2 Adjective + movement

Choose the more natural collocation:

1. Audiences were always spellbound by Nureyev's . . . . arm movements. *(beautiful / graceful)*

2. The . . . . movement of troops into the area brought a quick end to the days of rioting. *(rapid / fast)*

3. During the Second World War, we couldn't travel around the country. Our movements were very . . . . *(restricted / constrained)*

4. Our burglar alarm is activated by the . . . . movement in the house. *(smallest / slightest)*

5. Don't make any . . . . movement or you'll frighten the bird and it'll fly away. *(rapid / sudden)*

3 Verb + movement (group with a purpose)

Use the correct form of these verbs:

ban	be involved with	campaign
join	sympathise with	weaken

1. My brother . . . . heavily . . . . the animal rights movement and its campaign to stop animals being used in experiments.

2. Outraged by the inequalities between men and women in society Mrs Pankhurst . . . . the movement for equal rights.

3. Over the last thirty years the trade union movement in the UK has been . . . . by anti-union legislation.

4. Although I . . . . the nationalist movement, I don't approve of the use of violence.

5. When the peace movement began to gather strength, the military government saw it as a threat and took immediate steps to . . . . it.

6. The Green movement is . . . . for better recycling facilities in every town in the country.

4 Movement + preposition

Complete the sentences using these prepositions:

against	away from	for
of	in	towards

1. The police caught the last-known movements . . . . . . the terrorists on camera.

2. There's not been much movement . . . . . . crude oil prices for a number of years.

3. Since the death of Princess Diana, there seems to be a movement . . . . . . greater informality among members of the Royal Family.

4. There has been a mass movement . . . . . . government. The people hope to force the President out of office.

5. Recently, there has been some movement . . . . . . progressive methods of teaching and a return to more traditional ways.

6. There have been several movements . . . . . . reform of the voting system over the last century, but little real change has taken place.

Notes

1. Note this expression:
   The police have had the house under surveillance, but there have been no signs of movement for days.

2. Other movements are:
   The Arts and Crafts Movement, the Civil Rights Movement, the Anti-War Movement, the Ecumenical Movement, the Pro-Life Movement, etc.

3. Other kinds of movement are:
   the slow movement of his 5th Symphony
   troop movements

need

1 Verb + need

Use the correct form of these verbs:

eliminate   *feel*   *illustrate*
meet   *recognise*   *stress*

1. The theft of the Rembrandt last weekend clearly . . . . the need for better security measures at the Palace.

2. The main advantage of credit cards is that they . . . . the need to carry cash around.

3. The director . . . . the need for co-operation between workers and management if the company was to get out of its current difficulties.

4. More nurseries will have to be built to . . . . the need for high-quality child care.

5. The government says that it . . . . the need for immediate legislation to combat racism in the workplace.

6. I know you're getting out of hospital today, but you're welcome to come back and talk any time – if ever you . . . . the need.

2 Common adjective collocations

Complete the sentences below with the more natural adjective collocation:

constant   *desperate*
growing   *urgent*

1. United Nations officials say that the most . . . . need is for earth-moving equipment. *(urgent / anxious)*

2. My father's illness is long-term, so he's in . . . . need of treatment. *(continual / constant)*

3. Student numbers are increasing year by year, so there's a . . . . need for cheap rented accommodation around the university. *(growing / expanding)*

4. As winter approaches the refugees are in . . . . need of warmth, food and shelter. *(terrible / desperate)*

5. There's a . . . . need for more help for old people living at home on their own. *(big / clear)*

6. When the second Gulf War ended, there was a . . . . need for clean water, medical supplies and stable government. *(pressurised / pressing)*

3 Expressions with prepositions

Use a suitable preposition in the sentences:

1. Our organisation tries to help those most . . . . need of psychiatric help.

2. I'm going outside. I'm in need . . . . some fresh air.

3. There's no need . . . . all this shouting. Can't we discuss this quietly?

4. I think we're all . . . . need of a break.

4 Different needs

Complete the sentences below with the following:

basic   *emotional*   *future*
individual   *energy*   *special*

1. My wife teaches children with . . . . needs. Many of them have severe learning difficulties.

2. A family in Eritrea doesn't need much money to survive. About £10 a week is enough to cover all their . . . . needs.

3. The government is investing in training so that the country will be able to meet the . . . . needs of industry.

4. Without an increase in the number of nuclear power stations, I don't see how our existing system is going to meet the . . . . needs of this country in ten years' time.

5. Our fitness trainers put together a personal programme to suit your . . . . needs.

6. Good parents are sensitive both to the physical and . . . . needs of their children.

Notes

1. A 'crying' need is very urgent:
   There's a crying need for more doctors.

2. Note this expression which means 'if necessary':
   I'll stay up all night if need be.

3. Note these common expressions:
   She's badly in need of some new clothes.
   The school roof is in dire need of repair.

4. Note this verb collocation:
   We will contact you again if the need arises.

---

number

1 Number + of + noun

Use these nouns in the sentences below:

advantages   factors   changes   occasions
problems   reasons   times   ways

1. Yes, I know George Robertson. We've met on a number of . . . .

2. I decided not to go to the party for a number of . . . . that I'd rather not talk about.

3. A significant number of . . . . have taken place since I was at Oxford.

4. Stop worrying. You can only be infected with HIV in a limited number of . . . . and shaking someone's hand isn't one of them!

5. There are a number of . . . . that could account for the differences between the scores.

6. A number of unforeseen . . . . have arisen and we've had to postpone the concert.

7. I've lost track of the number of . . . . Tony has asked me to lend him money.

8. Studying English in Britain has a number of distinct . . . . You can't escape it! It's everywhere!

2 Adjective + number of + noun

Use these adjective / noun pairs in the sentences:

appalling / casualties   alarming / complaints
total / votes   increasing / cases
huge / convictions   limited / places
high / accidents   record / replies

1. The . . . . number of . . . . in the First World War was due partly to incompetent officers.

2. The advertisement we placed in last week's paper has attracted a . . . . number of . . . .

3. The tour company is investigating the . . . . number of . . . . made against one of its hotels.

4. There's been an . . . . number of . . . . of measles among young children.

5. He's a known criminal. He has a . . . . number of previous . . . . for theft.

6. This latest result brings the . . . . number of . . . . for the Socialists to over twenty million.

7. We have a . . . . number of free . . . . on the course.

8. There's a very . . . . number of . . . . at this junction.

3 Verb collocations

Use the correct form of these verbs:

1. More and more young people are going on to higher education. The number has . . . . tenfold over the past decade. *(reached / risen)*

2. The government has launched a new road safety campaign in an attempt to . . . . the number of deaths on the road. *(cut / chop)*

3. The hospital . . . . the number of visitors a patient can have. Only two people are allowed in at one time. *(reduced / put down)*

4. The number of visitors to Stonehenge could soon . . . . saturation point. The authorities will have to start turning people away. *(reach / come to)*

5. The number of people out of work in the town has . . . . from 5000 last year to 3500. *(reduced / fallen)*

4 Common adjective collocations

Complete the sentences below with the following:

disproportionate   huge   wrong
maximum   unlucky   exact

1. A lot of people believe that thirteen is an . . . . number.

2. . . . . numbers of cattle have had to be slaughtered following the outbreak of foot and mouth disease.

3. The . . . . number of people killed in the train crash is not yet known.

4. Sorry, I must have dialled the . . . . number.

5. There's a . . . . number of men compared to women in the government. Something must be done to redress the balance.

6. There were over twenty people in the lift – five more than the . . . . number allowed.

Notes

1. Note the following expressions:
   a sharp increase in the number of women who smoke
   a dramatic decrease in the number of cats in the area
   Teachers are leaving in increasing numbers.
   Complaints were surprisingly few in number.

2. 'Odd numbers' are 1, 3, 5, 7 etc and 'even numbers' are 2, 4, 6, 8 etc.

---

occasion

1 Verb + occasion

Use the correct form of these verbs:

celebrate   dress   forget   use

1. Remember it's a wedding that you're going to. Make sure you . . . . for the occasion. Have you got a dark suit?

2. My husband is fifty next week. We're having a big party to . . . . the occasion.

3. The Prime Minister opened a new school in London and he . . . . the occasion to announce the government's intention to spend more money on primary schools.

4. They seem a very nice couple, don't they? I'll never . . . . the occasion when they screamed and shouted at each other in public.

2 Common adjective collocations

Complete the sentences below with the following:

festive   memorable   previous
special   serious   suitable

1. As my parents' golden wedding was an extra- . . . . occasion, we let off a lot of fireworks.

2. OK! I'll speak to him about his behaviour – but only if a . . . . occasion arises.

3. We listened to his speech and tried not to laugh – a funeral is meant to be a solemn and . . . . occasion.

4. Yes, I know Hans. We've met on two . . . . occasions, once in Hamburg, the other time in London.

5. I'm sure I'm speaking for everyone when I say that this has been both an enjoyable and a truly . . . . occasion. It's certainly one that I will never forget.

6. The Millennium was a very . . . . occasion. People were singing and dancing in the streets.

3 Common expressions

Complete the sentences below with these adjectives and determiners:

more   number   odd
one   particular   this

1. You usually beat Dave easily. How did he get the better of you on . . . . occasion?

2. My mother is now over 80 and can be very demanding. On . . . . occasion, she called me in the middle of the night asking me to come round to her house to make her a cup of tea!

3. Smith has been late now on . . . . than one occasion. I think we're going to have to speak to him.

4. Jane and I talk about lots of things, but I just can't remember what we were discussing on that . . . . occasion.

5. His work has been unsatisfactory now on a . . . . of occasions. If it happens again, we'll have no choice but to dismiss him.

6. I don't really smoke. I just have a cigar on the very . . . . occasion.

4 Noun + preposition + occasion

Use these nouns to complete the expressions:

keeping   sense   sparkle   spirit

1. The music, the flowers and the crowds gave the event a real feeling of importance. They gave the wedding a real . . . . of occasion.

2. I know she doesn't really like party games, but she decided to join in and she seemed to enjoy herself. She certainly entered into the . . . . of the occasion.

3. His behaviour during the awards ceremony was rude and inappropriate. It was definitely not in . . . . with the occasion.

4. The room was full of men in grey suits, but the presence of the Prime Minister's wife in a beautiful green silk dress added a much needed . . . . to the occasion.

Notes

1. Note these expressions:
   The team must rise to the occasion and win the cup.
   I've suggested that on numerous occasions.
   If the occasion arises, I'll ask for his autograph.
   I went out and bought a new dress just for the occasion.

2. 'On occasion' means not often:
   On occasion I have a cigar after a meal.

3. If something is 'an occasion', it means it is special in some way:
   Everybody was there. It was quite an occasion.

---

offer

1 Verb + offer

Use the correct form of these verbs:

accept   *make*   *turn down*
put in   *up*   *withdraw*

1. Marie must be mad! She's declined an offer of an all-expenses-paid weekend in Prague!
   > Yes, she . . . . a similar offer last year. I'd never refuse an offer like that!

2. It was well after midnight. Andrew suggested that I stay the night at his place and I . . . . the offer. I wouldn't usually do that, but he's got two spare rooms.

3. The company have offered us a 5% salary increase. However, if we don't agree within seven days, the offer will be . . . .

4. They were asking £100,000 for the house and we . . . . an offer of £110,000, but we didn't get it. Somebody else put in an offer of £150,000!

5. If I were you, I'd . . . . an offer which was about 5% more than the asking price.

6. I think if you're going to have any chance of getting this flat, you're going to have to . . . . your offer by at least £2000, to £122,000.

In examples 4, 5 and 6 'offer' means *financial offer*. The past tense of 'up' would be 'upped'.

2 Common adjective collocations

Use the following adjectives in these sentences:

better   *final*
tempting   *special*
kind

1. We've just been down to Tesco's. Melons are on . . . . offer. Buy two, get one free. I'm usually suspicious of offers like that, but they're delicious!

2. A week with Will and Sue at their Spanish villa sounds great.
   > Yes, it IS a very . . . . offer, but, much as I like Will, I couldn't take Sue for a whole week!

3. I'm sorry, but £250 is my . . . . offer. You can take it or leave it.

4. If you like, I can do your shopping for you.
   > That's a very . . . . offer. Are you sure?

5. I think the Germans expected us to jump at the offer they made for our business, but we decided to hold out for a . . . . offer.

3 Offer + of + noun

Complete the sentences with these nouns:

help   *lift*   *marriage*   *support*   *work*

1. When our house was flooded, we received several offers of . . . . from friends to clean it up.

2. We've received many offers of . . . . since we started our campaign to outlaw handguns.

3. You need to get a job some time, you know! You can't turn down offers of . . . . just like that.

4. I can't get a taxi, so could I take you up on your offer of a . . . . to the airport?

5. My aunt was very beautiful when she was younger. Everyone says she turned down lots of offers of . . . .

4 Common expressions

Complete the sentences with these expressions:

a. they made me an offer I couldn't refuse.
b. open to offers.
c. I might take you up on that offer someday.
d. on offer

1. The local college has a wide range of vocational courses . . . . I'm sure you'll find one that meets your needs.

2. Feel free to stay at our place whenever you're in town.
   > Thanks. . . . .

3. The asking price is £300, but I'm . . . .

4. Although I was perfectly happy with my previous job with Xenop, I moved to Easycopy because . . . .!

Notes

1. If something is 'on offer', it can mean it is available:
   The new flats will be on offer as from 1st March.

   or it can mean 'available at a reduced price':
   Beans are on special offer this week.

2. We talk about job offers:
   I've been to several interviews, but I haven't had any job offers yet.

opinion

1 Verb + opinion

Use the correct form of these verbs:

influence   *respect*   *form*   *give*

1. Could you read this essay and . . . . me your opinion on it before I hand it in to my tutor?

2. I always value our teacher's opinion. He's a man whose opinion I . . . .

3. What do you think of this new government? > It's too early to say. I haven't really . . . . an opinion yet.

4. There can be no doubt that television and newspapers do . . . . public opinion.

express   *ask*   *revise*   *share*

5. The fact that he passed the exam has made me . . . . my original opinion of him. He's obviously more intelligent than I thought he was.

6. Would anyone like to . . . . an opinion on this matter?

7. I know what you think, but do the other members of the team . . . . your opinion?

8. If you . . . . my opinion, there's a danger I'll disagree with you – so it's better not to ask!

2 Noun + of + opinion

Match the two halves of these situations:

1. Their marriage is almost at an end. Over the years
2. Zidane is the greatest footballer the world has ever seen.
3. The government needs to find out what the
4. Most people are fed up with the congestion and pollution that traffic brings.
5. Over the last twenty years there has been a distinct

a. *A substantial body of opinion* supports the idea of banning all cars from the city centre.

b. *That's a matter of opinion.* I think Pele was a better player.

c. *shift in opinion* on the issue of abortion. More and more people seem to approve of it these days.

d. *irreconcilable differences of opinion* have developed between them. They can't seem to agree on anything.

e. *current climate of opinion* is before it makes any changes to the tax on fuel. It's important that they know what people generally think.

3 Adjective + opinion

Use the following adjectives in the sentences:

honest   *popular*   *second*   *strong*

1. Many people have very . . . . opinions on capital punishment. My father, for example, thinks that all murderers should be executed.

2. The article accurately reflects . . . . opinion. It's what the majority of people think.

3. I'm grateful for his advice, but I really need to get a . . . . opinion before I make a final decision. I don't want to do something that I might regret.

4. OK, if you want my . . . . opinion, I think the dress looks awful. It just doesn't suit you.

considered   *high*   *personal*   *expert*

5. I have a very . . . . opinion of Mark's abilities as an actor, but a very low opinion of him as a father. He hardly saw his children as they grew up.

6. Prime Minister, we have discussed the present crisis in depth and it is our . . . . opinion that for the good of the country you should resign.

7. . . . . opinion is divided on the issue of how to treat this condition. Some doctors would operate; others favour drugs.

8. My . . . . opinion doesn't really matter here. We need to decide for the good of everyone.

Notes

1. If someone thinks too highly of themselves, we say:
   He's got too high an opinion of himself.

2. Note these expressions:
   The general opinion is that the new traffic scheme is a good thing.
   The doctor was of the opinion that an operation was not necessary.
   Everybody is entitled to their own opinion!
   Opinion is deeply divided on this issue. I can see little hope of reaching any sort of agreement.

3. Note this very common expression:
   In my opinion, interest rates are going to go up.

4. Newspapers often carry out 'opinion polls' to find out the opinions of lots of people on the popularity of political parties.

opportunity

1 Verb + opportunity

Use the correct form of these verbs:

come up	deny	give
grab	take	miss

1. You can't let an opportunity like a trip to Australia go by. It's simply too good to . . . .

2. I'd like to . . . . this opportunity to thank you all for coming.

3. This programme . . . . the public the opportunity to make their voices heard. So get on the phone straightaway!

4. Make sure you . . . . the opportunity with both hands! You won't get another one like it for years.

5. An opportunity as good as this . . . . only once in a lifetime.

6. I would have liked to have learnt Spanish at school, but I was . . . . the opportunity. Only French and German were taught.

2 Common adjective collocations

Complete the sentences below with the following:

ample	great	missed	ideal
possible	rare	golden	right

1. We need to make an appointment with you for further tests. Please contact this office at the earliest . . . . opportunity.

2. Don't worry. You will have . . . . opportunity to ask questions after the talk. The speaker intends to stay behind for about an hour.

3. This is a . . . . opportunity to see all the painter's work together in one place. There hasn't been an opportunity like this for 20 years.

4. Look, this is the right job for you! It's a . . . . opportunity. Who else do you know gets the chance to work in New York for two years?

5. I'm not changing jobs at the moment but when the . . . . opportunity comes along, I intend to take it.

6. You mean he came to the club and I could have got his autograph! Another . . . . opportunity!

7. If you don't invest now, you'll miss a . . . . opportunity to double your money.

8. Club 18–25 offers an . . . . opportunity for you to meet other single people on holiday.

3 Determiner and quantifiers

Complete the sentences with these words:

only	much	no
this	every	an

1. Sue isn't the best company to be with. She talks about her children at . . . . possible opportunity!

2. Since we started a family we don't get . . . . opportunity to go out dancing.

3. If I have . . . . opportunity, I'll take your books back to the library for you this afternoon.

4. She's just in town for the day. This may be your one and . . . . opportunity to meet her.

5. The Professor left straight after his lecture, so there was . . . . opportunity to find out why he held such weird ideas.

6. I'd like to take . . . . opportunity to thank all of you for your support.

"We don't get much opportunity to go dancing any more!"

Notes

1. In 1-5 'arises' is also possible.

2. Note this expression:
   Make sure you make the most of this opportunity.

3. Note these ways of talking about great opportunities:
   I'll have a wonderful opportunity to practise my Italian when I'm in Rome.
   From the company's point of view, this is an excellent opportunity to expand into Europe.
   We see this agreement as an exciting opportunity for both companies to work together.

4. Note these two common expressions:
   All over the world women are demanding equal opportunities in the workplace.
   Job opportunities for women have improved greatly.

order

1 Verb + order (command)

Use the correct form of these verbs:

be under   come   disobey   receive   take

1. You're not my boss! I'm not .... orders from you.
2. In the army I was punished for .... orders. I was made to clean the toilets for a week.
3. The troops .... orders to attack the city at dawn.
4. I'm afraid you can't come in. We .... orders not to allow anybody into the building.
5. The order .... direct from the Minister to release the murderer from prison two years early.

2 Giving and obeying orders

Match the two halves of these sentences:

1. Soldiers learn to obey orders
2. Don't blame me! I'm only carrying out
3. The ship was sinking fast so the captain issued
4. Instead of stopping to think,
5. It was clear she was furious with us when
6. The sergeant barked out a series of orders
7. He was arrested for refusing

a. the order to abandon ship.
b. we just blindly followed orders.
c. without questioning them.
d. to the new recruits.
e. she gave orders that she wasn't to be disturbed.
f. someone else's orders.
g. to comply with a court order to leave the city.

Go back and underline all the verbs used with order or orders.

3 Common expressions

Use these words to complete the sentences:

doctor's   marching   strict   tall

1. All employees are under .... orders not to talk to the press. They will be sacked if they do.
2. Getting this job done on time will be a .... order. I don't know how we will be able to meet the deadline.
3. She was useless and unreliable, so she got her .... orders! She's looking for a new job.
4. He's under .... orders to cut down on his smoking and drinking.

4 Verb + order (business / restaurant)

Use the correct form of these verbs:

cancel   deal with   lose
place   send   take

1. I wish a waiter would come and .... our order!
2. We're thinking of .... a rather large order. What kind of discount could you offer?
3. I .... you my order two weeks ago, together with a cheque for £60.
4. We will .... your order immediately. Goods are generally dispatched within 24 hours of receipt of order.
5. Unfortunately, we .... an important order worth hundreds of thousands of pounds because the workers went on strike.
6. I'm afraid you will lose your deposit if you decide to .... your order.

5 Adjective + order (arrangement)

Use these adjectives in the sentences:

alphabetical   chronological   reverse
pecking   particular   running

1. Write down the events in .... order, that is, in the order in which they happened.
2. They read out the names of the winners of the competition in .... order – third, second and then first.
3. My name is Zavaroni – so I'm always at the bottom of every list, arranged in .... order!
4. The .... order for a concert is the order in which each singer or band will play.
5. The files are arranged in no .... order. If you can think of one, let me know.
6. I've just started with the company so I'm at the bottom of the .... order. I'm the last person to get a share of any of the good jobs that come up.

Notes

1. Note these adjective expressions:
   I think I'll have a side order of french fries.
   The coffee machine is out of order again!
2. Note the expression 'law and order'.

---

person

1 Determiners and quantifiers

Complete the sentences with these words:

each	first	last
one	only	single

1. When my car broke down on the motorway, not a . . . . person stopped and offered to help me.

2. My best friend is about the . . . . person that I can trust my secrets to.

3. Allow about 200gms of rice for . . . . person.

4. Democratic systems are based on the principle of . . . . person, one vote.

5. The . . . . person to give the correct answer wins the competition.

6. I wouldn't go out with Damien if he were the . . . . person on earth!

2 Common adjective collocations

Match the two halves of these situations:

1. Federico's a very private person.
2. Tom strikes me as a very humble person.
3. Bill's a very insecure person.
4. Angie seems to be a responsible person.
5. Liz is the wrong person to talk to.
6. Harry's not a very organised person.
7. Simon's a lively, talkative person.
8. Jo will be remembered as a caring, thoughtful person.

a. I think we can rely on her to finish the job.
b. You'll enjoy his company.
c. He always arrives late for meetings.
d. He was always doing things for other people.
e. She can't keep a secret for more than a minute.
f. He keeps himself to himself.
g. He's got a lot of hang-ups and low self-esteem.
h. He never talks about his achievements.

Now use these adjectives in the sentences below:

average	difficult	guilty	poor
reasonable	right	stupid	easy

9. After a difficult few months, there seems to be general agreement that Melanie is the . . . . person for the job.

10. It is a fact that the . . . . person in the street is much better-off today than they were twenty years ago.

11. The new finance director is not an . . . . person to deal with, is she?
    No, I'm finding her fairly . . . . , too.

12. The police are sifting through the evidence in an effort to find the . . . . person.

13. What . . . . person left the oven on all night! We could all have burnt to death!

14. What a state the room was in at the end of the party. I pity the . . . . person who had to clean the mess up.

15. Any . . . . , right-minded person can see that this decision is not fair.

3 Kinds of person

Match up these people with the definitions:

1. a morning person
2. a displaced person
3. a missing person
4. an outdoor person
5. a people person

a. somebody who has disappeared
b. somebody who gets on well with almost anybody
c. someone who is at their best before lunch
d. somebody who likes walking, climbing etc.
e. somebody who has been forced to leave their own country and has not found asylum in another country

---

Notes

1. Note this useful way of talking about someone:
   He's the type of person who always offers to help.

2. Note these expressions:
   It gave me a big thrill to meet Sting in person after the concert.
   Can I speak to the person in charge, please?
   Police think they have found the person responsible for the attack.
   Reactions to the treatment vary from person to person.
   Rooms cost from £20 per person.
   Customs officers found drugs concealed about his person.

3. This is a common question:
   What's Linda like as a person?

---

place

1 Verb + place

Use the correct form of these verbs:

earn   change   find   look for
mark   take   save   hold

1. Sorry, we're late. It took us ages to . . . . a parking place.

2. I'm fed up living with my parents, so I'm . . . . a place of my own.

3. It's quite common for people to . . . . their place in a book they're reading by turning down the corner of a page.

4. Come and sit here beside us. We've . . . . a place for you.

5. If you want to . . . . a place in this team, you'll have to prove you're worth it!

6. Would you like to . . . . places with me so that you can sit beside your husband?

7. Ataturk . . . . a very important place in the minds of all Turks.

8. Last-minute talks are . . . . place in an attempt to avert a strike by workers on the underground.

Notice the different meaning of 'place' in no 8. What does 'place' mean in these sentences?

a. Please state your place of birth.

b. Let's take our places round the table.

c. It's not my place to remind you of your duty.

d. I've just heard I've got a place at Oxford.

e. We had lunch at a very nice place in the centre.

f. Van Nistelroy has lost his place in the team.

2 Verbal expressions

Now complete the sentences below with these phrasal verbs:

get the feel of   turn into
come round to   get out of

1. I'll . . . . your place about nine if that's OK with you.

2. We were only in Bristol for one night, so we didn't really . . . . the place.

3. Let's . . . . this place! The food and the music are awful.

4. Those chairs blocking the fire exits could easily . . . . this place . . . . a death trap.

3 Common adjective collocations

Use the following adjectives in these sentences:

quiet   conceivable   decent   public
right   safe   uninviting   unlikely

1. I was very lucky to get this job. I just happened to be in the . . . . place at the right time.

2. I've looked in every . . . . place for my wallet, but I can't find it anywhere.

3. Remember to put your passport in a . . . . place.

4. This is a very . . . . place during the winter months, but the place is really busy in July.

5. The organisation ASH have mounted a campaign to ban smoking in all . . . . places.

6. You find things in the most . . . . places. For example, I found my shoe in the fridge the other day. It must have been my two-year-old!

7. Is there a . . . . place to eat round here?

8. The hotel was cold, empty and damp. It was a most . . . . place!

4 Place + of + noun

Use these nouns to complete the sentences:

birth   interest   safety   work   worship

1. Stonehenge is a place of great historical . . . .

2. A place of . . . . is a building used for religious services, such as a church, temple or mosque.

3. Migrating birds return every year to their place of . . . . to lay their eggs.

4. The hostel for battered wives offers a place of . . . . and refuge for women who are assaulted by men.

5. In an emergency the hospital may need to contact you at your place of . . . .

Notes

1. Note the following expressions:
   Ely is a great place for a day out.
   This is no place to bring up children.
   There was rubbish all over the place.

2. A way of talking about your home is 'my place':
   Shall we go back to your place or mine?

---

plan

1 Verb + plan

Use the correct form of these verbs:

announce	approve
change	go ahead with
make	scrap
get	wreck

1. It's important that you all look ahead and . . . . plans for the future.

2. We had to . . . . our holiday plans at the last minute, when my mother was taken into hospital.

3. The school was forced to. . . . . its plans for a new library due to a lack of financial support.

4. I'm afraid the picnic had to be cancelled. The bad weather . . . . all our plans.

5. The committee unanimously . . . . the plan. Not one person opposed it. Everybody supported it.

6. Yesterday the government . . . . plans to create thousands of new jobs.

7. If I . . . . my plan to open a restaurant, can I count on your support? I'll need good advice and some financial backing to . . . . my plans off the ground.

2 Common adjective collocations

Use the following adjectives in these sentences:

audacious	contingency	crazy
detailed	future	original

1. Although . . . . plans were drawn up for a new housing development, it didn't get planning permission.

2. What a . . . . plan! It'll never work. Who on earth thought this one up?

3. Managers have drawn up a . . . . plan to keep the factory running if there is a power failure.

4. We looked at a number of different plans for a bridge over the river, but after much discussion we decided to stick with the . . . . plan of building a tunnel under it.

5. The interviewer asked me what my . . . . plans were. I could only tell him that they were dependent on getting this job!

6. The prisoners put together an . . . . plan to escape from prison using a helicopter.

3 Noun + preposition + plan

Complete the sentences with these nouns:

beauty	change	details
favour	opposition	success

1. There's been a . . . . of plan. We're leaving next week instead of this week.

2. We expect to come up against a lot of . . . . to the plan. A number of people have voiced their objections to it already.

3. Remember that the . . . . or failure of the plan depends on you.

4. Everybody wants to know how the government is going to pay for its ambitious proposals, but the PM wouldn't give away any . . . . of their plan.

5. The government pledged its support for the plan to build a new runway at Gatwick airport. However, none of the local residents are in . . . . of the plan.

6. The . . . . of this plan, what makes it so good, is that it won't cost the members of the club a penny!

Notes

1. In 1-3 'cancel' and 'drop' are also possible. In 1-4 'spoiled' and 'scuppered' are also possible.

2. Note these ways of expressing opposition to a plan:
   We remain strongly opposed to these new plans.
   Parents are fiercely opposed to the plan to close the local primary school.
   I am totally opposed to the plan to legalise the use of cannabis for personal use.
   We are all fundamentally opposed to this plan to change the voting system.
   The workers are bitterly opposed to the plan to increase the length of the working day.

3. Note these expressions:
   There was an airline strike, so all our plans fell through at the last minute.
   I don't have any plans for the weekend.
   Your best plan would be to take the train.
   If everything goes according to plan, we should arrive around midday.
   It soon became obvious that plan A wasn't going to work, so we had to resort to plan B.

position

1 Verb + position (place)

Use the correct form of these verbs:

jostle for   occupy   change   take up

1. Government troops have . . . . defensive positions around the capital.

2. I get cramp in one leg when I drive, so I have to keep . . . . position on long journeys.

3. The castle . . . . a commanding position at the top of a hill with unrivalled views of the surrounding countryside.

4. People in the crowd . . . . the best positions to see the princess as she arrived at the theatre.

2 Verb + position (job)

Use the correct form of these verbs:

abuse   apply for   strengthen
rise   hold   fill

1. Our sales manager is leaving, and I'm thinking of . . . . the position.

2. She has . . . . the position of chief accountant since 1994.

3. This latest move is clearly intended to . . . . the President's position as head of state.

4. I'm afraid it's too late to apply. The position has already been . . . .

5. The Minister was sacked for . . . . her position by giving jobs to her friends and cronies.

6. I started as a clerk, but I've . . . . to a senior position in a government office.

3 Verb + position (attitude or opinion)

Use the correct form of these verbs:

make   reconsider   soften   take

1. This new evidence on the vaccine has forced the medical profession to seriously . . . . its position on the use of multiple vaccines for young children.

2. I have . . . . my position as clear as I can. Nothing will change my mind.

3. My parents always . . . . the position that children need lots of love rather than strict discipline.

4. The authorities are still taking a hard line on asylum seekers. They show no signs of . . . . their position.

4 Common adjective collocations

Use these adjectives in the sentences:

awkward   enviable   prominent   upright
sheltered   similar   vulnerable

1. Don't plant these bulbs in an exposed place where the wind can get at them. The plants will only thrive in a . . . . position.

2. Don't lay the box on its side. Make sure it is kept in an . . . . position at all times.

3. My parents are in the . . . . position of having enough money to retire.

4. You should display new books in a . . . . position at the front of the shop where they can be easily seen.

5. The council put me in contact with other single mothers who are in a . . . . position to me.

6. I can't understand why they built houses in such a . . . . position on the slopes of the volcano.

7. You've put me in a very . . . . position. Both candidates are my friends, so I really don't want to get involved in deciding which one gets the job.

"The position may be a bit vulnerable, but the sunsets are amazing!"

Notes

1. Note the following expression:
   I'm afraid that as I have no money, I am not in a position to help you.

2. We talk about a 'sitting, kneeling, or standing position'.

3. The question 'What's your position?' can mean either *what is your job* or *what is your stance on this issue*.

---

possibility

1 Verb + possibility

Choose the more natural collocations:

1. Keep trying. Don't give up until you have . . . . every possibility. (explored / discovered)

2. Look, we've been investigating this case for almost two years now. I think we've . . . . all the possibilities. (tried / exhausted)

3. I'm afraid that we can't give you an exact date for the completion of the building. We have to . . . . the possibility that bad weather may hold up progress. (allow for / prevail on)

4. This new breakthrough . . . . the possibility of finding a cure for MS. (raises / lifts)

5. We can't . . . . the possibility that the child was swept out to sea by a huge wave. (forget / rule out)

6. Hundreds of police were present at the Cup Final to . . . . any possibility of a repetition of last year's fighting between rival fans. (evade / avoid)

7. Let's . . . . a few other possibilities before we book the hotel. We might find somewhere a bit more convenient. (examine / discover)

8. The conviction of John Faulkner . . . . the possibility that other crimes might be solved through the use of DNA evidence. (opens up / suggests)

2 Considering and rejecting possibility

Mark the sentences C if they mean 'considering the possibility' and R if they mean 'rejecting':

1. They are examining the possibility of a complete five-year ban on fishing in the North Sea.

2. It's not likely to happen but I wouldn't rule out the possibility.

3. Have you decided how you'll travel to the meeting?
   > No, I'm still considering the possibilities.

4. At this stage of our investigation we can't exclude the possibility that he may have been murdered.

5. We are also looking at the possibility of converting the old school into a hotel.

6. Before the election the President refused to entertain the possibility of defeat.

3 Likely or unlikely possibilities

Mark the sentences below L if they are likely to happen and U if they are unlikely to happen:

1. I think we should postpone our trip to the seaside. There's a strong possibility of rain this afternoon.

2. We need to do a number of further tests as there is a remote possibility that it could be cancerous.

3. Cloudy skies are forecast so there's only a faint possibility that you will see the eclipse of the sun.

4. If sales of our products don't improve soon, I'm afraid job losses remain a real possibility.

5. There's a distinct possibility that I will be in London next week. Perhaps we can meet up.

4 Common expressions

Complete the sentences below with the following:

every   various   any   one   endless

1. In order to clear your debts, you have a number of options open to you. Selling your car is just . . . . . . possibility.

2. Is there . . . . . . possibility of you giving me a lift to the station tomorrow night?

3. Have you decided what to do?
   > No, I'm still considering the . . . . . . possibilities.

4. The cottage is surrounded by huge areas of open countryside. There are . . . . possibilities for hill-walking and fishing.

5. There is . . . . . . possibility that we will be able to complete the work on time. We're almost certain to meet the deadline.

Notes

1. Note this expression:
   We might holiday in space one day – it's not beyond the bounds of possibility.

2. If something 'has possibilities', it means it has potential:
   The house is a bit run down, but it has possibilities.

3. Both 'for' and 'of' can be used after 'possibility':
   There's a possibility of snow.
   The place has possibilities for development.

---

power

1 Verb + power

Use the correct form of these verbs:

use	*fall from*	*give*
return to	*seize*	*have*

1. The authorities . . . . the power to cancel the march if they think it will lead to civil disobedience.
2. The police . . . . their powers under the Public Order Act to remove the protesters who were blocking the entrance to the nuclear power station.
3. When one politician . . . . power, another comes to power in their place.
4. After four years out of government, the Socialist Party is expected to be . . . . power in the forthcoming election.
5. The President was ousted from power yesterday when rebel soldiers . . . . power in a bloodless coup.
6. The aim of the new legislation is to . . . . people more power over their own lives.

2 Noun + preposition + power

Use these nouns in the sentences:

rise	*hunger*
balance	*trappings*
grip	*positions*
abuse	

1. The mayor has been arrested on charges of corruption and . . . . of power.
2. He enjoyed the . . . . of power, such as chauffeur-driven cars and five-star hotels.
3. Her rapid . . . . to power surprised many people.
4. There is certainly a shortage of women in . . . . of power, but plans are being made to change this.
5. Like so many politicians, he had an insatiable . . . . for power.
6. The new employment laws mean that the . . . . of power has shifted away from workers towards employers.
7. The army refuses to hand over power to the civilian government. It is obviously reluctant to relax its . . . . on power.

3 Common adjective collocations

Complete the sentences below with the following:

creative	*destructive*	*enormous*
mysterious	*absolute*	*sweeping*

1. The . . . . power of modern weapons is terrifying.
2. She held a senior position and wielded . . . . power over the Prime Minister.
3. I don't know why Helen does everything Mark says. He seems to have some . . . . power over her.
4. During the crisis, the security forces were given . . . . powers to search people and their homes.
5. As an artist, he was at the height of his . . . . powers in his forties.
6. Mugabe was a ruthless dictator who ended up exercising . . . . power over Zimbabwe.

4 Power(s) + of + noun

Complete the sentences with these words:

advertising	*concentration*
positive thinking	*speech*

1. Chess is a game that requires great powers of . . . .
2. No one can doubt the persuasive power of . . . . – especially on TV.
3. My father had a stroke and lost the power of . . . . for a few months, but he can communicate quite well now.
4. He claims that his recovery from illness demonstrates the power of . . . . – the power of the mind over the body.

Notes

1. Note the following expressions:
   The government has promised to do everything in its power to combat terrorism.
   There's a power struggle going on at the top of the Labour Party.
2. We talk about 'nuclear power, steam power' etc.

problem

1 Verb + problem

Use the correct form of these verbs:

appreciate   ignore   pose   have
wrestle with   tackle   solve   flee from

1. We've been . . . . a few problems with our air conditioning recently.

2. Asylum seekers may be . . . . problems at home, but they often meet very serious problems when they finally settle somewhere else.

3. No one has . . . . the problem of what to do with radioactive waste.

4. We simply can't afford to avoid the problem of teenage pregnancy. I think that we need to . . . . it head on.

5. I fully . . . . your problem, but I'm afraid there is little I can do to help you.

6. Are you seriously suggesting that we should just . . . . the problem? Just turn a blind eye to it?

7. The professor . . . . the problem for weeks, but he finally had to admit defeat.

8. I'm glad Dave and Gill and the kids are coming to stay, but it . . . . the problem of where they are all going to sleep!

2 Common adjective collocations

Choose the more natural collocations below:

1. Smoking seems a . . . . problem among teenage girls, in particular. Every year more and more are getting hooked. *(growing / rising)*

2. I'm afraid this is a very . . . . problem which requires prompt attention. *(serious / large)*

3. There are a number of reasons why Geoff is not suitable for the job, but the . . . . problem is that he is famous for rubbing people up the wrong way! *(simple / basic)*

4. One of the most . . . . problems facing cities today is traffic congestion. *(pressing / important)*

5. I believe that traffic congestion in large cities is an . . . . problem. I can see no way round it. And it's only going to get worse and worse. *(unsolvable / insurmountable)*

6. I wish there was a simple answer to this issue, but it's a very . . . . problem, and it will require a complex solution. *(complicated / complete)*

3 Noun + preposition + problem

Use these nouns to complete the sentences:

extent   answer   root
nature   approach   view

1. We must get to the . . . . of this problem. We need to discover the cause of it before too much damage is done.

2. There isn't a straight . . . . to the problem because it just isn't that simple.

3. We aren't getting anywhere. I feel we need to take a fresh . . . . to the problem.

4. The full . . . . of the problem became clear when the pilots realised that the plane was almost out of fuel.

5. We need to take an overall . . . . of the problem. We need to consider all parts of it.

6. If you think that our profitability will improve simply by making staff cuts, then you misunderstand the . . . . of the problem.

Notes

1. In 1-8 'create' is also possible.
   In 3-1 'bottom' is also possible.

2. Note these expressions:
   This problem won't just disappear overnight.

3. If you think someone is going to disagree, you can ask: *Do you have a problem with this?*

4. Note the prepositions with 'problem':
   The government is looking for new ways to deal with the problem of homelessness.
   Unemployment is a serious problem for a lot of young people in this area.

5. Note that we use the expression 'No problem' to mean something is OK:
   Can you look after the shop for an hour or so?
   > No problem!

6. A 'thorny problem' is a difficult problem to which there is no obvious and easy solution.

7. Note these kinds of problems: *personal problems / health problems / a drink problem / a weight problem / an attitude problem.*

8. A 'problem child' or family is one which causes problems for other people.

9. Note the useful expression: 'the only problem is':
   The only problem with this car is it's incredibly expensive!

process

1 Verb + process

Use the correct form of these verbs:

begin   *develop*   *repeat*
reverse   *speed up*   *streamline*

1. For perfect boiled rice, wash and rinse the rice with cold water, then . . . . the process until the liquid is clear.

2. The company have . . . . a new process for producing microchips more cheaply.

3. Going to the passport office in person . . . . the process of renewing my visa. Instead of taking three weeks I had a new visa within two days.

4. Unfortunately, ageing is one process that we cannot . . . . !

5. If we don't . . . . our production process, we are going to end up inefficient and uncompetitive.

6. When the sperm enters the egg, it . . . . the process of fertilisation and the creation of a new life.

2 Common adjective collocations

Use the following adjectives in these sentences:

painful   *lengthy*   *delicate*

1. My friend Dave was badly burned in the accident. The doctors say that recovery from these injuries will be a long and . . . . process.

2. Removing a piece of dirt from somebody's eye is a very . . . . process. It needs to be done very carefully to avoid damaging the eye.

3. It was a . . . . process recovering from my operation. It really took the best part of 2 years!

natural   *gradual*   *complicated*

4. I thought buying a house would be easy and straightforward but it turned out to be a long and . . . . process. I've lost count of the number of forms I've had to complete and sign.

5. I didn't just wake up one day and decide to become a Buddhist. My conversion was a very . . . . process which took place over a number of years.

6. Learning our mother tongue is a . . . . process. It just happens! Many of us wish it could be the same when learning a second language later in life!

3 Types of process

Complete the sentences with these words:

decision-making   *healing*   *democratic*
manufacturing   *peace*   *selection*

1. Our yoghurt is tested several times during the . . . . process to ensure that it is of the highest quality.

2. When choosing a holiday, I think it is best if all the family are involved in the . . . . process.

3. You will be asked to perform a number of tasks during the . . . . process. These activities are designed to test your drive and initiative.

4. This latest bombing incident has de-railed the . . . . process. The representatives of both governments have gone home.

5. Many sick people believe that positive thinking can accelerate the . . . . process. Some people claim that it can even cure cancer.

6. The attack on the polling station was widely denounced as an attack on the . . . . process itself.

"Trying to reverse the ageing process!"

Notes

1. Note the following common expressions:
   Taking responsibility for yourself is an important part of the process of growing up.
   Making mistakes is an essential part of the learning process.

2. You reject other solutions if you make a decision 'by a process of elimination':
   We decided that the culprit had to be Ted – by a careful process of elimination.

3. Note this useful expression:
   The hospital is in the process of modernisation.
   We are in the process of moving to new premises.

progress

1 Verb + progress

Use the correct form of these verbs:

bring	*discuss*
make	*follow*
hold up	*monitor*

1. At the end of each school term parents . . . . their child's progress with a teacher.

2. Since he moved to his new school, William has . . . . a lot of progress.

3. I remember my Uncle George took a personal interest in my education. He . . . . my progress closely and gave me help and a lot of encouragement.

4. The British were enthusiastic builders of railways. They believed railways . . . . progress and civilisation to less developed countries.

5. Each student's progress is closely . . . . We use a system of regular tests to measure their progress.

6. Fallen trees are . . . . the progress of the rescue workers.

2 Common adjective collocations

Use the following adjectives in these sentences:

disappointing	*good*
rapid	*real*
slow	*steady*

1. We are making slow but . . . . progress. The job should only take about a day longer than we anticipated.

2. There has been such . . . . progress in computer technology over the last few years that I can hardly keep up with the speed of change.

3. They are having great problems trying to reach the trapped men. Progress is painfully . . . .

4. Fortunately, there wasn't much traffic on the roads, so we made . . . . progress and arrived with plenty of time to spare.

5. The police have made no . . . . progress in the investigation and detectives are now appealing to the public for help.

6. No agreement has been reached after five days of discussions. Progress has been . . . . – to say the least!

Go back and underline the adjective collocations.

3 Expressions with prepositions

Choose the correct preposition for each sentence:

in	*of*	*on*

1. We are frustrated at the lack . . . . progress.

2. Although she's recovering from her illness, her rate . . . . progress is quite slow.

3. In order to continue your financial assistance, we will need regular updates . . . . your progress.

4. John's teacher says that his reading and writing is showing signs . . . . progress.

5. Now that the project has started, we will need a weekly meeting for the next two months to keep a close check . . . . progress.

6. There has not been much progress . . . . the border dispute between the two countries.

7. Political observers noted that there had been a lot of progress . . . . human rights.

8. A concert was . . . . progress in the school hall, so we looked for another room.

9. The college will be closed while maintenance work is . . . . progress.

What is the meaning of 'progress' in nos 8 and 9?

Notes

1. In 1-1 'review' is also possible.

2. We talk about *economic* and *technological* progress:
   The country has made significant economic progress in recent years.
   Technological progress has allowed scientists to build smaller and smaller computers.

3. We use the following expression to say that not all progress is good:
   We are destroying the planet with our technology – all in the name of progress.

4. Note the following ways of expressing 'holding up' progress:
   His progress was hindered by his lack of experience.
   The inability of management to decide what it wants has hampered the progress of the plan.
   Continuing disagreement is impeding progress towards reform of the educational system.
   By refusing to operate the new machines, the print workers were accused of standing in the way of progress.

promise

1 Verb + promise

Use the correct form of these verbs:

break   *have*   *make*   *keep*

1. I'll try to get back in time for the party, but I'm not . . . . any promises.

2. Do I . . . . your promise that you won't tell anyone else about this?

3. As expected, the government failed to . . . . its promise to improve health care.

4. David, my ex-husband, keeps promising the kids he'll take them out, and then he rings to say he can't come round. I wish he'd stop . . . . his promises. The kids get so disappointed.

extract   *hold to*   *give*   *go back on*

5. Can you . . . . us a promise that the work will be completed on time?

6. After months of complaining, and after dozens of letters and phone calls, we eventually . . . . a promise from the travel agency that they would refund the full cost of our holiday.

7. British car workers were furious that the parent company had . . . . its promise to build the new model in the UK.

8. The opposition is determined to force the government to . . . . its election promises. They say they will not let it go back on any of the promises it made during the election campaign.

2 Promise (uncountable)

Promise also means a sign that a person or thing will be successful. Choose the more natural collocation in each sentence:

1. Our younger son, Jack, took up the violin a couple of years ago. He's . . . . a lot of promise and his school wants him to have extra tuition.
(holding / showing)

2. It's a good example of a film which was . . . . promise, but bombed at the box office.
(full of / filled with)

3. This actor had a brilliant early career, but he failed to . . . . his early promise. Now he's lucky if he gets any work at all.
(fulfil / fill)

3 Common adjective collocations

Choose the more natural adjective in the following sentences:

1. She made a . . . . promise to him when they were married that she would give up smoking.
(serious / solemn)

2. If I were you, I wouldn't be too disappointed if Mike doesn't turn up. He's famous for making . . . . promises that he never keeps.
(empty / blank))

3. The politicians made . . . . promises about tax cuts but they refused to discuss them in any detail when asked for more information.
(large / big)

4. After a string of . . . . promises, it is becoming clear that the company cannot provide the level of service and reliability that we need.
(broken / unkept)

5. Before they went bankrupt, ECO Transport made all sorts of . . . . promises, but fortunately nobody believed them.
(wild / crazy)

6. Think carefully before committing yourself. Try to avoid making any . . . . promises that you may regret later.
(rash / fantastic)

"Showing promise!"

Notes

1. Note the following expressions:
   I'll tidy up my room before I go out tonight.
   > Is that a promise?
   True to his promise, Paul returned my notes before the next class.

2. We talk of election promises:
   The government is facing criticism for failing to carry out its election promises.

proposal

1 Verb + proposal

Use the correct form of these verbs:

approve	*consider*	*change*
back	*put forward*	*ditch*

1. Your new proposals are excellent. Make sure you have costed them carefully before you . . . . . . them . . . . at the next meeting of the board.

2. In the present economic climate, it will be an uphill struggle to get the new proposals for an increase in research spending . . . .

3. The President was forced to . . . . his proposals for a new space programme after Congress rejected it.

4. Now that I've had a chance to . . . . your proposal in more detail, I'm not so sure it's such a good idea after all.

5. The original proposals for the superstore had to be . . . . after objections were lodged by local residents.

6. I hope you're going to . . . . my proposal to have the staffroom redecorated. I need your support.

Go back and underline the verb collocations.

2 Proposal + verb

Use the correct form of these verbs:

aim at	*allow*	*go ahead*
backfire	*meet with*	*work*

1. These new proposals would . . . . more people to buy their own homes.

2. Your proposal is all very well in theory, but I don't think it will . . . . in practice.

3. The proposal to increase the managing director's salary by 50% . . . . stiff opposition from shareholders at the company AGM.

4. I don't think the latest proposals, ... breaking the political stalemate in the Middle East, have much chance of success.

5. Despite strong objections from the public, the proposal to de-nationalise water . . . . and now we're all paying more for it.

6. The Progressive Party's proposal to hold an enquiry into corruption . . . . when it was disclosed that several party officials have been arrested on suspicion of accepting bribes!

3 Noun + preposition + proposal

Complete the sentences with these expressions:

concern over	*consideration of*	*in favour of*
close look at	*reactions to*	*support for*

1. After careful . . . . your proposal, I regret to say that we were unable to give it our approval.

2. A recent poll suggests there is widespread . . . . the proposal to spend more on the health service.

3. So far, ... the proposal for a new community newspaper have been favourable.

4. Leading scientists have voiced their . . . . proposals to build five more nuclear power stations before 2020.

5. Everyone . . . . this proposal, please raise your hand.

6. We will be taking a . . . . the latest proposals in the next few weeks to see if they are viable in the long term.

"All those in favour of the proposal?"

Notes

1. In 1-2 *accepted* is also possible.

2. Note the following expressions:
   Under the original proposal, most families would have been £30 a week better off.

3. Note the verb-adverb collocations in the following:
   The party voted overwhelmingly against the proposal to increase taxes.
   The proposal for a new theatre was unanimously approved by the city council. They gave it their full backing.

4. A *proposal* also means an offer of marriage:
   Martin was heartbroken when I rejected his proposal.

quality

1 Verb collocations

Use the correct form of these verbs:

vary	*affect*	*test*
deteriorate	*improve*	*suffer*

1. My father's quality of life has . . . . dramatically since his operation. He can now see things he couldn't see before.
2. The increase in class sizes will adversely . . . . the quality of education in our schools.
3. The restaurants on the seafront . . . . a lot in terms of price and quality.
4. We . . . . the quality of the sea water every week during the summer to make sure it is safe for bathing.
5. We may be better off nowadays, but there is no question that our quality of life has . . . .
6. The company is cutting costs, so the quality of its products will definitely . . . . as a result.

2 Noun + preposition + quality

Use one of these prepositions in the sentences:

in	*for*	*on*

1. The company has a worldwide reputation . . . . the quality and reliability of its products.
2. We can no longer have confidence . . . . the quality of the food we eat. It contains so many added chemicals these days.
3. The main emphasis should always be . . . . quality rather than quantity.
4. John's work has shown a marked improvement . . . . quality this year.

3 Different qualities

Match up these ideas with the ideas below:

a. *air quality*	e. *water quality*
b. *personal qualities*	f. *managerial qualities*
c. *leadership qualities*	g. *medicinal qualities*
d. *negative qualities*	h. *artistic qualities*

1. Army officers must have good . . . .
2. Famous painters have excellent . . . .
3. A lot of disease is caused by poor . . . .
4. The boss of a big firm needs good . . . .
5. An interviewer is looking for your . . . .
6. The water at the spa has excellent . . . .
7. Too much traffic causes poor . . . .
8. Nobody is proud of their . . . .

4 Common adjective collocations

Choose the more natural adjective below:

1. The acting was of very . . . . quality. There were some great performances but Peter Daley was terrible. *(variable / different)*
2. The fact that something is cheap doesn't necessarily mean it's of . . . . quality. *(poor / weak)*
3. I'm so impressed by the . . . . sound quality of CDs that I've stopped buying audio cassettes. *(superior / better)*
4. A new seafood restaurant has just opened. The food and the service are of the . . . . quality. *(best / highest)*
5. No smoker doubts the . . . . quality of tobacco. *(habitual / addictive)*
6. The cheese from the region has a . . . . quality and flavour not found anywhere else. *(unique / uniform)*

"We only use ingredients of the highest quality."

Notes

1. Note these 'quality of' expressions:
   These new drugs will improve the quality of life for cancer patients.
   He takes great pride in the quality of his work.

2. Quality or qualities can also refer to personal characteristics:
   The essential quality of a good teacher is patience.
   What quality do you most admire in others?

3. Note these quality + noun expressions:
   I've started working part-time so that I can spend more quality time with my children.
   I only read quality newspapers, like The Times or The Guardian.
   The market for quality cars like Volvos or BMWs remains strong.
   We only use top-quality ingredients in our cooking.

question

1 Verb + question

Use the correct form of these verbs:

answer	avoid
expect	invite
repeat	have
raise	misunderstand

1. Please read the instructions carefully, then . . . . the following questions.

2. Do you mind if I . . . . the embarrassing question of expenses? How much do we get?

3. The Prime Minister wasn't . . . . a question about his private life and it caught him completely off guard.

4. For the benefit of those who weren't listening the first time, I will . . . . the question.

5. I'm afraid you've completely . . . . my question.

6. At the end of his talk, the speaker . . . . questions from the audience.

7. Just answer the question I asked and stop trying to . . . . it!

8. Does anyone . . . . any more questions?

2 Common adjective collocations

Use the following adjectives in these sentences:

burning	innocent
open	personal
straight	unexpected

1. I expect a straight answer to a . . . . question, so don't give me any rubbish about having to consult your colleagues first!

2. Do you mind if I ask you a rather . . . . question? It's about your relationship with Paula. > Sure, go ahead.

3. Whether we move to London or not is still an . . . . question. We're having problems making our minds up.

4. The speaker was clearly caught off balance by the . . . . question.

5. I only asked a perfectly . . . . question, and he came out with all this abuse! I don't know what he got all upset about!

6. The . . . . question at the moment is – will interest rates go up and by how much?

Go back and underline the adjective collocations.

3 Noun + preposition + question

Complete the sentences with these nouns:

barrage	kind	reply	series

1. His vague . . . . to my question was somewhat unsatisfactory.

2. At the public meeting, the speaker was faced with a . . . . of angry questions from the floor.

3. You work your way through the program by answering a . . . . of yes/no questions.

4. Asking this . . . . of question could get you into deep trouble.

"Popping the question!"

Notes

1. In 1-3 'anticipating' is also possible.
   In 1-7 'evade' and 'sidestep' are also possible.

2. If you 'pop the question', you ask somebody to marry you!

3. Note the following verbs which follow 'question':
   Questions remain about the President's honesty.
   The final question completely foxed the panel of experts.

4. Note the following adjectives used to describe difficult questions:
   Children often ask awkward questions about sex.
   I felt he dealt well with a very tricky question.

5. Note these expressions:
   The audience was invited to put questions to both the speakers.
   Journalists bombarded the President with questions about the war.
   We will win the cup. There is no question about it.
   I'm afraid a day off tomorrow is out of the question.

6. A 'searching' or 'probing' question is one which someone usually doesn't want to answer:
   In court he was asked searching questions about the nature of his private life.

---

rate

1 Adjective + rate (speed)

Use the following adjectives in these sentences:

tremendous   *own*   *present*
average   *this*   *steady*

1. Babies don't grow at a . . . . rate. They grow in fits and starts.

2. Throughout my teaching I've always let my students work at their . . . . . . rate.

3. The car was going at a . . . . rate as it passed us. It must have been doing over 150 kilometres an hour.

4. If the numbers of pandas continue to decrease at their . . . . rate, they will be extinct in ten years.

5. Most of us walk at an . . . . rate of about 5 kilometres an hour.

6. We'll be lucky if we get there by midnight at . . . . rate! Can't you go any faster?

2 Rate (money)

Complete the sentences with these words:

interest   *exchange*
flat   *going*
variable   *inflation*
hourly   *concessionary*

1. What are people usually paid for this kind of work?
   > I've no idea what the . . . . rate is.

2. We offer special reduced rates for students and pensioners. These . . . . rates are also available to the unemployed.

3. Please note that our rates are . . . .
   If you make a call during peak hours, it is charged at a higher rate.

4. We charge a . . . . rate of £2 per hour for internet access, unlike some companies which charge you double before six pm.

5. I need to change these pounds into dollars. What's the current . . . . rate?

6. . . . . rates are at their lowest for 40 years.

7. There has been a further fall in the rate of . . . . this month.

8. The . . . . rate for hotel and restaurant workers can be as low as £4.50. That's not enough to live on.

3 Other types of rate

Complete the sentences with these words:

birth   *crime*
divorce   *dropout*
heart   *success*
death   *survival*

1. She is a highly-paid lawyer because she has a high . . . . rate in the cases she handles.

2. The university has a very low . . . . rate. Only 2% of students fail to complete their courses.

3. He argued that the . . . . rate would be reduced if the police were armed, but few people agreed with him.

4. You attach this machine to your finger and it measures your . . . . rate.

5. With new medicines, the . . . . rate for people who have this disease is now an amazing 92%.

6. The . . . . rate has risen steeply in recent years as more and more women have the financial resources to support themselves.

7. In Southern Africa the . . . . rate from AIDS is getting worse and worse.

8. The national . . . . rate remained static for a decade, then it started to fall steadily as the standard of living increased.

Notes

1. Note this expression:
   Figures published today show another rise in the rate of unemployment.

2. We talk about 'high' and 'low' rate of something:
   We put the low crime rate in the area down to good policing.

3. We talk of *bank rates, interest rates, hourly rates* and *daily rates.*
   Banks have increased interest rates by half of one per cent.

4. We talk about *birth rates, death rates* and *infant mortality rates.*

5. In the UK 'rates' sometimes means local taxes. For example: *water rates.*

reaction

1 Verb collocations

Use the correct form of these verbs:

affect	give	predict	get
be	require	vary	watch

1. I always loved to .... the reactions of my children when they opened their Christmas presents.

2. Driving after drinking even a small amount of alcohol is difficult as it .... your reactions.

3. It is often difficult to .... people's reactions to a new idea in advance.

4. What sort of reaction did you .... when you told them you were the new inspector?

5. The President .... his reaction to the crisis in a carefully-worded press statement.

6. Table tennis is a sport that .... very fast reactions.

7. I understand there's .... no reaction to my letter.

8. People's reaction to the film .... a lot. Some loved it, while others simply hated it.

2 Common adjective collocations

Use these adjectives in the sentences:

angry	delayed	favourable	immediate
violent	instinctive	mixed	natural

1. The proposal has received a generally .... reaction. Most people seem to accept the need for change.

2. There has been a very .... reaction to the plans to cut benefits to single mothers.

3. When I heard the news of my friend's death, my .... reaction was one of utter shock.

4. There has been a .... reaction to the new timetable. Some people like it, but others don't.

5. Don't worry. Everyone feels lonely when they first leave home. It's a perfectly .... reaction.

6. I fainted twenty minutes after leaving the doctor's surgery. I suffered a .... reaction to the injection the doctor had given me.

7. When things go wrong the .... reaction of most people is to look for somebody to blame.

8. As soon as he took the medicine, he had a .... reaction to it, and died within hours. It was tragic.

3 Types of reaction

Match up the meanings with these different types of reaction:

1. an allergic reaction
2. a chain reaction
3. a gut reaction
4. a knee-jerk reaction
5. a subconscious reaction

a. one event which sets off lots of linked reactions
b. a reaction in yourself which you are not aware of
c. an instinctive reaction
d. a negative medical reaction eg a rash
e. an immediate and automatic reaction

Now use the collocations in 1–5 in these sentences:

6. Whenever there is a report of some particularly brutal attack on children or old people, there is the usual .... reaction, demanding the return of the death penalty.

7. I don't know what your reaction to all this malicious gossip is, but my .... reaction is to ignore it completely and hope it will go away.

8. Drinking milk can cause an .... reaction such as a running nose or coughing in children, while eating peanuts can trigger a very violent and even fatal reaction.

9. There is a danger that this local dispute could set off a .... reaction that would endanger the whole of the world.

10. I am sure that all these headaches I've been having are just a .... reaction to all the stress I've been under recently.

Notes

1. In 2-3 'first' and 'initial' are also possible.

2. Note the following:
   You can imagine my reaction when I met my mother for the first time in 30 years.
   A relief fund was set up in reaction to the disaster in order to help the victims and their families.

3. A 'chemical reaction' is a natural process that takes place between chemicals:
   The energy is generated by a chemical reaction between hydrogen and oxygen.

reason

1 Verb + reason

Use the correct form of these verbs:

> explain   have
> give   understand
> know   see

1. Mel and Frank . . . . every reason to be unhappy. He lost his job last year and now she's been told she might lose hers!

2. I . . . . no reason for us to depart from our usual practices in this hospital. We will treat the Prime Minister just like any other patient.

3. I could . . . . you any number of reasons for not going to Elizabeth's party. But just tell her that I'm not feeling very well.

4. I'd like to . . . . the reason why you're so late.

5. He died suddenly at the age of 21 and the doctors are at a loss to . . . . the reason for his sudden death. A second autopsy will have to be held.

6. I don't . . . . the reason why computers can't repair themselves. I would have thought someone could write a program.

Go back and underline the verb collocations.

2 Common adjective collocations

Use the following adjectives in these sentences:

> apparent   main
> particular   simple
> sentimental   valid

1. Our son isn't going to university for the . . . . reason that he can't afford it. And neither can we.

2. Why do you want to know her name?
   > Oh, no . . . . reason. I was just wondering.

3. She kept all her late husband's letters and diaries for . . . . reasons. They reminded her of all the good times that they had together.

4. Do you have a . . . . reason for being absent from work or did you just take a day off?

5. For no . . . . reason, the man opposite me in the train suddenly got up and started screaming and shouting. I think he must have been ill.

6. *The Guardian* may be left-wing, but that's not why I buy it. The . . . . reason I read it is because it reports places that other papers don't.

3 Common expressions

Complete the sentences with these words:

> for   to   why

1. The wonderful weather in the winter is our main reason . . . . choosing to live in Portugal.

2. There's no earthly reason . . . . you should feel guilty. The accident had nothing to do with you.

3. There's no reason . . . . be concerned. He has a temperature, but he'll be fine in the morning.

4. There's no rhyme or reason . . . . her behaviour. One day she's nice, the next she's really nasty.

5. I expect there's some good reason . . . . them not turning up. I'm sure they'll phone.

6. There's no reason . . . . we shouldn't win. We have the best players and they're on top form.

7. Sue had every reason . . . . be angry. Jerry shouldn't have taken her car without her permission.

Notes

1. When you can't explain something, you can use these expressions:
   For some reason, I just didn't like him.
   For some unaccountable reason, my letter of application never arrived at the office.
   For some obscure reason, he keeps his money in his left shoe.
   He's desperately ill, but for some perverse reason he refuses to see a doctor.

2. Note these types of reason:
   She wants to change her job for purely personal reasons.
   The man cannot be named for legal reasons.
   There's no compelling reason to act. (really important)

3. Note the following expressions:
   For obvious reasons we have changed the names of the people in the article.
   The building has been closed for reasons of public safety.
   Due to reasons beyond our control, the 4.15 flight to Edinburgh has been cancelled.
   For reasons best known to herself, she gave up her job and left town.
   Why do you ignore him?
   > I have my reasons. (which I'm not telling you.)

record

1 Verb + record (highest / best)

Use the correct form of these verbs:

break	hold	reach
knock	set	stand

1. The footballer Rivaldo . . . . a new record for the amount of money paid for a footballer when he joined the Barcelona team.

2. Unemployment has . . . . an all-time record of 4 million.

3. Maurice Green . . . . the world record for the 100 metres and for a time was the fastest man on earth.

4. The movie *Titanic* . . . . all box-office records, making more money than any other film before.

5. Everyone knew she was going to beat the world marathon record, but she actually . . . . over two minutes off it!

6. The world long jump record . . . . for over 20 years until Bob Beamon smashed it with one enormous leap at the Mexico City Olympics.

2 Noun + noun collocations

Use these nouns to complete the sentences:

turnout	time	number	low

1. There's been a record . . . . of applications for the job.

2. I left an hour earlier than usual and I got to work in record . . . .

3. The euro was down again. In fact it hit a record . . . . against the pound at the close of trading yesterday.

4. There's a record . . . . for this year's London marathon. More than 50,000 want to run the race.

audience	profits	temperatures	levels

5. Drug use amongst young people has risen to record . . . .

6. This year's Glastonbury rock festival attracted a record . . . . with 40,000 fans flocking to hear their favourite bands.

7. The company has made record . . . . this year.

8. We've seen record . . . . this summer – the highest since records began.

3 Adjective + record (written account)

Use the following adjectives in these sentences:

accurate	confidential	dental	official

1. Many of the bodies recovered from the crash could only be identified by their . . . . records.

2. . . . . records must be kept in case the tax authorities arrive to inspect us.

3. Your medical records are strictly . . . . Only you and your doctor have access to them.

4. All births, deaths and marriages are entered in the . . . . records. Most of these records have been computerised in recent years.

4 Adjective + record (the past)

Complete the sentences with these words:

clean	criminal	past
poor	safety	track

1. The country has been criticised for its very . . . . record on human rights.

2. I have no doubts about investing in this company. They have a proven . . . . record.

3. He has a . . . . record as long as your arm, so he's well-known to the police!

4. I'd never fly with an airline that has a bad . . . . record, would you?

5. The defendant got off relatively lightly because the judge took his . . . . record into account when passing sentence.

6. I can't see him getting the job. His . . . . record will weigh heavily against him.

> ### Notes
>
> 1. To get to the truth is to 'set the record straight':
>   *I'm determined to set the record straight this time!*
>
> 2. If something is 'in the records', it is in the archives:
>   *If you search the records, you'll find he was married.*
>
> 3. Record also has another meaning:
>   *Some people still prefer vinyl records to CDs.*
>
> 4. If you speak 'off the record', it is not official:
>   *Off the record, he has no hope of getting this job.*
>
> 5. If something is 'on record', it is on file:
>   *The PM is on the record as saying he is pro-Europe.*

relationship

1 Verb + relationship

Use the correct form of these verbs:

build up	*fall apart*
have	*break off*
improve	*work*

1. I saw Millie and Jake walking hand in hand. They must be . . . . some sort of relationship.

2. Fortunately the relationship between the police and the local community has . . . . since last month's riots.

3. Let's call it a day! I don't think our relationship is going to . . . . We don't agree on anything.

4. Our business has grown and grown because we concentrated on . . . . good relationships with all our clients – big and small.

5. When Jane discovered that her new boyfriend was still in touch with his old girlfriend, she . . . . the relationship immediately.

6. Liz and Harry have split up. Their relationship . . . . after Harry started travelling in his work.

2 Common adjective collocations

Complete the sentences with these words:

close	*lasting*
love–hate	*physical*
stable	*working*

1. Many of the staff find our new MD difficult to work with and don't get on with him. However, I seem to have established a good . . . . relationship with him right from the start.

2. I have a very . . . . relationship with my youngest brother. I had to look after him when he was a boy. We still spend a great deal of time together.

3. I have a . . . . relationship with my job! Sometimes I find my work very interesting while at other times I just want to be somewhere else.

4. They've never fallen out with each other in twenty years of marriage. They obviously have a very . . . . relationship.

5. They see a lot of each other but their relationship is strictly platonic. They have no kind of . . . . relationship as far as I know.

6. Sadly, our affair was brief. It did not develop into a . . . . relationship.

3 Positive and negative relationships

Mark the expressions in colour P (positive relationship, or B (bad relationship):

1. I enjoy a fairly harmonious relationship with my children. It's always been friendly and peaceful.

2. I have a rather uneasy relationship with my mother-in-law. I'm not comfortable with her and I find it quite a strain having her to stay with us.

3. I feel sorry for Marie. She's had a string of disastrous relationships since the breakup of her marriage.

4. They appear to have a healthy relationship – they can talk about most things and they remain on good terms even when they disagree.

5. They have a stormy relationship. One minute they are looking lovingly into each other's eyes, the next they are shouting and arguing with each other.

4 Expressions with prepositions

Complete the sentences below with these nouns:

breakdown	*details*	*nature*
questions	*strain*	

1. She's applied for a divorce. Money problems have put a severe . . . . on their relationship.

2. He deliberately misled us about the . . . . of their relationship. He said they were just good friends, but they've been having an affair for years.

3. The most common cause of depression today is the . . . . of a close relationship.

4. The local police chief dodged . . . . on his relationship with the local drugs mafia.

5. The Sunday papers were full of pictures of the bishop plus all the sordid . . . . of his relationship with the actress.

Notes

1. In 1-3 'last' is also possible.
   In 1-4 'establish' is also possible.

2. Note the question:
   What's your relationship to Bill? > He's my nephew.

3. Note the following relationship:
   Trust is a key factor in the doctor–patient relationship.

4. 'In a relationship' means to have a lover:
   No, I'm not married, but I'm in a relationship right now.

---

report

1 Verb + report

Use the correct form of these verbs:

blame	deny
highlight	publish
recommend	give

1. The committee are due to . . . . their long-awaited report on the health service next week.

2. A spokesman refused either to confirm or . . . . the reports that bank rates were about to rise.

3. I've got to . . . . a report on our financial situation to the board meeting on Friday.

4. The report . . . . some of the problems in schools today. In particular, it identifies the main causes of violence and lack of discipline.

5. The report calls for a total ban on smoking in night clubs. It also . . . . that all buildings be fitted with smoke detectors.

6. Initial reports . . . . the train driver for the accident, but the official report released yesterday exonerated the driver from all responsibility.

Go back and underline all the verb collocations.

2 Common adjective collocations

Use the following adjectives in these sentences:

biased	live
damning	detailed
eye-witness	unconfirmed

1. In a few minutes we hope to bring you a . . . . report from the games in Australia via satellite.

2. A . . . . and in-depth report on the Prime Minister's resignation will follow shortly.

3. The government complained that the BBC's reports of the war were . . . . It expected the BBC's reporting to be objective and impartial.

4. The version of events given by the army was contradicted by . . . . reports from locals.

5. The committee published a . . . . report on the running of the company. In particular, it is highly critical of senior management.

6. . . . . reports said that at least eighty people had been killed in riots. However, a government spokesman claimed that these reports were greatly exaggerated.

Go back and underline all the other interesting collocations in this exercise.

3 Noun + preposition + report

Complete the sentences with these nouns:

recommendations	contents	light
publication	touches	copy

1. The government has accepted the key . . . . in Lord Talbot's recently published report on drug-taking among school-age children.

2. I will send you a . . . . of the report as soon as it is ready.

3. There will be an investigation to find out who leaked the . . . . of the report to the press.

4. The government has decided that . . . . of the report would be contrary to the public interest.

5. I spent all morning putting the finishing . . . . to my report.

6. The company will have to revise some of its health and safety procedures in the . . . . of this report.

4 Types of report

Match the two halves of these sentences:

1. Tune into Radio 4 while driving – the traffic and weather reports are

2. The judge will delay his verdict until he receives a medical report

3. Can you give us a progress report

4. The chairman of the company presented the annual report

5. She dismissed the newspaper reports of the break-up of her marriage

a. on the offender.
b. on what has happened so far?
c. always up to the minute.
d. as pure speculation.
e. to the shareholders.

Notes

1. Note these expressions:
   According to news reports, there was only one survivor.
   We're getting reports from the scene of the crash that about 20 cars were involved.

2. You may hear this on the television news:
   The following report contains images which some viewers may find upsetting.

---

request

1 Verb + request

Use the correct form of these verbs:

deal with   ignore
grant   make
meet with   receive
agree to   refuse

1. I don't get on with my boss, so I've . . . . a request for a transfer to another department.

2. She's such a nice person that I couldn't bring myself to . . . . her request.

3. The box office has been inundated with requests for tickets. We've . . . . over one thousand requests since the telephone lines opened at 9 this morning.

4. I applied for two months' unpaid leave to travel around India, but I'm afraid my request has . . . . a flat refusal!

5. Please be patient. We are a bit understaffed today. Your request will be . . . . in due course.

6. We've just had a request for help from a hospital in Zimbabwe. I don't think we can . . . . it.

7. The judge . . . . the request for a break when some startling new evidence suddenly came to light.

8. The deposed president's request for political asylum has been . . . . , so he will be able to remain in France indefinitely.

2 Common adjective collocations

Use the following adjectives in these sentences:

special   last   reasonable
popular   repeated   urgent

1. I've made . . . . requests to my neighbours to turn their music down, but they just think I'm mad.

2. My father's . . . . request was that there should be no flowers at his funeral.

3. You've nothing to lose by asking for a rise. It seems a perfectly . . . . request to make.

4. He received an . . . . request to meet the Prime Minister and left for London immediately.

5. I've got a . . . . request. Could you play 'All you need is love'?

6. The film is on TV every Christmas by . . . . request.

3 Expressions with prepositions

Complete the phrases in italics with a suitable preposition:

1. I'm here . . . . *the request of* my boss. He couldn't make the meeting and asked me to take his place.

2. Full details are available . . . . *request.* Just send a stamped addressed envelope to the address below.

3. The writer's name was withheld, ... *request.* Given the content of the article, the author feared for his safety.

4. We've had lots of *requests . . . . more information* about visa requirements for Tibet.

"Your request will be dealt with in due course, Sir. We're under quite a lot of pressure today."

Notes

1. In 2-6 note the fixed expression 'by popular request'. Something happens by popular request if lots of people ask for it.

2. Note the phrasal verbs in the following:
   The bus company turned down a request for reduced prices for pensioners. (refused)
   He put in a request for a week's extra holiday, but he doesn't hold out much hope of the boss granting it. (made)

3. In 3-2 if something is available on request, you have to write for it specially.

4. If you ask for something for yourself, you do so 'at your own request.'
   The footballer, Ali Smith, has been put on the transfer list at his own request.

---

response

1 Common adjective collocations

Use the following adjectives in these sentences:

disappointing   enthusiastic   initial
mixed   positive   satisfactory

1. The response to the proposal, in the main, has been very . . . . Everyone I've spoken to is in favour.

2. There was an . . . . response to my suggestion that we go camping for the weekend. Everybody's really excited about the idea.

3. When I heard what he said about me, my . . . . response was one of anger.

4. If I don't receive a . . . . response from you, I will be forced to put this matter into the hands of my solicitor.

5. The council's decision to subsidise public transport has met with a . . . . response. Those who use the buses think it is a great idea, but most car owners are against it.

6. The response to our appeal for help has been rather . . . . Very few people have come forward.

Match up the following adjective collocations with the meaning opposite:

7. a. quiet   an immediate response
   b. fast   a lukewarm response
   c. not enthusiastic   a favourable response
   d. good   a muted response

2 In response to . . . .

Complete the sentences with these words:

appeal   complaints   criticism   pressure

1. The school has changed some of its teaching methods in response to . . . . in the latest report by government inspectors.

2. Millions of people gave freely in response to the . . . . for the victims of the famine in East Africa.

3. In response to . . . . about the number of minor accidents in its factory, the company has decided to review its safety procedures.

4. Management have reduced the working week to 38 hours in response to . . . . from the unions.

Go back and underline these noun collocations.

3 Expressions with prepositions

Match up the halves of these sentences:

1. The school is delighted with
2. The marketing people are disappointed with
3. I was totally unprepared for
4. Have you had any response yet to
5. What's the response been like from

a. the people you work with?
b. the response to its appeal to raise £10,000.
c. your letter of resignation?
d. his response. He actually hit me!
e. the poor response to their TV adverts.

"A favourable response!"

Notes

1. Note the verbs that we use to describe getting a response:
   Plans to reduce the workforce have produced an angry response from union leaders.
   The speech provoked an angry response from teachers and community leaders.
   The proposed shopping centre met with an angry response from local residents.

2. Notice these examples of an initial / immediate response:
   When anything goes wrong, his immediate response is to blame other people. I wish he would stop and think before opening his mouth!
   What do you think the initial response will be to this announcement?

3. If you *make no response* to somebody, you ignore them or say nothing.

4. Note this formal expression in business letters:
   I am writing in response to your letter of May 12th.

responsibility

1 Verb + responsibility

Use the correct form of these verbs:

accept   *assume*   *claim*
deny   *have*   *lie*

1. As security officer, I . . . . the responsibility for ensuring that nothing is stolen from the office.

2. The club does not . . . . responsibility for loss of or damage to club members' personal property.

3. No terrorist organisation has yet . . . . responsibility for this latest bomb outrage.

4. The problem is out of my hands now that Derek Winton has . . . . responsibility for the business. He took over full responsibility for the running of the firm last week.

5. The rail company are trying to evade responsibility for the disaster. I don't know how they can possibly . . . . responsibility for an accident which involved their trains.

6. We must be clear about where the responsibility . . . . Personally, I think the responsibility for the present crisis rests squarely on the government.

2 Common adjective collocations

Use the following adjectives in these sentences:

diminished   *equal*   *extra*
full   *huge*   *overall*

1. Being the captain of the team is a . . . . responsibility. A lot rests on your shoulders. I think it takes a special kind of person to deal with such a heavy responsibility.

2. I'm only in charge of the lower school. The person with . . . . responsibility for the whole school is the headmaster.

3. I don't feel ready to take on new or . . . . responsibilities at the moment.

4. I think that working parents should take . . . . responsibility for their children's upbringing and education. They need to share the responsibility.

5. I won't try to make any excuses. I accept . . . . responsibility for my mistake.

6. The accused pleaded not guilty on the grounds of . . . . responsibility. He claimed that he had been under a lot of stress at the time of the crime.

3 Noun + of + responsibility

Complete the sentences below with these nouns:

abdication   *area*   *delegation*
position   *range*   *sense*

1. The job is a demanding one, involving a wide . . . . of responsibilities.

2. For a person in a . . . . of such responsibility, the managing director's conduct at the meeting was unacceptable.

3. We hope that their visit to the retirement home will instill in the children a . . . . of responsibility towards the elderly in the community.

4. I'm afraid you're complaining to the wrong person. This matter is outside my . . . . of responsibility.

5. There had been a complete . . . . of responsibility in the ferry company. Nobody will accept any responsibility for the disaster in which 350 people lost their lives.

6. A key factor in managing a successful business is the . . . . of responsibility.

Notes

1. In 1-3 'admitted' is also possible.

2. Note the expression 'sole responsibility':
   Our office has sole responsibility for UK sales.

3. Note the following ways of accepting responsibility:
   Remember. It's your decision and you must bear the responsibility if things go wrong.
   Each of us must take responsibility for our own health.
   He's an adult now and he has to learn to face up to his responsibilities.
   It is usually women who shoulder the major responsibility for the care of elderly relatives.
   Which government minister carries responsibility for the police?

4. We talk of *legal, social,* and *moral responsibilities.*

5. Note how we use responsibility to talk about duties:
   Your responsibilities will include answering the phone and dealing with the mail.
   A doctor's first responsibility is to his patients.
   The kitchen is your responsibility, so keep it clean.
   He couldn't accept his family responsibilities and left his wife and young son.

result

1 Verb + result(s)

Use the correct form of these verbs:

await	depend on
know	have
predict	see

1. With both France and Italy playing well it is difficult to . . . . the result of the match between the two teams.

2. He is anxiously . . . . the results of medical tests.

3. I don't know if I will be going to university next year. Everything . . . . the results of my examinations.

4. This new diet relies on eating less food in order to obtain results. I've been following the diet for a month and I'm just beginning to . . . . some results.

5. Have you . . . . the results of your blood test yet?

6. I finished my exams yesterday, but I won't . . . . the results for a month. It's going to be a nail-biting time until I hear the results.

Go back and underline the verb collocations.

2 Results + verb

Use the correct form of these verbs:

confirm	exceed
indicate	prove
represent	support

1. Early results . . . . that the government will be returned to power with a big majority.

2. The results of the tests . . . . my worst fears – I'm losing my sight.

3. We're delighted at the results our students achieved. These results . . . . all our expectations.

4. The results of these latest experiments seem to . . . . the theory that music can help people to think better. I think I'll start listening to Mozart while I'm doing my homework!

5. These results . . . . a major breakthrough in the treatment of AIDS.

6. I don't think these latest results . . . . that one school is better than any other.

Go back and underline the verb collocations.

3 Common adjective collocations

Use the following adjectives in these sentences:

best	direct	disappointing
disastrous	end	inevitable

1. There was little the doctors could do to save the woman. She died as a . . . . result of the injuries she received in the crash.

2. I tried to put up a bookshelf with . . . . results! I only succeeded in making two large holes in the wall!

3. I'm not quite sure what the . . . . result of all these meetings is. I just hope that something constructive will come out of it!

4. Long traffic jams were the . . . . result of the decision to ban cars from the city centre.

5. For . . . . results, bake the pie at a low temperature.

6. The team should have done much better – what a . . . . result!

"Disastrous results!"

Notes

1. Note these common expressions:
   There is no fixed salary. Your income will be decided on the basis of the results that you achieve.
   In view of these poor results, it is impossible for us to consider a pay rise at this time.

2. Notice this adjective collocation:
   I'm sure we can achieve the desired result.

3. Note these two common expressions:
   Stephen wasn't at school last week – with the result that he missed a couple of important exams.
   Jane was ill and, as a result, she missed the party.

4. Note these common noun collocations:
examination results	*election result*
a surprise result	*the football results*

right

1 Verb + right

Use the correct form of these verbs:

campaign for   give   know
stand up for   have   abuse

1. Just because you're older than me doesn't . . . . you the right to tell me what to do!
2. Don't let them push you around. You've got to . . . . your rights.
3. You can't arrest me without charging me. I . . . . my rights. So, what am I meant to have done?
4. Reports suggest that human rights are being systematically . . . . in their prisons.
5. Martin Luther King . . . . civil rights for black people in the US in the 1960's.
6. Everyone . . . . the right to freedom of speech.

Now match the two halves of these sentences:

7. The police officer told the prisoner that he had the right
8. The management of this club reserve the right
9. We must respect the rights of independent states
10. Our company has been granted the exclusive rights
11. When the Prince married a divorced woman, he gave up his right

a. to become king.
b. to govern themselves.
c. to distribute Heinle books in India.
d. to refuse entrance to anyone under the influence of alcohol.
e. to remain silent.

2 Common expressions

Match these halves:

1. I have a lot of respect for
2. I don't know
3. You can't walk along this path.
4. I don't agree with some of the tactics of
5. You have no right

a. to treat anyone like that!
b. It's not a right of way.
c. the animal rights people.
d. the civil rights movement.
e. the rights and wrongs of the situation.

3 Common adjective collocations

Use the following adjectives in these sentences:

automatic   basic   equal
every   legal   human

1. In a democratic society free speech is a . . . . right.
2. Why should people who are found guilty have the . . . . right of appeal? I just don't understand!
3. How can the government claim to support . . . . rights when there are so few women in important positions in the party?
4. I would check with a lawyer first, if you're unsure of your . . . . rights.
5. After the way you've been treated, you have . . . . right to complain.
6. Food, shelter, education, clothing, health care are all basic . . . . rights.

4 Noun + preposition + rights

Use the prepositions in the sentences below:

on   within   to   for (x2)   of

1. The new government affirmed its commitment . . . . . equal rights.
2. Should we intervene in the internal affairs of countries where there are serious abuses . . . . . human rights?
3. For many years Germaine Greer has been an indefatigable campaigner . . . . . women's rights.
4. There is a lot of competition between airlines . . . . . the right to fly between London and New York.
5. The President vigorously defended his country's record . . . . . human rights.
6. I think if you refuse to pay the bill, you are acting well . . . . . . your rights. After all, the TV doesn't work!

Notes

1. Note the following:
   The house belongs to me by right. I inherited it from my grandfather.

2. Note how we say someone's behaviour is wrong:
   You have no right to park in front of my house!

risk

1 Verb + risk

Use the correct form of these verbs:

carry	consider
pose	outweigh
reduce	take

1. A fatty diet increases the risk of heart disease whereas a low fat diet . . . . the risk.

2. We cannot afford to . . . . risks when people's lives are involved.

3. Boxing is a contact sport which . . . . a high risk of injury. However, wearing protective headgear can help minimise the risk of head injury.

4. The chemicals in food are not dangerous. They . . . . little risk to health.

5. I've . . . . all the risks of having the operation and I've decided to go ahead.

6. All things considered, the benefits of this treatment . . . . the risks.

2 Common adjective collocations

Use the following adjectives in these sentences:

calculated	potential
real	unnecessary

1. I must warn you that there is a small, but . . . . risk that something could go wrong.

2. The director took a . . . . risk, giving the film's main role to an unknown actor, but it paid off. The film was a great success.

3. The information in this leaflet warns young people of the . . . . risks to health associated with drug use.

4. You are exposing yourself to . . . . risks by walking through the park alone at night.

3 Common expressions

Use these words to complete the sentences:

aware	own	prepared
small	worth	

1. I want to take no risks, however . . . .

2. That's a risk I'm not . . . . to take.

3. If we buy these shares, we might lose all our money! It's just not . . . . the risk.

4. It's OK. I'm fully . . . . of the risks involved.

5. You leave your bike here at your . . . . risk.

4 How big a risk?

Mark the following sentences (B) if they describe a big risk and (S) if they describe a small risk:

1. Hygiene is so bad in this hospital that there is a serious risk of infection.

2. There is a slight risk of side-effects with this drug. You may feel a little sick or dizzy at times.

3. Please remember that any financial investment contains an element of risk, but it's only a minimal risk as far as we are concerned.

4. He sold his house and invested the money in the stock market. It was a huge risk to take, but it proved worthwhile in the end. He's now a millionaire.

5. You've got to wear protective goggles as the light is very strong and there's a high risk of damage to your eyesight.

6. Lots of war correspondents carry out their work at great risk to themselves.

"At great risk!"

Notes

1. If people's lives have been 'put at risk', they have been put into a dangerous situation.

2. Note the common expression: run the risk of -ing:
   If you don't put a coat on, you'll run the risk of catching a cold.
   Unless his performance improves, he runs the risk of losing his job.

3. We talk of a health, fire, and security risk:
   Some people think red meat is a serious health risk.
   Campers and picnickers pose the biggest fire risk in the forests in the summer.
   The Pope decided to travel in an open car – despite the security risk.

role

1 Play a role in + verb

Use the correct form of these verbs:

> build up   campaign for
> educate   influence
> open   remove

1. President Clinton played a pivotal role in . . . .
   channels of communication between the leaders
   of the two countries.

2. Television has a crucial role to play in . . . .
   young people. That's why we need more
   documentaries and fewer game shows.

3. Your kidneys play a vital role in . . . . waste
   products from your blood.

4. Nobody would deny that the media play a major
   role in . . . . people's opinions.

5. He played a key role in . . . . the company
   into the success it is today.

6. She played a leading role in . . . . equal
   opportunities for women.

**Go back and underline all the adjectives used to
describe an _important role_.**

2 Common adjective collocations

Use the following adjectives in these sentences:

> active   dual
> minor   peace-keeping
> clear   traditional

1. He is finding his . . . . role as composer and
   conductor quite demanding.

2. Most of the top management positions are held by
   men. Women seem to play relatively . . . .
   roles in the running of the organisation.

3. Every member of staff must have a . . . .
   role. Everybody needs to know what is expected
   of them.

4. United Nations troops are only deployed in a
   . . . . role. They do not fight wars, they try
   to prevent them.

5. I think our government should be playing a more
   . . . . role in promoting human rights. It
   needs to do more.

6. Many women have abandoned their . . . .
   role as wife and mother. For many the pursuit of a
   career is more important.

Go back and underline the adjective collocations.

3 Verb + role

Use the correct form of these verbs:

> examine   reverse
> see   play
> find   take on

1. When my mother died when I was five, my older
   sister had to . . . . her role.

2. My parents looked after me when I was young, but
   now the roles are . . . . and I look after
   them.

3. I . . . . my role as that of a mediator, helping
   other people to work out their problems
   together.

4. The report . . . . the changing role of
   women in modern society.

5. Because most parents work nowadays,
   grandparents are . . . . a more and more
   important role in bringing up children.

6. In the reorganisation of the company, my old boss
   hasn't really . . . . a role for himself.

"Grandpa playing an important role!"

Notes

1. Role also refers to an actor's part in a play or film:
   _I auditioned for the leading role, but I ended up with
   only a tiny part in the film._

2. Note the following examples:
   _She's acting in an advisory role.
   Sports stars need to remember that they are role models
   for thousands of young people.
   The main role of the police is to enforce the law.
   Now that I'm a patient and not the doctor, it feels like
   role reversal!_

rule

1 Verb + rules

Use the correct form of these verbs:

change   come into effect
enforce   stipulate

1. There is no point in having rules unless they are
   . . . .

2. In the UK school rules often . . . . that no
   pupil is allowed out of school during school hours.

3. The new rules for handling meat products . . . .
   . . . . from Monday next week.

4. The proposal to . . . . the rules was
   narrowly defeated by 403 votes to 401. Things
   will remain as they were.

2 Noun + of + rules

Complete the sentences with these nouns:

adherence   exceptions
set   violation

1. When our daughter started at her new school,
   she had to learn a whole new . . . . of
   rules.

2. The investigation showed that the pilot of the
   crashed plane had not broken any rules or
   regulations. In particular, there had been no
   . . . . of air safety rules.

3. There are always . . . . to grammar rules,
   but maybe that means there's something wrong
   with the rules!

4. The new manager's strict . . . . to the
   rules made him unpopular. Sometimes you have to
   bend the rules a little!

3 Obeying and disobeying rules

Underline the 10 verbs that collocate with *rules*:

1. There are stiff fines for breaking the rules.

2. If competitors do not follow the rules, their team
   will lose points.

3. Safety rules are routinely flouted on the building
   site. It's dangerous to disregard them.

4. I'm sorry, madam, but we have to go by the rules.
   I can't change them just for you.

5. Staff must abide by the new rules. Those who
   refuse to comply with them will be dismissed.

6. Do we have to stick rigidly to the rules? Can't you
   bend them just a little?

Now divide the above verbs into two groups:

a. obey: . . . .
b. disobey: . . . .

4 Common adjective collocations

Use these words to complete the sentences:

ground   hard and fast   petty
present   strict   first

1. Before we can even begin to settle this dispute,
   we need to agree the . . . . rules first.
   Without these basic rules in place, we'll get
   nowhere!

2. Under the . . . . rules, you can bring 1,000
   cigarettes into the country. A few years ago you
   were only allowed 200.

3. There are rules which are not official, but which
   people accept and obey. For example, you can
   wear what you like to my work. There's no
   . . . . rule that says you can't
   wear jeans. It's just that most people don't.

4. Orthodox Jews will only eat kosher food which
   has been prepared according to very . . . .
   rules.

5. The students complain that they are subjected to
   too many . . . . rules. For example, many
   think that having to walk up steps one at a time
   is mad!

6. The . . . . rule of good management is –
   learn to delegate!

Notes

1. Note the expression 'as a rule':
   *We don't travel business class – as a rule – but it
   depends on the length of the flight.*

2. Workers who 'work to rule' do what they must do,
   but nothing extra. For example:
   *The work-to-rule by postal workers has meant that some
   deliveries are not taking place as part of their action.
   It means there is an overtime ban.*

3. If you 'bend' or 'stretch' the rules, you do something
   that is not normally allowed:
   *I might be able to bend the rules just this one time and
   because it's you. I wouldn't do it for anyone else, you
   know!*

safety

1 Verb + safety

Use the correct form of these verbs:

compromise   guarantee   improve   reach

1. Army officers told the journalists it was such a dangerous area that they could not . . . . their safety.

2. The refugees walked for nearly a week until they . . . . safety.

3. Railway companies have dismissed fears that staff cuts will . . . . safety. They say they are not putting profit before people's lives.

4. These new measures are designed to . . . . safety in our schools.

2 Expressions with prepositions

Complete the sentences with these expressions:

*for the safety of
from the safety of
for your own safety
in safety
to safety*

1. In the crowded streets of the city centre it is difficult to find a place where children can play . . . .

2. The boat sank about a hundred metres from the shore, but we all managed to swim . . . .

3. The police are concerned . . . . a three-year-old boy who has been missing for two days.

4. In the safari park you can watch the lions . . . . your car.

5. Smoking and the use of mobile phones are not permitted on board this plane . . . .

3 Safety + noun

Complete the sentences below with these nouns:

*features   precautions   procedures
reasons   regulations   record*

1. Farmers need to take safety . . . . and wear protective clothing when spraying pesticides onto their crops.

2. The area in the park near where the children play has been fenced off for safety . . . .

3. This hall does not conform to safety . . . . That's why we can't let the public use it.

4. Very stringent safety checks are carried out on all our planes. That's why this airline has such an excellent safety . . . .

5. Our engineers have incorporated all the latest safety . . . . into the design of this car.

6. As the plane prepared for take-off, the cabin crew demonstrated the safety . . . .

4 Noun + preposition + safety

Cross out the wrong preposition in these sentences:

1. There is growing concern about / on the safety of mobile phones.

2. German cars have a reputation on / for safety and reliability.

3. In the interests of / in safety, smoking is forbidden in the cinema.

4. This latest accident has raised doubts in / about the safety of the aircraft.

5. The firemen led the women out of the burning building to a place of / in safety.

6. With no thought to / of her own safety, she dived into the river to save the drowning child.

Notes

1. Note this expression:
   There's safety in numbers, so it's better to walk home with a friend late at night.

2. Note these adjective collocations:
   *The thick glass walls allow you to watch these wild animals in perfect / complete safety.
   The car is fitted with side bars for extra safety.*

3. Note this expression:
   The fireman carried the child to safety.

4. Note the following noun collocations:
   *All employees are issued with health and safety guidelines.
   The reduction in the speed limit is part of a new road safety campaign.*

5. By law, companies have to have a 'Health and Safety' expert, who is responsible for all matters relating to the safety of employees.

situation

1 Verb + situation

Use the correct form of these verbs:

comment on   depend on   handle
review   misunderstand   improve

1. John's calm approach prevented a nasty argument from developing during the meeting. You have to admire the way he . . . . the situation.

2. It would be unwise to . . . . the situation in Kashmir without knowing all the facts.

3. Would you come to my aid if somebody attacked me?
   > Well, it would . . . . the situation.

4. I thought the man you were with was your husband. I didn't realise he was your brother. I'm so sorry. I totally . . . . the situation.

5. The refugees have no fresh water or sanitation. There's little anyone can do to . . . . the situation.

6. Before we throw any more money at the problem, I think we should . . . . the situation and see what worked and what didn't.

2 Common adjective collocations

Complete the sentences with these adjectives:

current   desperate   delicate   ideal
impossible   Catch-22   volatile   difficult

1. We're trying to buy a house, but everywhere is too expensive for us. We're in an . . . . situation.

2. You'll need to handle this very sensitively. It's a very . . . . situation.

3. We can't allow the . . . . situation to go on any longer. We need a change.

4. The news report from the Sudan showed the . . . . situation people are in. They have no food, very little water and no medical supplies.

5. I think she coped admirably with a very . . . . situation. It was a real 'can of worms'.

6. I can't get the job because I don't have the right experience and I can't get the experience until I get a job. It's a . . . . situation.

7. The house we want to buy is in an . . . . situation with wonderful views of the mountains.

8. The political situation is very . . . . – the army could start a coup at any time.

3 Situation + verb

Use the correct form of these verbs:

arise   calls for   continue
return   turn   deteriorate

1. The situation . . . . prompt action. We must do something quickly.

2. Let's get out of here. The situation could . . . . nasty at any moment.

3. The situation is . . . . day by day. Soon, there will be no food, water or medical supplies left.

4. This situation can't . . . . I simply won't allow it to go on any longer.

5. Three days after the riots the situation has . . . . to normal.

6. I don't have the time to think about it now. I'll worry about it when the situation . . . .

4 Noun + of + situation

Complete the sentences with these nouns:

advantage   facts   handling
misunderstanding   gravity   side

1. I don't think you fully realise the . . . . of the situation. We could all lose our jobs.

2. Our school has been closed for repairs, so we are taking full . . . . of the situation and going on a short holiday.

3. I'm glad you can see the funny . . . . of the situation. Not many people would.

4. It's important that we don't let our prejudices blind us to the . . . . of the situation.

5. Her . . . . of the situation was masterly. She dealt with the problem very professionally.

6. His inappropriate reaction was obviously based on a complete . . . . of the situation.

Notes

1. Note the following expressions:
   I'm in a no-win situation. Whatever I do will be bad.

2. Note this question:
   What would you have done in my situation?

3. We talk about the *economic / political / social situation.*

size

1 Expressions with prepositions

Use these prepositions in the sentences:

into   in (x3)   on   up   to (x2)

1. Over the last ten years, the village has greatly increased .... size. In fact, the population has almost doubled.

2. The wood needs to be cut .... size before it is nailed into place.

3. The eggs of this bird vary .... size from 5 to 10 cms.

4. In the factory, the fruit is sorted .... different sizes by machine.

5. A college principal can earn anywhere between £35,000 and £100,000 a year, depending .... the size of the college.

6. Radiotherapy has managed to shrink the tumour .... the size of a pea.

7. People come .... all sorts of shapes and sizes. If you don't believe me, come to my exercise class!

8. I think the next time I buy trousers, I'll need to go .... a size. I've put on some weight.

2 Common adjective collocations

Cross out the wrong adjective in the following:

1. The sheer / big size of the country makes it difficult to govern.

2. Despite its minimal / small size, the car is surprisingly comfortable.

3. This bag is a handy / right size for carrying my sports equipment.

4. These plants grow to a maximum / full size of 50 cms in two years.

5. When I was stung by a bee, my foot swelled up to twice its average / normal size.

6. There was a life-size model of Napoleon at the exhibition which showed the actual / normal size of the man. I never realised how small he was.

7. The bathroom is a bit small, but the kitchen is a good / bad size.

8. Our house is quite a workable / manageable size. Some people think it's too big.

9. Paper comes in standard / common sizes.

10. The very / great size of the Palace is what makes it so impressive.

3 Common situations

Complete the situations with these words:

*your   my   several   collar
French   take   up to   half*

1. What's your ...... size?
   > My shirts are usually 15s.

2. This is a lovely flat. Mine is only ...... the size!

3. Did you find a new skirt?
   > No, I couldn't find one in ...... size that I liked.

4. I'm sorry I don't have any in ...... size in stock at the moment.

5. This pullover isn't just too big. It's .... sizes too big. I don't know why you bought it!

6. Have you got a size 16?
   > I'm sorry, this style only goes .... size 12.

7. What size of battery does it ......?
   > I think it takes those double As.

8. If it's a ...... 85, that means it's a UK size 32.

"It was twice its normal size!"

Notes

1. Note the following expressions:
   The towns are similar in size, but different in character.

2. Note the following verb collocations:
   In my opinion, reducing the size of classes would improve educational standards.
   The company has had a successful year and has decided to increase the size of its workforce.

3. Note the following comparisons:
   Their house is about the same size as ours.
   The wheels are different in size / different sizes.
   The planet Venus is roughly the same size as the Earth.

space

1 Verb + space

Use the correct form of these verbs:

make   provide   save   take up

1. I think we can . . . . a bit of space if we get rid of some of these books.

2. Can we . . . . space for an extra chair so that John can join us?

3. We'll need to get rid of that old desk. It's . . . . too much space.

4. Print your name and address clearly in the space . . . .

clear   stare into   find   make use of

5. I think we can . . . . better . . . . the space if we shift this desk over to the window.

6. She just ignored everyone. She just sat there . . . . space.

7. I couldn't . . . . a space in the car park big enough for my 4 x 4.

8. We need to . . . . some space in our spare room. We've got people coming to stay.

2 Common adjective collocations

Complete the sentences with these adjectives:

blank   confined   extra   storage

1. Now that the children have left home, we've got a lot of . . . . space.

2. There's a . . . . space at the bottom of the form for you to sign your name.

3. It's cruel to keep animals in such a . . . . space. They should be in much larger enclosures where they can roam free.

4. There's a lot of . . . . space up in the loft so we can put your suitcases up there.

advertising   enclosed   open   narrow

5. Do not use this substance in an . . . . space. Make sure all doors and windows are open when working with it.

6. I eventually found a place to park but it was such a . . . . space that I had difficulty getting my car into it. It was very tight!

7. Paris is a city with fine buildings and plenty of . . . . spaces. It is a great place for a holiday.

8. We financed our student magazine by selling . . . . space.

3 Noun + of + space

Complete the sentences with these nouns:

amount   sense   shortage   plenty

1. It's a big car with a generous . . . . of space inside.

2. The light colours and the big windows give the room a real . . . . of space.

3. No, you don't need to move. I've got . . . . of space.

4. There's a . . . . of office space in the centre of town at the moment, but there are plans to build a new block.

"A confined space!"

Notes

1. Note this way of creating space:
   We moved the furniture around to create more space.

2. Note the following uses:
   After working all morning without a break, I need a breathing space before starting the next job.
   I left the party because I needed space to think things through.

3. Note these time expressions:
   It was a lot to absorb in a short space of time.
   In the space of 24 hours, I had flown halfway round the world to Australia.

4. *Outer space is outside the Earth's atmosphere.*
   Wasn't Gagarin the first man in space?

5. Note these different kinds of space:
   parking spaces   floor space   working space
   living space   wall space   shelf space

6. People talk about their 'personal space':
   Our office is very crowded. I need more personal space.

standard

1 Verb + standard

Use the correct form of these verbs:

fall   maintain   raise
enjoy   reach   set

1. Our job is not just to . . . . standards – our job is to make sure they improve!

2. He failed to . . . . the required standard, and did not qualify for the race.

3. Do you think that reducing class sizes would . . . . standards in our primary schools?

4. It's hard for others to come up to the standards our head of department . . . . for herself.

5. The standard of service has . . . . steadily since the company was taken over a year ago. It's now so bad, something will have to be done.

6. Today most people in this country . . . . a standard of living which their parents could only dream about.

2 Common adjective collocations

Complete the sentences with these adjectives:

approved   falling
high   low
minimum   modern
same   usual

1. My boss demands extremely . . . . standards from the people that work for him. In fact some people think he is unrealistic.

2. I was disappointed when I took some friends to my favourite restaurant and neither the food nor the service were up to the . . . . standard.

3. Not everyone judges success by the . . . . standards. Unlike you, I think that happiness is more important than the size of your car.

4. Parents are always complaining about . . . . standards in schools.

5. A number of Britain's beaches fail to meet the . . . . standards laid down by the EU.

6. This special mark shows that the product conforms to an . . . . industry standard.

7. We decided that it would be our first and last trip to the island. The hotels and restaurants were all of a very . . . . standard.

8. By . . . . standards, the plumbing in our hotel was totally inadequate!

3 Standard + of + noun

Complete the sentences below with these nouns:

behaviour   care   hygiene
singing   living   workmanship

1. Some countries simply don't provide proper standards of . . . . for the elderly.

2. Inspectors criticised the kitchen staff for poor standards of . . . .

3. I had my windows replaced, but I'm not very pleased with the standard of . . . .

4. There's been a progressive increase in the standard of . . . . over the last five years. People are now much better off.

5. The school insists on strict standards of . . . . on school trips.

6. Although it was an amateur production, the standard of . . . . was excellent.

4 Expressions with prepositions

Use these prepositions in the sentences:

of   to   up   below   by   in

1. The work has been done . . . . a professional standard.

2. Students will be sent home if their behaviour falls . . . . an acceptable standard.

3. The first computers were very slow . . . . today's standards.

4. Universities deny that there has been a decline . . . . academic standards.

5. The report is highly critical . . . . safety standards at the factory.

6. The teacher said that my essay was not . . . . to standard and that I would have to do it again.

Notes

1. In 2-8 you can also say 'by today's standards':
   By today's standards, Shakespeare was a rich man.

2. Note the use of *safety standards* and *moral standards*:
   The airline's maintenance programme did not conform to the high safety standards set by the industry.
   The Minister did not live up to the high moral standards expected of him.

3. If someone has 'double standards', they are guilty of condemning something, while doing it themselves.

---

state

1 Common adjective collocations

Use these adjectives in the sentences:

fit	*mental*	*original*	*real*
untidy	*financial*	*advanced*	*sorry*

1. I'll drive. You're in no . . . . state!

2. Some people believe that an analysis of your dreams can reveal details of your . . . . state.

3. They complained about the . . . . state that the flat had been left in.

4. The company is in a dangerous . . . . state. We are on the point of bankruptcy.

5. By the time she arrived for her interview, she had worked herself up into a . . . . state. I've never seen her so nervous before.

6. The experts believe that they will be able to restore the painting to its . . . . state.

7. The dog was in a very . . . . state when we found it – cold and thin and abandoned.

8. I've looked at your roof and I'm sorry to tell you that the wood is in an . . . . state of decay. You need a new roof.

2 State + of + noun phrase

Use these expressions in the sentences:

poor state of repair	*state of health*
state of emergency	*sad state of affairs*

1. The house was in a very . . . . when we bought it.

2. It's a . . . . when two adults argue over who gets to sit beside the chairman!

3. After the disaster the government declared a . . . .

4. Regular exercise can make a big difference to your . . . .

high state of alert	*state of total chaos*
state of the economy	*state of decline*

5. Security forces are on a . . . . because of the terrorist threat.

6. Ever since our secretary left, the office has been in a . . . .

7. Since the civil war the economy has been in a . . . .

8. Economists are painting a grim picture of the current . . . .

3 States of emotion

We often use 'state' when describing feelings and emotions. Complete the sentences below:

nervous exhaustion	*fear*
panic	*shock*

1. After the accident the driver just sat in the car, unable to speak. He was in a state of . . . .

2. The news of the outbreak of war threw investors into a state of . . . . Many tried frantically to sell their shares.

3. We lived for years in a perpetual state of . . . . in Sarajevo. You could be shot by a sniper at any time.

4. She was in a state of . . . . , so her doctor signed her off work and told her to take a complete rest for a month.

"You're in no fit state!"

Notes

1. Note how we describe a very bad state:
   We were shocked at the appalling state of the hospital.
   Inspectors condemned the shocking state of the prison.
   The engine is in good condition, but the bodywork is in a terrible state and needs some attention.
   The kitchen was in a disgusting state when they left.
   The rail system is in a bit of a sorry state at the moment.

2. If something is in a 'state of flux', it is constantly changing.

3. 'State' also means country:
   In 1947 India became an independent state.
   The United States is made up of 'states'.

4. The 'welfare state' is the system which provides health care, unemployment benefit, old age pensions etc.

story

1 Verb + story

Use the correct form of these verbs:

believe	*check*
make up	*read*
sell	*stick to*

1. He says he was at home at the time of the crime. We'll need to . . . . his story. See if you can find someone who can back it up.

2. Your mother will never . . . . that story about you missing the last bus. Just tell her the truth!

3. No, I didn't . . . . the story . . . . . . I've told you the whole thing is true!

4. When mum and dad ask us how the window was broken we must all . . . . the same story if we want them to believe us!

5. In my opinion, criminals should not be allowed to make a fortune by . . . . their stories to the newspapers.

6. Did your parents . . . . you stories before you went to bed?

2 Common adjective collocations

Complete the sentences with these adjectives:

complicated	*full*
gripping	*same old*
likely	*true*

1. That TV series about a doctor working in Africa in the 1920's is based on a . . . . story.

2. I don't think that we've heard the . . . . story of the Prime Minister's resignation yet. I think there's a lot more to come.

3. He said he found the video recorder under a tree! That's a . . . . story! How can he expect anybody to believe that!

4. It was such a . . . . story that the children wouldn't leave until they had heard how it ended.

5. I'll tell you about my childhood some other time. It's a long and . . . . story and I don't have time to go into it all just now.

6. It's the . . . . story wherever you go – the rich get richer and the poor get poorer. The world doesn't change.

Go back and underline all the useful collocations in exercises 1 and 2.

3 Noun + of + story

Complete the sentences below with these nouns:

moral	*part*	*point*	*side*

1. I couldn't make much sense of the story. In fact, I couldn't see the . . . . of it at all.

2. We've all read about it in the papers, but before we make any judgements I think we should hear his . . . . of the story first.

3. The main lesson or . . . . of the story is that crime doesn't pay.

4. Some crucial facts have been missed out. We've only heard . . . . of the story!

4 Noun + noun collocations

Complete the sentences below with the following nouns and noun phrases:

cock-and-bull	*hard-luck*	*success*
rags-to-riches	*love*	*real-life*

1. Lots of companies have gone out of business during the recession. The Green Shoe company is a rare . . . . story.

2. I can always tell when Pete is lying. He gave me some . . . . story about helping a friend decorate his living room – a highly unlikely story! Pete has never used a paint brush in his life!

3. The beggar told me some . . . . story about being cheated out of his inheritance.

4. The film was based on the . . . . story of General Patton.

5. He was brought up in poverty in a Glasgow slum, but through hard work and a bit of luck he became the millionaire owner of a huge supermarket chain. It's a classic . . . . story.

6. Why do all . . . . stories have happy endings?

Notes

1. A story is also a report in a newspaper:
   The Times has a story about that bribery scandal.

2. If we say that something is 'only a story', we mean that it is not true.

3. We say 'to cut a long story short' when we don't want to go into details.

4. We talk about *detective, horror, ghost* and *love stories.*

---

subject

1 Verb + subject

Use the correct form of these verbs:

> change   come up
> deal with   drop
> get onto   talk about

1. Can we . . . . a different subject please? I really don't like talking about other people behind their backs.

2. When I asked him about his job, he just . . . . the subject like a hot potato!

3. How did we . . . . the subject of your mother? I thought we were discussing holidays.

4. His poems often . . . . the subject of death.

5. I asked Richard about the money he owed me, but he just . . . . the subject and started talking about his health problems.

6. We didn't intend talking about his divorce. The subject just . . . . in conversation.

2 Common adjective collocations

Use these adjectives in the sentences:

> cheerful   chosen
> pet   complex
> taboo   touchy

1. Death is a . . . . subject in many western societies. People tend not to talk openly about it.

2. Can we talk about a more . . . . subject? Funerals aren't a very happy thing to talk about.

3. Once he gets onto his . . . . subject of football hooligans, there's no stopping him. So don't encourage him or he'll talk for hours.

4. I can't understand why the break-up of her marriage is still such a . . . . subject. Surely she can talk about it now without getting upset.

5. In the examination, each candidate has to talk for two minutes on their . . . . subject.

6. Whether scientists should be free to experiment on human embryos is a very . . . . subject.

These examples deal with a different meaning:

> favourite   core   compulsory

7. Everybody has to take English. It's a . . . . subject in our school system.

8. Chemistry and biology are my . . . . subjects.

9. You have to take six . . . . subjects and two optional ones.

3 On the subject

Use these words to complete the sentences:

> authority   briefly   information
> holidays   nothing   views

1. I have . . . . further to say on the subject of your wedding. As far as I'm concerned, the matter is closed.

2. We only touched . . . . on the subject of salaries during the meeting.

3. The Pope's . . . . on the subject are well known.

4. She's the leading . . . . on the subject of South American butterflies. She knows pretty well everything there is to know on the subject.

5. I've read every scrap of . . . . I can find on the subject.

6. Oh, on the subject of . . . . , have you thought where we could be going this summer?

4 Be the subject of

Use these nouns in the sentences:

> concern   debate   discrimination   speculation

1. The Minister's controversial views on immigration have been the subject of much . . . . in the media.

2. We encourage any employee who has been the subject of . . . . to report it immediately.

3. Her private life is the subject of much . . . . in the press at the moment.

4. The huge number of heavy vehicles passing through the village has been a subject of . . . . this year.

Notes

1. Note these verbs used to introduce a subject:
   By tacit agreement, the subject was never mentioned.
   At some point we've got to discuss money but I don't know quite how to broach the subject with him.
   Don't blame me. It was you who brought up the subject, not me.
   I'm glad you raised the subject of safety. I think it is very important.

2. If you 'know your subject', you are an expert on it.

success

1 Verb + success

Use the correct form of these verbs:

achieve	attribute
have	make
guarantee	owe
prove	wish

1. I've been looking for a job for some time now, but I haven't . . . . much success in finding one.

2. Liz needs to pull her socks up and work harder if she is going to . . . . a success of her career.

3. I'd like to take this opportunity to . . . . you every success in your new job.

4. How do you account for the success of brands like Coke and Nike?
   > They . . . . their success to good advertising.

5. My efforts to become an actor have met with little success, but my brother has . . . . success beyond his wildest dreams. He's now filming in Hollywood.

6. What do you put your success down to?
   > I . . . . my success to hard work and, of course, a little luck.

7. The novel . . . . such a success that the author quickly followed it up with another, based on the same characters.

8. This treatment can't . . . . success, but at least 70% of women who have used it have seen significant loss of weight in the first three months.

2 Expressions with prepositions

Use these nouns to complete the expressions:

chance of	degrees of	key to
sign of	measure of	taste of

1. I've tried a number of different medicines, with varying . . . . success.

2. The doctors told us that the operation only has a fifty-fifty . . . . success.

3. Confidence is the . . . . all success.

4. We've achieved some . . . . success with our new product range.

5. They are still enjoying the sweet . . . . success after their championship win.

6. The opening of two new outlets in the town is yet another . . . . the continuing success of the supermarket chain.

3 Great success

Match the two halves of these situations:

1. The party was a spectacular success.
2. Mr Hughes, to what do you ascribe the phenomenal success of your new play?
3. His latest novel is already a roaring success.
4. The good weather helped to make the occasion a resounding success.
5. Abba have enjoyed success on a scale unparalleled by any previous pop group.
6. The World Cup theme tune 'Nessun Dorma' has proved an out-and-out success.

a. It's sold over three thousand copies in a week.
b. Except the Beatles, of course.
c. A good time was had by all.
d. Nobody quite knows why.
e. Was it the production?
f. There wasn't a drop of rain.

Go back and underline the adjective collocations.

Notes

1. Note the different verbs we use to say that something is considered a success:
   The evening was deemed a success by everyone.
   The play was an overnight success. It was rated a success after only one performance.
   The event was voted a success and it is now certain that it will be held again next year.
   The new scheme has been hailed as a success by the general public.

2. Note the expression 'without success'.
   I tried to ring him, but without success.

3. Books, films, pop groups can be 'an immediate success' or 'an overnight success'.

4. Operations have a 'success rate':
   The success rate for this operation is 90%.

5. If a play or a film is a 'box-office success', lots of people go to see it.

6. You may want to ask someone:
   What is the secret of your success?

7. If you are the 'victim of your own success', something negative has accompanied your success:
   Bill was the victim of his own success. As his company grew, he worked longer and longer hours until one day he just dropped dead – the richest man in the graveyard!

suggestion

1 Verb + suggestion

Use the correct form of the verbs:

agree to	have
ignore	reject
make	welcome

1. Can I . . . . a suggestion? Try turning the key in the opposite direction. I'm sure that'll work.

2. Have you got a few minutes to spare? I . . . . a suggestion I want to put to you.

3. I know it's not a good idea. I only . . . . her suggestion in order not to upset her.

4. Please use the form provided to make any comments on your stay at our hotel. We would . . . . any suggestions you have for improving our services to our customers.

5. You can . . . . my suggestion if you like, but do any of you have a better idea?

6. It may seem silly to suggest that we go back to the planning stage again, but I don't think we should . . . . his suggestion without thinking seriously about it.

Go back and underline the verb collocations.

2 Common adjective collocations

Use the following adjectives in these sentences:

better	tentative
bizarre	best
serious	useful

1. OK, the food isn't that great, but it's the only place I know that's open. Have any of you got a . . . . suggestion?

2. Why are you laughing? This is a perfectly . . . . suggestion!

3. I know this new plan is only . . . . at the moment, but I think we should take it seriously and adopt it.

4. The report contained no . . . . suggestions on how to improve the company's performance and profitability. What a waste of money!

5. A fancy-dress bike ride! What a . . . . suggestion! Don't we have any more sensible ways of raising money?

6. Sack the boss! Now that's the . . . . suggestion we've had all morning!

Go back and underline all the collocations.

3 Good and bad suggestions

Divide the sentences below into two groups:

a. those describing good suggestions
b. those describing bad suggestions

1. To be perfectly honest, I think that suggestion is utterly ridiculous!

2. I was mocked for making such a stupid suggestion.

3. That's the first sensible suggestion he's made since he started working here.

4. That's an excellent suggestion! Why didn't I think of that myself!

5. What an absurd suggestion! Nobody will agree to that!

6. Thank you. That's a very constructive suggestion.

7. Your suggestion is preposterous! Nobody can afford a 10% pay rise!

8. The suggestion that I have been having an affair with our secretary is outrageous! I've never heard anything like it!

Notes

1. Note the difference in meaning between the two underlined expressions:
   I have a few favourite dishes that I tend to order but I'm always open to new suggestions
   (I am willing to try something new.)
   I am a good listener and I'm always open to suggestion.
   (I am willing to listen to and to consider other people's suggestions.)

2. Note the following ways of rejecting suggestions:
   I don't think my boss values me at all. He knocks every suggestion I make.
   Well, your suggestion that we take a cut in salary to help the company went down like a lead balloon.
   My suggestion was dismissed out of hand. It was given no thought or consideration at all.
   I shall treat that suggestion with the contempt it deserves.

3. If there is 'a suggestion of something', it means there is a suspicion or possibility that it is true:
   The police have denied any suggestion of involvement in the prisoner's death.
   The company rejected any suggestion that it was to blame for the accident.

system

1 Verb + system

Use the correct form of these verbs:

devise   *break down*
introduce   *model on*
reform   *work*

1. The government have proposed a whole raft of measures to . . . . the health service.

2. Can you explain how the security system . . . . ?
   > Ask Jack. He knows the system inside out.

3. When we . . . . the new booking system, no one believed it would work.

4. We need to . . . . some sort of system whereby staff can meet regularly with each other.

5. The country's legal system is . . . . the British system.

6. The recently-installed computerised system keeps crashing and the telephone system has also . . . . We can't talk to anybody!

2 Common adjective collocations

Use the adjectives to complete the sentences:

complicated   corrupt   excellent   current

1. Germany has an . . . . rail system, making it easy to travel around the country. It is the envy of many other countries.

2. The whole system is . . . . – every official you deal with demands money before helping you.

3. We've called in consultants to identify what is wrong with our . . . . management system.

4. The new system is quite . . . . , I'm afraid. It takes quite a bit of getting used to.

sophisticated   outdated   unfair   inefficient

5. Why does it take three men to do the job that one could do? What a hopelessly . . . . system!

6. We still operate an . . . . filing system with paper files and filing cabinets. What we need is a modern, state-of-the-art computer system.

7. Something must be done to help poorer children get to university. Our system is very . . . .

8. The museum is protected by a very . . . . system of burglar and fire alarms. It contains priceless treasures from Ancient Greece.

Go back and underline all the other useful collocations in this exercise.

3 Noun + preposition + system

Complete the sentences with the following:

access   advantages   injustices   overhaul

1. The government report on salaries exposes the . . . . of the current system of wages – with women still being paid less than men for the same job.

2. She was at great pains to stress the . . . . of the new system over the old one.

3. There are calls for a radical . . . . of the tax system.
   >Yes. Changes to the system are long overdue.

4. You need a password to gain . . . . to the computer system.

Notes

1. Note the following useful expression:
   Under the new system, student grants have been scrapped and replaced by loans.
   Pregnant women are exempt from dental charges under the current health system.

2. System collocates with lots of nouns:

banking system	*alarm system*
heating system	*education system*
legal system	*railway system*
prison system	*road system*
welfare system	*support system*
digestive system	*immune system*
telephone system	*sprinkler system*
canal system	*school system*
public address system	*public transport system*

3. If you talk about your 'sound system', you mean your home stereo system.

4. If you use a computer, you will be used to 'installing, booting up, and re-booting the system' and using 'system software'.

5. If you talk about 'the system', you mean all the rules and laws of the country:
   You can't beat the system!

---

thing

1 Verb + things

Use the correct form of these verbs:

make   need   pack   wash up

1. We'll have to stop at the supermarket. We . . . . a few basic things like bread and milk.

2. My dad's a sculptor. He . . . . things out of wood he finds on the beach.

3. Peter, you haven't . . . . the breakfast things yet. Do them before you go to school, please.

4. . . . . your things. We're leaving in 10 minutes.

accept   look at   make   think   turn out

5. He's not sure what he's going to do, so he's taken a few days off to . . . . things over.

6. You should try to change the situation rather than . . . . things as they are.

7. I don't know if things are going to work out between John and me.
   > Don't worry. I'm sure things will . . . . OK.

8. You're only . . . . things worse by ignoring her. I think you two need to talk things over.

9. Try to . . . . things from my point of view for a change.

2 Do + thing

Match the halves of these situations:

1. I'll be late home tonight.
2. Philip is definitely different!
3. The phone never stops ringing!
4. I'm sorry I've got to get on with some work.
5. I know people who cheat in exams.

a. *That's why it's impossible to get things done.*
b. *I'd never do a thing like that.*
c. *Yes, he does have a funny way of doing things.*
d. *I've got loads of things to do at work.*
e. *I've got better things to do than stand chatting!*

6. I can't get the video to work.
7. I rang and told him what I thought of him!
8. I wish I had listened to you!
9. The Minister's resigned!
10. He asked me how much I earned.

f. *It's just not the done thing to ask that.*
g. *Good. It was the proper thing to do.*
h. *Yes, it was a foolish thing to do.*
i. *I would have done the same thing myself.*
j. *I've done all the right things! I think it's broken.*

3 Verb + not + thing

Use the correct form of these verbs:

do   eat   miss   say   see

1. I'm sorry, I can't . . . . a thing without my specs. Could you read the menu out to me?

2. I'm going to the party as early as I can. I don't want to . . . . a thing.

3. They have cheated you out of your money, but I'm afraid you can't . . . . a thing about it.

4. I'm absolutely starving. I haven't . . . . a thing all day.

5. I heard that Frank is losing his job. I haven't . . . . a thing about it to anyone.

4 Common adjective collocations

Use these adjectives to complete the sentences:

bad   funny   good
last   main   slightest

1. It's a . . . . thing you remembered to bring the bottle opener! I completely forgot !

2. He's easily upset. He loses his temper at the . . . . little thing.

3. Too much exercise can be a . . . . thing. You can easily damage your body.

4. The . . . . thing in this type of situation is to remain calm.

5. A . . . . thing happened to me on the way to work this morning.

6. I only want to help you. The . . . . thing I want to do is to make you unhappy.

Notes

1. Note the following common expressions:
   Try not to let things get you down. Remember the saying, 'Things can only get better!'
   She offered to help me, but I assured her that I had things under control.
   I demanded a meeting with the manager to get a few things straight.

2. Notice this expression:
   Books may one day become a thing of the past.

3. This expression is used when you make a mistake socially:
   Oh, sorry, I've just said the wrong thing, haven't I?

thought

1 Verb + thought

Use the correct form of these verbs:

have	*gather*	*go out to*
hear	*occur*	*spare*

1. Have you given the new proposal any thought yet? We're keen to . . . . your thoughts.
2. The President was taken aback by the question and took a minute to . . . . his thoughts.
3. . . . . a thought for all those who are homeless on a cold night like this.
4. I've just . . . . a thought! Why not have a party?
5. Our thoughts . . . . all those families who lost relatives in the disaster.
6. The thought just . . . . to me that it's mum's birthday tomorrow and we haven't got her a card.

2 The thought of . . .

Use these words to complete the sentences:

injection	*eating meat*	*dying*
meeting	*examination*	*going home*

1. The very thought of my final . . . . fills me with dread!
2. As a vegetarian, just the thought of . . . . makes me feel sick.
3. We all became very excited at the thought of . . . .
4. I was shocked at the thought of all those people . . . .
5. I was trembling with fear at the thought of the . . . .
6. She shuddered at the thought of . . . . the man who had attacked her.

3 Noun + preposition + thought

Use the following expressions in the sentences:

> *great deal of thought*
> *freedom of thought*
> *school of thought*
> *train of thought*

1. Sorry, where was I? I've lost my . . . .
2. Some places still don't encourage . . . .
3. Shirley doesn't devote a . . . . to her appearance.
4. One . . . . contends that modern man originated in Central Africa.

4 Common adjective collocations

Use these adjectives in the sentences:

comforting	*morbid*	*negative*
original	*second*	*secret*

1. As soon as I got onto the plane, I began to have . . . . thoughts about leaving. Was I doing the right thing?
2. If you want to win, think positively. Try not to let . . . . thoughts take over.
3. Many people use a diary to record their . . . . thoughts.
4. As I waited for the results of the tests, my mind was filled with . . . . thoughts of death.
5. It's a . . . . thought that we'll be sleeping in our own beds this time tomorrow night.
6. He doesn't have an . . . . thought in his head. He just steals other people's.

"Trembling with fear at the thought of the injection!"

Notes

1. If you thought something was unimportant, you say:
   I didn't give it a moment's thought.

2. Note these expressions with *thought + verb*:
   The thought occurred to me that he might . . .
   The thought suddenly struck me that . . .
   That thought had never crossed my mind.

3. To ask someone's opinion, you can say:
   What are your thoughts on the matter, Alan?
   Any thoughts on what we should do?

4. If you don't want to lose something or somebody:
   I couldn't bear the thought of losing my dog.

5. Thought is also used to mean 'caring':
   He's always in my thoughts.

time

1 Verb + time

Use the correct form of these verbs:

afford	*kill*	*make*
save	*spend*	*take*

1. It can . . . . quite a long time to get used to living in a different country.
2. People who . . . . too much time together usually end up getting on each other's nerves.
3. It'll take you about half an hour to walk to the station. Get a taxi. Think of the time you'll . . . . !
4. I arrived two hours early for my interview, so I . . . . some time in the National Gallery and then I looked around a bookshop.
5. You keep saying you don't have enough time. That's not good enough! You've simply got to . . . . time!
6. I'd love to come out with you tonight, but I can't . . . . the time. I have a report to finish for the morning.

2 Common adjective collocations

Use these adjectives in the sentences:

convenient	*quality*
smashing	*spare*

1. We had a . . . . time at Sarah's party. Everybody really enjoyed themselves.
2. She quit her job so that she could spend more . . . . time with her children.
3. I enjoy gardening in my . . . . time. As soon as I go into the garden, I forget all about work.
4. I'm sorry, I seem to have called at a bad time. When would be a . . . . time to call back?

ample	*precious*
good	*rough*

5. She's having a . . . . time at work.
   >Yes, there's talk of redundancies. And I think her boss has been giving her a difficult time.
6. She claims that she didn't have enough time to prepare for the interview, but like all other candidates we feel she had . . . . time.
7. Make sure you're at the station in . . . . time. The train won't wait for you! It leaves at 9, so the rest of us are going to be there at 8.45.
8. Hurry up! You're wasting . . . . time! We only have a few hours left!

3 Noun + of + time

Use these nouns in the sentences:

amount	*course*	*length*
matter	*space*	*waste*

1. These meetings are a complete . . . . of time. Nothing is ever decided!
2. Children seem to spend an inordinate . . . . of time watching TV – up to ten hours a day!
3. This new strain of flu is out of control. It's only a . . . . of time before it arrives here.
4. Standing on one leg for any . . . . of time is quite difficult for most people.
5. His injuries are severe but they will heal in the . . . . of time. He just needs to be patient.
6. Within a very short . . . . of time he had lost his title. He was champion for under a month.

4 Expressions of time

Use the following expressions in the sentences:

the whole time	*the first time*	*next time*
my usual time	*a specific time*	*some time*

1. She kept on talking . . . . ! She didn't stop for a minute.
2. The body had been in the water for . . . . which made it difficult to determine the exact time of death.
3. I met my girlfriend's parents for . . . . last week.
4. Could we arrange . . . . to discuss this problem? How about 10 tomorrow?
5. I'd try a different approach . . . . You might be more successful.
6. Although I was on holiday I still got up at . . . .

Notes

1. If you arrive 'in the nick of time', you arrive just in time.
2. Note these expressions:
   There's no hurry. We've got all the time in the world.
   Time is running out to save the survivors.
   Time's up! Stop writing. (said in an examination)
   You took your time! I've been waiting here for hours!

trouble

1 Verb + trouble

Use the correct form of these verbs:

ask for	get into
give	have
save	store up

1. I'm sorry I'm late. I . . . . a lot of trouble finding somewhere to park.
2. Parking in London is a nightmare! You'd . . . . yourself a lot of trouble by taking the train.
3. My car is . . . . me a lot of trouble at the moment. I think it's the cold weather.
4. Anybody who drives a car at 150 kilometres an hour is simply . . . . trouble.
5. If you don't deal with this problem, you're only . . . . trouble for yourself in the future.
6. He . . . . a lot of trouble for writing on the walls of the school toilets.

2 Noun + of + trouble

Use these nouns in the sentences:

amount	end
least	share

1. I've had more than my fair . . . . of trouble this week – certainly more than I deserved!
2. You wouldn't believe the . . . . of trouble I've had with this video recorder. It's never worked!
3. Buying you a birthday present is the . . . . of my troubles. I can't even pay my rent!
4. I've had no. . . . . of trouble finding a hotel room. There's a big conference on in town.

3 Adjective + trouble

Match up the sentence with the situation:

1. I've got engine trouble.
2. I'm in financial trouble.
3. I'm in serious trouble with the police.
4. I've got back trouble.
5. I'm in big trouble at school.
6. I went to enormous trouble to help her.

a. I did everything I could.
b. I was caught drinking and driving.
c. I hurt it on a skiing holiday.
d. My car won't start.
e. I have debts of over £20,000!
f. I didn't turn up for a recent exam.

4 Verb + trouble

Trouble is also used to describe a situation in which people argue or fight. Use the correct form of these verbs:

break out	look for	stay out of
brew	stir up	want

1. My sister is always trying to . . . . trouble between me and my boyfriend. I think she's jealous.
2. My parents warned me to steer clear of trouble. > Yeah. Mine told me if I didn't . . . . trouble they wouldn't let me go out at night.
3. I don't . . . . any trouble in this bar, so if you don't mind, just finish your drinks and leave.
4. There have been riots in the capital, and trouble has also . . . . in other cities.
5. He says he doesn't . . . . trouble, but he always seems to be getting into fights.
6. I think trouble is . . . . I overheard a couple of people talking about a strike.

Notes

1. Note in 3-4 _trouble_ is also used to talk about health problems:
   He has heart trouble.
   She's having trouble with her legs.

2. Note how we describe being in a lot of trouble:
   He's in real trouble. He was caught stealing money.
   She'll be in big trouble if she crashes that car.
   Tony landed in terrible trouble for breaking the church window.
   You'll get into deep trouble if you keep arriving late.
   The company ran into serious trouble when it lost its biggest contract.

3. Note these expressions:
   I managed to change my flight without any trouble.
   Making your own bread is more trouble than it's worth.

4. We use the expression 'it's no trouble' to mean that something is not a problem:
   I can wait. It's no trouble.

5. We also use _trouble_ when we have made a special effort:
   They went to a lot of trouble to set up this meeting.
   I always take the trouble to learn names quickly.

truth

1 Verb + truth

Use the correct form of these verbs:

come out	distort
expose	face up to
hide	tell

1. She didn't have the courage to . . . . him the truth about his friend.

2. Newspapers are often guilty of . . . . the truth.
   > Yes, it's a well-known fact that some of them bend the truth to sell more copies.

3. You'll have to . . . . the truth some time. You're just too old for this job. Why don't you think about retiring?

4. As a journalist it's my job to uncover and . . . . the truth.

5. I don't think the truth about President Kennedy's assassination will ever . . . .
   > I think you're right. It's all so long ago now. We'll never know the truth now.

6. Since I became a politician I have never tried to . . . . the truth about my past.

2 Finding and telling the truth

Match the two halves of these sentences:

1. The real reason people buy our paper is that
2. Before we start blaming anyone, it's important that
3. The police forced him into admitting
4. It will be difficult to discover
5. It was some time before I realised
6. The doctors thought it best not to reveal

a. *the truth of what he had done.*
b. *the truth about who my real parents were.*
c. *it speaks the truth.*
d. *the truth about her parents, but she is determined to leave no stone unturned.*
e. *we establish the truth about what went on.*
f. *the truth to him until he was strong enough to deal with the news of his parents' death.*

Now list 6 verbs from the exercise which mean:

find out the truth	tell the truth
1. . . . . the truth	4. . . . . the truth
2. . . . . the truth	5. . . . . the truth
3. . . . . the truth	6. . . . . the truth

3 Common adjective collocations

Use these adjectives in the sentences:

sad	honest	painful	whole

1. I didn't take your pen! That's the plain and . . . . truth!

2. I don't think you're telling us the . . . . truth about what happened, are you?

3. My father has always been independent but the . . . . truth is that, at 89, he's no longer able to manage by himself.

4. The truth may be . . . ., but there's not much you can do about it!

4 Noun + preposition + truth

Use these expressions in the sentences:

distortion of the truth	moment of truth
quest for the truth	ring of truth
scant regard for the truth	

1. The instructor gave me the controls. It was the . . . . ! Could I fly the plane myself?

2. Nothing will stop them in their . . . . They will not be satisfied until they find out exactly how their son died in a police cell.

3. I'm inclined to believe Laura. Her story has a . . . . about it.

4. The film was a gross . . . . It bore little resemblance to what actually happened.

5. I wouldn't trust him. He has . . . . He will lie if he needs to.

Notes

1. Note these ways of saying there is a small amount of truth in something:
   a measure of truth   a certain degree of truth
   an element of truth   a grain of truth

2. These mean there is no truth in something:
   Don't listen to her! There's not a jot / an iota / a vestige / an ounce of truth in what she's saying.

3. Note this expression to introduce an idea:
   To tell you the truth, it doesn't really matter.

4. To deny something:
   Nothing could be further from the truth!

5. 'Home truths' are ideas to bring someone back to reality:
   It's time someone told him a few home truths.

use

1 Verb + use

Use the correct form of these verbs:

introduce   ban   have   lose
recommend   share   make

1. I'm afraid she can't walk. She .... the use of her legs in a road accident a few years ago.

2. As there is a shortage of practice facilities, both teams will have to .... the use of the gymnasium.

3. In order to reduce pollution we need to .... more use of the energy provided by the sun and the wind.

4. Let's go for a drive. I .... the use of my father's car for the weekend.

5. Doctors discourage the use of fats in cooking and .... the use of oils instead.

6. The United Nations should .... the use of all chemical weapons.

7. The aim of the course is to .... you to the uses of the internet.

2 Noun + preposition + use

Complete the following expressions with the correct preposition, then use them in the sentences below:

guidelines .... the use   ease .... use
increase .... the use   range .... uses
restrictions .... the use   years .... use

1. The steep .... of mobile phones in recent years has led to a dramatic reduction in the use of phone boxes.

2. The steps in the castle had been worn away by ....

3. Our organisation has to follow very strict .... and storage of personal details on computers.

4. During the war there were .... of cars and many people travelled everywhere by bicycle.

5. Buy a food processor. It has a .... in the kitchen. It can mix, chop and juice.

6. It's very user-friendly. There is a large handle at the front of the device for ....

3 Common adjective collocations

Choose the more natural collocation in each sentence:

1. This medicine is for *external / outside* use only. It should not be taken internally.

2. This entrance is in *constant / full* use. Please do not park in front of it.

3. Your son is very clever, but he doesn't make *complete / full* use of his abilities. He is capable of much better results.

4. I thought I'd give my tennis racket to Andy since I've no *remaining / further* use for it. I'm just too old to play now.

5. The sign next to the fire alarm said 'Penalty for *improper / wrong* use – £200'.

6. The *everyday / widespread* use of antibiotics is causing a lot of unexpected health problems. As a result doctors are beginning to restrict their use of these drugs.

7. This shampoo is very mild and doesn't dry your hair out. It's ideal for *everyday / widespread* use.

8. Members of the club have *constant / unlimited* use of the swimming pool at weekends.

Notes

1. Note the following useful expressions:
   Organic vegetables are grown without the use of chemical fertilisers.
   All of the equipment must be sterilised before use in the operating theatre.
   Teenage drug use is on the increase.

2. If something is used a lot, we say:
   heavy use   extensive use

   If something is used normally, we say:
   normal use   ordinary use

   If something is used a little, we say:
   occasional use   limited use

3. If something is *of little use*, it is no longer useful and may even be useless.

4. The question *What's the use?* means *What's the point?* For example:
   What's the use of complaining? Nobody listens!

---

value

1 Verb + value (money)

Use the correct form of these verbs:

assess   *depend on*   *fall*
hold   *offer*

1. The value of most cars depreciates quite quickly, but sports cars tend to . . . . their value well.

2. Everything is included in the price. This holiday certainly . . . . value for money.

3. The exact value of the vase will . . . . its condition. You can expect around £3000 if it's in perfect condition.

4. When we decided to sell our house, an estate agent came round to . . . . the value of the property.

5. The value of the pound . . . . against the dollar and other major currencies yesterday.

2 Value (interesting quality)

Use these words to complete the sentences:

nutritional   *sentimental*   *novelty*   *shock*

1. It's a not an expensive watch, but it's of great . . . . value to me. It belonged to my grandfather.

2. A lot of junk food is tasty, but much of it has no . . . . value whatsoever.

3. The game has a certain . . . . value – it's new and interesting – but I think people will get bored with it quite quickly.

4. The sex wasn't necessary in the film. I think it was included purely for its . . . . value.

3 Different values

Values (plural) means a set of beliefs. Match the following:

1. People from the same culture tend to share
2. Older people tend to regret the loss of
3. The main political parties say they stand for
4. Lots of people reject

a. traditional values. But they often forget that the 'good old days' were often not very good!

b. similar values. Maybe this is less true today than it used to be.

c. middle-class values as not relevant to them.

d. family values. It's an easy thing to say!

4 Common adjective collocations

Use these adjectives in the sentences:

face   *great*   *incalculable*
market   *original*   *street*

1. Tickets were changing hands at many times their . . . . value. I had to pay £20 for a £5 ticket.

2. The thieves took a few small things, but nothing of . . . . value.

3. I had to sell my car well below its . . . . value. It was worth a lot more than I got for it.

4. Last night customs officers at Heathrow airport seized drugs with an estimated . . . . value of £5 million.

5. These ancient paintings are of . . . . value. It's simply impossible to put a price on them.

6. The present value of these shares is £4000 – they're now worth ten times their . . . . value.

"The exact value is difficult to estimate, but I would insure it for about £3,000!"

Notes

1. *Value* is often used to talk about something important or useful:
   I don't think parents should set too high a value on exam results.
   The discovery of these old letters will be of great value to historians.

2. Note the following *preposition + value* phrases:
   Jewellery to the value of three million pounds was stolen.
   The pound dropped in value yesterday.
   Their house has increased in value by about £20,000.
   Do not leave any articles of value in your hotel room.

view

1 Verb + view

Use the correct form of these verbs:

take　　　*express*　　　*hear*

1. The Prime Minister . . . . his views on the war during a live television broadcast.

2. We would be interested to . . . . your views on this subject. So what do you really think?

3. I have always . . . . the view that we are each responsible for our own actions.

air　　　*represent*　　　*hold*

4. My grandfather . . . . the view that corporal punishment is good for children.

5. The comments by the leader of our group do not . . . . the views of all of us.

6. We're holding this meeting so that everyone can have the chance to . . . . their views.

reflect　　　*exchange*　　　*agree with*

7. I don't . . . . Jason's view that we should ignore this letter. We must reply.

8. The main purpose of this session is so that people from different departments within the company can . . . . views on the takeover.

9. I don't think your ideas . . . . the views of the majority of us.

2 Common adjective collocations

Use these adjectives in the sentences:

extreme　　　*personal*
opposing　　　*outspoken*
prevailing　　　*strong*

1. The Foreign Minister was careful to point out that these were his . . . . views and not those of the government.

2. My father holds . . . . views on marriage. He thinks everybody should be married in church.

3. Bill says exactly what he thinks even if it offends people. His . . . . views make him unpopular.

4. She thinks that all gays should be put in prison. Nobody shares such . . . . views.

5. The . . . . view is that the men are innocent. Everybody thinks they should be released.

6. My father and I have sharply . . . . views on politics. He's a conservative and I am a socialist.

Go back and underline the adjective collocations.

3 Point of view

Match the the following:

1. OK. Has everyone had a chance to
2. That's a highly
3. I think if you are going to discuss things, you have to be willing to
4. They stoutly
5. They don't agree with the proposals at the moment, but don't worry, they'll . . .

a. *listen to other people's points of view.*
b. *come round to our point of view* eventually.
c. *put their point of view or is there somebody who still wants to speak?*
d. *subjective point of view. It's not based on the facts.*
e. *defended their point of view and refused to change it in any way.*

4 View of a place

Match the following:

1. The best view of the city
2. We had a grandstand view of the cyclists
3. We have a wonderful view
4. We had a terrible view of the stage
5. Our view was blocked by a woman

a. *as they passed.*
b. *wearing a large hat.*
c. *is from the castle.*
d. *from our sitting room window.*
e. *from our seats in the back row.*

Notes

1. Note these ways of describing opposing views:
   My father and I have sharply conflicting views on lots of issues.
   The book explores contrasting views of the writer's work.
   They hold differing views on money.

2. Note this way of introducing your view:
   In my view, we need a new government.

3. Note these adjective collocations:
   Looking at it from an economic point of view . . .
   From a scientific point of view . . .
   From the point of view of road safety . . .
   It's written from a child's point of view.

violence

1 Verb + violence

Use the correct form of these verbs:

condemn   *condone*

contain   *resort to*

stir up   *threaten*

1. If they have to, the group are prepared to .... violence to get what they want.
2. The leader of the gang was accused of using racist language to .... hatred and violence.
3. The President .... the violence and appealed to the rioters to refrain from further violence.
4. As a pacifist, I deplore all violence. I can't .... violence in any shape or form.
5. When I was .... with violence, I handed over my passport and credit cards.
6. Violence flared up again last night in many areas. Police in riot gear struggled to .... the violence.

2 Common adjective collocations

Use these adjectives in the sentences:

domestic   *excessive*

gratuitous   *mindless*

racial   *widespread*

1. The police deny that they used .... violence while arresting the accused.
2. Unfortunately, ... violence is a regular occurrence in some families.
3. A group of white youths were accused of instigating .... violence by taunting the two Asian boys.
4. The high tax on food led to .... violence throughout the country.
5. There's too much .... violence on TV. Most of it is totally unnecessary.
6. Police said that the horrific attack on the old woman was an act of .... violence.

drug-related   *sectarian*   *endemic*

7. In parts of India the communal violence seems to be .... It's gone on for generations.
8. Northern Ireland has seen less .... violence in recent years.
9. In most big cities most violence is ....

3 Noun + of + violence

Use these nouns in the sentences:

history of   *outbreak of*   *scenes of*

upsurge of   *use of*   *victims of*

1. It is a fact that women are still the main .... domestic violence.
2. Our group believes in political change, but it does not advocate the .... violence.
3. In India, fifty people were reported killed today in a fresh .... inter-racial violence.
4. There were unprecedented .... violence in the city's main square as rival football fans clashed.
5. There's been an .... violence in the city recently, and this sudden rise is being linked to increased unemployment.
6. He has a long .... violence and is considered to be a danger to society.

4 Noun + preposition + violence

Complete the sentences below with a suitable preposition:

to (2)   *about*   *in*

1. Among psychologists, there is growing concern .... violence on television.
2. They have called for an end .... violence and a return to peace.
3. Security at benefit offices is being stepped up to deal with the recent increase .... violence.
4. There are hopes that the conflict can be resolved without resort .... violence.

Notes

1. Note the following expressions with prepositions:
   violence against women
   violence within the family
   violence between different ethnic groups

2. Violence in a community or among a large group of people 'erupts' – like a volcano:
   Widespread violence has erupted since the government was overthrown by the rebels.

3. An outbreak of violence can be 'quelled' (ended).

---

warning

1 Verb + warning

Use the correct form of these verbs:

give	heed
ignore	issue
serve as	shout

1. Doctors have . . . . a warning against eating shellfish from the polluted beaches.

2. Many people continue to . . . . warnings about the dangers of sunbathing. They think it'll never happen to them.

3. They can't complain. They were . . . . adequate warning that the factory was in danger of closing.

4. He . . . . a warning as the piece of wood started to fall towards me.

5. They failed to . . . . the warnings about the dangerous currents in the river. Both of them drowned.

6. After passing sentence, the judge said that the punishment would . . . . a warning to all politicians who thought they were above the law.

2 Common adjective collocations

Use these adjectives in the sentences:

advance	health
final	dire

1. All cigarette packets must carry a government . . . . warning.

2. The referee gave the player a . . . . warning. Next time, he would be sent off.

3. I can prepare the food for the party. Just give me . . . . warning of how many people to expect.

4. Environmentalists are always issuing . . . . warnings to us about global warming.

prior	stern	written	clear

5. By law, employers have to give you a . . . . warning before they can dismiss you.

6. Paragliding can be dangerous, so all participants get a . . . . warning of the risks involved.

7. The judge sent the driver to prison and issued a . . . . warning about drinking and driving.

8. The whole class agrees that we should be given . . . . warning of a test. It's not fair just to spring it on us without any warning.

3 Expressions with prepositions

Use these prepositions in the sentences:

to	without	for	of

1. The soldiers opened fire . . . . warning.

2. Just a word . . . . warning – there are speed cameras about 5 miles outside Bideford.

3. That's what happens when you work too hard. Let it be a warning . . . . you!

4. Thanks. I would have crashed into the car in front, but . . . . your warning.

"I can't really give you a clearer warning of the risks involved!"

Notes

1. Note the following:
   The warning sign said 'Caution – Danger of Ice'.
   The police fired warning shots above the heads of the crowd, but the protesters took no notice.

2. Note the following:
   I was stopped by the police for speeding, but I was let off with a warning.

3. If you 'heed' a warning, you pay attention to it:
   The company consistently failed to heed warnings about the safety of its equipment.

4. An 'early warning system' is a defence system that warns of imminent attack.

5. Nowadays we get warnings about: *the dangers of smoking / speeding / eating too much etc.*

6. Note the expression – *as a warning to:*
   The prisoners were publicly flogged as a warning to others not to try to escape.

way

1 Verb + way

Use the correct form of these verbs:

> admire   change
> criticise   develop
> look at   see

1. The committee is always . . . . new ways to improve the services the club provides.

2. I wasn't pleased when she . . . . the way I ran the office. I felt her comments were so unfair.

3. The internet has . . . . the way we do business. In fact, it has revolutionised it.

4. This job has to be completed today, but I can't . . . . any way of finishing it before five.

5. I . . . . the way she carried on when she had no chance of winning the race.

6. We're trying to . . . . new ways of treating people for depression without the use of drugs.

> keep out of   make   lose   push

7. If you . . . . your way, just use your mobile.

8. I think it's best if you . . . . Rachel's way for a while. She's fairly annoyed with you.

9. After driving through miles of forest, we . . . . our way past some incredibly beautiful lakes.

10. Just . . . . your way to the front of the queue!

Go back and underline all the verb collocations.

2 Common adjective collocations

Use these adjectives in the sentences:

> efficient   hard   novel
> proper   one sure   various

1. Why do you insist on doing things the . . . . way? Life is difficult enough!

2. We looked at . . . . ways of solving the problem, but they were all unsatisfactory.

3. E-mail provides an . . . . way of communicating with people that's fast and cheap.

4. Keeping a cow in the garden is certainly a . . . . way of keeping the grass short!

5. There is only . . . . way of getting him to tidy his room and that is to pay him to do it!

6. The . . . . way to lay the table is something you learn from your parents. I can't understand why some people don't have a clue how to do it!

Go back and underline all the collocations above.

3 Way (manner of doing something)

Use these adjectives in the sentences:

> disgusting   leisurely   meaningful
> great   possible   shoddy

1. When you tell Philip that you don't want to go out with him, please try to do it in the nicest . . . . way. You don't want to hurt him.

2. Did you see the . . . . way she ate her food? Some people have no table manners!

3. He looked at me and raised his eyebrow in a . . . . way, but I'm not sure what he was trying to say to me.

4. There was no rush, so we walked through the park in a . . . . way.

5. They didn't even explain why they were sacking her after 40 years working for them! In my opinion, that's a pretty . . . . way to treat an employee.

6. We went on this fantastic trip to Lake Victoria. It was a . . . . way to end our holiday.

Notes

1. Notice the structures 'way to' and 'way of':
   We need to come up with ways to save money.
   We need to come up with ways of saving money.
   We need new ways to promote our products.
   We need new ways of promoting our products.

2. Notice these expressions:
   The twins are different in every way.
   I like getting my own way!
   You have a very nice way of life here.

3. Examples 7-10 in exercise 1 have a literal meaning for 'way'. Here are some more expressions with this meaning:
   Their house is a bit out of the way. (remote)
   Can you tell me the way to the pub?
   Sorry, my bags are in your way.
   Let's stop for a meal on the way.

4. Here are other common expressions:
   Our anniversary is still a long way off.
   Try turning it the other way up and see if you can open it.
   You always take the easy way out!
   I could tell by the way she looked at me that she was irritated by my comments.

word

1 Verb + word

Use the correct form of these verbs:

breathe	*choose*
exchange	*find*
look up	*say*
send	*understand*

1. I've . . . . the word in every dictionary and I still don't know how to use it!

2. He ignored us. He just walked by without . . . . a word.

3. It was supposed to be an introductory talk about computing, but I couldn't . . . . a word of it.

4. It's sometimes very difficult to . . . . the right word to express precisely what you want to say.

5. No, she's not here yet. She . . . . word that she would be about an hour late.

6. What I just told you is private and confidential so please don't . . . . a word of it to anyone.

7. In order not to upset him, she . . . . her words with great care.

8. The Queen shook hands and . . . . a few words with the winner of the competition.

Now use these phrasal verbs:

get in	*take down*	*go back on*	*get out*

9. She has . . . . her word and decided not to lend me the money after all.

10. She talks so much it's impossible for anybody to . . . . a word . . . . . . edgeways.

11. Reporters . . . . every word of the Prime Minister's speech.

12. If word . . . . about the affair, the President will have to resign.

2 Common adjective collocations

Use the following adjectives in these sentences:

exact	*four-letter*	*kind*	*own*
right	*overused*	*single*	*quick*

1. Can I have a . . . . word before the meeting starts? It'll only take a few minutes.

2. You haven't been listening to a . . . . word I've been saying for the past ten minutes!

3. The play is full of . . . . words. Why do modern writers need to use so many swear words?

4. Take your time and in your . . . . words tell the court exactly what happened.

5. I can't remember the teacher's . . . . words, but he said something along those lines.

6. 'Nice' is a very . . . . word. Can't you think of a better word?

7. Teachers sometimes forget that a few . . . . words at the right time can make all the difference to a student's confidence.

8. Is this the . . . . word that fits in this sentence?

3 Word + of + noun

Use these noun expressions in the sentences:

words of apology	*words of comfort*
words of encouragement	*word of mouth*
a word of warning	

1. Just . . . . before you go out – these streets can be dangerous at night.

2. All the orders were given by . . . . to avoid leaving any written evidence which might be discovered later.

3. He wasn't looking forward to the exam, but he brightened up at the teacher's . . . .

4. My brother muttered a few . . . . for his appalling behaviour, then left the room.

5. After the funeral, a lot of people came and offered . . . . to members of my family.

Notes

1. If you 'have a word' with someone, it means you have spoken to them for some purpose:
   I'll have a word with Alex and ask him if he can pick you up before the meeting.

   If you 'have words' with someone, it means you have had a disagreement or argument:
   Have you and your father had words?

2. If you have to give a speech, this expression is very useful:
   Good morning, I'd just like to say a few words.

3. Notice the following expressions:
   I was so shocked. I was lost for words.
   He left in the middle of the meeting – without a word.
   He's not good at putting his ideas into words.
   Give me your word you won't be late back tonight.
   (give your word = promise)

work

1 Verb + work

Use the correct form of these verbs:

check	complete
do	face
make	give up
find	involve

1. I'd . . . . work if I could afford to.

2. I'm still looking for a job. It's so difficult to . . . . work in the present economic climate.

3. There's plenty of work to be . . . . in the garden at this time of year.

4. I just couldn't . . . . work yesterday, so I took the day off.

5. Payment will be withheld until the work is . . . . to my satisfaction.

6. As a salesman my work . . . . a lot of driving.

7. Make sure you . . . . your work before handing it in. Silly mistakes can lose marks.

8. These new regulations have . . . . a lot of extra work for me.

Now use these phrasal verbs in the sentences:

put ... into	get on with	get off
get down	go into	go out

9. Stop talking and . . . . your work. I want this finished by the end of the lesson.

10. After the baby's born, I won't have to . . . . to work any more – at least not for a few years.

11. Can you try to . . . . work early tomorrow so that we can visit Sue in hospital?

12. He's . . . . a lot of work . . . . improving his maths. He studies for hours most nights.

13. A tremendous amount of work has . . . . the preparations for the wedding.

14. I've been avoiding . . . . to work all day. I just feel so tired and lifeless at the moment.

2 Common adjective collocations

Use these adjectives in the sentence:

back-breaking	extra	hard
monotonous	hard day's	skilled

1. There is no doubt that teaching is . . . . work, but it can be very fulfilling.

2. Washing dishes all day is pretty . . . . work.

3. I'm afraid we can't take on any . . . . work at the moment. We're already working to capacity.

4. Furniture-making is very . . . . work and involves years and years of training.

5. Digging the garden is . . . . work. It's so physically demanding.
   > Then, why not get your son to do it for you!

6. After a . . . . work, it's nice to get home and put your feet up.

3 Noun + of + work

Use these nouns to complete the sentences:

backlog of	rewards of	piles of
pressure of	search of	standard of

1. Many young people travel to the large cities in . . . . work.

2. Sorry, I can't come to the meeting this evening. I've got . . . . work to do for tomorrow.

3. It was good to see her reaping the . . . . all her hard work.

4. The . . . . his written work is extremely high. His speaking is less good.

5. The only way to clear this huge . . . . work is to take on more part-time staff.

6. The . . . . work is beginning to get to him. Unless he cuts down the time he's at the office, his health will suffer.

Notes

1. Note the following expressions:
   His work is satisfactory / up to standard / up to scratch.
   His work is unsatisfactory / of a poor standard / shoddy / sloppy.

2. If you are *out of work*, you are unemployed.
   If you are *in work*, you have a job.
   My brother's been out of work for 5 years.
   There are a lot more people in work than there were 10 years ago.

3. We talk about part-time / full-time / casual / freelance / voluntary work.

4. If you have too much work, you are *up to your ears in work*.

5. Note the proverb: Many hands make light work!

6. If you have a particularly difficult task to do, you 'have your work cut out!'

Of expressions

'**Of**' is one of the smallest words in English and one of the most common. It also plays an important role in the structure of many common noun phrases. This section helps you with some of the most important of these phrases.

Don't forget when you finish each exercise to go back and underline the complete expressions.

an act of

an amount of

a copy of

a great deal of

a feature of

a lack of

a level of

a list of

a loss of

a matter of

a part of

a piece of

a range of

a sense of

a series of

a set of

a sign of

a stage of

a supply of

a waste of

an act of

Act of + noun

Complete the sentences with these nouns:

generosity   terrorism
revenge   mercy

1. The hijackers released two elderly hostages as an act of . . . . Both had serious heart conditions and needed urgent medical attention.

2. The gift of his whole art collection to the nation was an act of incredible . . . .

3. Police believe that the murder of two policemen last night was an act of . . . . for the shooting of two gangsters in the recent bank robbery.

4. The attacks of September 11th were the worst acts of . . . . ever committed on American soil.

faith   desperation
treason   God

5. Colonel Briggs was found guilty of selling information to the enemy. The punishment for such an act of . . . . could only be execution by firing squad.

6. I'm not sure that your project has much chance of succeeding, but as an act of . . . . I will lend you the money you require to get started.

7. In order to escape from the hunters, the tiger leapt from a 100-metre cliff into the river below. It was an act of sheer . . . .

8. We're insured against things like fire, burglary, earthquakes or what insurance companies call an act of . . . . !

"It cost an incredible amount of money!"

an amount of

1 A large amount of

Use the correct form of these verbs:

cost   do   drink   make
get through   need   spend   store

1. When the temperature reached 40, we were sweating profusely. We . . . . huge amounts of water to replace lost fluids.

2. Sorry, I can't make the party tonight. I've got an enormous / a massive amount of work to . . . .

3. A huge amount of information can be . . . . on a computer's hard disk.

4. Mary . . . . an inordinate amount of time in the bathroom in the morning.

5. The new house . . . . a substantial amount of work done to it before we can think about moving into it.

6. We . . . . an unbelievable amount of food each week. We'll need to cut down. We simply can't afford it.

7. Their wedding . . . . an incredible amount of money. No expense was spared.

8. The students above me were . . . . a tremendous amount of noise last night.

2 Common adjective collocations

Use the following adjectives in these sentences:

average   excessive
maximum   generous
limited   total

1. . . . . amounts of alcohol can damage your liver.

2. The . . . . amount of pocket money which teenagers get is around £15 per week.

3. It's a big car with a . . . . amount of space in the back.

4. Land mines are designed to cause the . . . . amount of harm to anybody who stands on them.

5. The . . . . amount of money raised so far for the charity is approaching one million pounds.

6. We only have a . . . . amount of time to complete this task – we can't continue indefinitely. So let's get a move on!

a copy of

1 Copy of + noun

Complete the sentences with these nouns:

unauthorised   *free*   *well-thumbed*   *poor*

1. . . . . copies of the leaflet on scholarships are available from the Department of Education.

2. I still have my . . . . copy of Shakespeare's Sonnets somewhere in the house. I'll go and get it for you.

3. Making an . . . . copy of this article is against copyright law.

4. It's such a . . . . copy of the original painting. Surely nobody would be taken in by such an obvious fake.

advance   *back*   *true*

5. Any photocopies you send must be certified as . . . . copies of the original documents.

6. I have over 200 . . . . copies of the magazine. I don't think I missed an issue.

7. . . . . copies of a book are usually sent to reviewers before it appears in the shops.

2 Verb + copy of

Use the correct form of these verbs:

enclose   *get hold of*   *keep*
print   *make*   *sign*

1. I think we'd better . . . . twenty copies of the agenda and bring them to the meeting.

2. We . . . . file copies of all official letters that we send out just in case we need to refer to them at a later date.

3. Please remember to . . . . a copy of your birth certificate with your application form.

4. Bruce Witlon will be . . . . copies of his latest book straight after this talk.

5. I finally managed to . . . . a copy of that book you were looking for. I picked one up in a second-hand bookshop.

6. The publishers only . . . . 500 copies of the book. They don't think it will be a big seller.

a great deal of

A great deal of + noun

Deal – used on its own – is not a common word, but *a great deal of* is used in many different situations. Complete the sentences with these words:

concentration   *controversy*
soul-searching   *publicity*
time and effort   *truth*
work   *trouble*

1. Fox-hunting is a sport which arouses a great deal of . . . . in the UK.

2. This job requires a great deal of . . . . You can't relax for a minute.

3. We have invested a great deal of . . . . in setting up this meeting. I hope it was all worth it in the end.

4. Her decision to give up her baby for adoption came after a great deal of . . . . She spent weeks thinking about it, but in the end she knew she wouldn't be able to cope.

5. You've caused me a great deal of extra . . . . Try not to make any mistakes next time.

6. There has been a great deal of . . . . surrounding the team captain's arrest for drunk driving.

7. There is undoubtedly a great deal of . . . . in your arguments, but I still can't agree with you.

8. You've really gone to a great deal of . . . . for us. We don't know if we'll ever be able to thank you enough.

"Fox-hunting arouses a great deal of controversy!"

a feature of

1 Feature of + noun
Complete the sentences with these nouns:

building   elections
landscape   life

1. High mountains and deep valleys are natural features of the Afghan . l . . . .
2. High stress levels are a feature of . . life . . for people working in the stock market.
3. In recent years television debates between party leaders have become a regular feature of general . . el . . .
4. The dominant feature of the old l . . . . . . was its huge wooden door.

2 Adjective + feature of
Use the following adjectives in these sentences:

key   familiar   redeeming
special   safety   striking

1. The old castle is the most sp . . . . . feature of the city – it's the sight most tourists will take away with them.
2. Electric windows and central locking are standard features on most cars these days. Among other sa . . . . . features of this car are anti-lock brakes and passenger airbags.
3. Remember that teamwork is the . . . k . . . . feature of a successful organisation.
4. The one f . . . . feature of the plan is its low cost. If it wasn't for that, we wouldn't be going ahead.
5. Windmills are a . f . . . . . feature of the Dutch landscape.
6. A . . st . . . . feature of this year's Book Festival is the appearance of the world-famous children's writer and former EFL teacher, J K Rowling.

a lack of

1 Lack of + noun
Complete the sentences with these nouns:

experience   sleep
facilities   progress
understanding   practice

1. I've lost some of my skiing skills through lack of . . . p . . . . I haven't skied for the last two winters.
2. We complained to the local authority about the lack of recycling . . . . f . . . . . . in the town.
3. The lack of . s . . . . finally caught up with me, and I began to doze off in the meeting.
4. His comments showed a complete lack of . un . . . . . . of the problem.
5. The President expressed his disappointment at the lack of . pros . . . . . in the peace talks.
6. Lack of . exp . . . . . will generally count against you in a job interview.

2 Lack of + noun
Complete the sentences with these nouns:

enthusiasm   self-confidence
exercise   investment

1. A lack of . . . i . . . . . . over the years has led to a general decline in public transport.
2. Her lack of . s c . . . . makes her feel awkward and uncomfortable in social situations.
3. A lack of regular . ex . . . . . increases the risk of heart disease.
4. Naturally, his parents are concerned at his lack of ent . . . . . for school.

interest   people   privacy   respect

5. He shows a lack of . . . r . . . . . . for authority and is always getting into trouble.
6. Lots of film stars complain about the lack of . pr . . . . in their lives, but there's nothing they like better than publicity.
7. The concert has been cancelled owing to a lack of . . in . . . . from the public.
8. When we appealed for volunteers to help clean up the beach, there was no lack of . . pea . . . who came forward to offer their time.

a level of

1 Verb + level of

Use the correct form of these verbs:

measure   reach   reduce   require

1. After two years of study he has . . . .
   a reasonable level of competence in English.
2. He works as an air-traffic controller. It's a job that
   . . . . a high level of concentration.
3. Few people would disagree that something should
   be done to . . . . the level of crime in
   the area.
4. A breathalyser is a device used by traffic police to
   . . . . the level of alcohol in the blood.

2 Level of + noun

Complete the sentences with these nouns:

frustration   violence   pollution   fitness

1. We have exercise classes which cater for all levels
   of . . . .
2. I think that children today are exposed to
   unacceptable levels of . . . . on television.
3. The results of a recent survey show a growing
   level of . . . . among hospital doctors.
   Many are thinking of leaving the profession.
4. Increased levels of air . . . . in the city
   centre represent a major health hazard to the
   local residents.

   anxiety   expertise
   difficulty   unemployment

5. It is difficult to find good staff with the level of
   . . . . required for this job.
6. Many patients experience high levels of . . . .
   before a major operation.
7. What is the government doing about the high
   level of . . . . in this country?
8. After the exam all the students complained about
   the level of . . . . of the maths test. Most of
   them couldn't even attempt half of the questions.

a list of

1 Verb + list of

Use the correct form of these verbs:

make   find   leave
cross   publish   memorise

1. We were burgled last night. The police have asked
   us to . . . . a list of everything that's missing.
2. At the back of your handout you will . . . .
   a list of the books that I have referred to during
   the lecture.
3. The English teacher made us . . . . the
   whole list of irregular verbs. It took ages!
4. Every year *The Times* . . . . a list of the 30
   richest people in the UK.
5. My wife went off on holiday and . . . . an
   endless list of things for me to do around the
   house.
6. After his dreadful behaviour at dinner the other
   night, I have . . . . Tim off my list of friends.

2 List of + noun

Complete the sentences with these nouns:

priorities   candidates   complaints

1. We didn't enjoy our holiday one bit. We have a list
   of . . . . as long as your arm!
2. I've drawn up a list of . . . . that I'd like to
   interview. I've narrowed it down to five people.
3. Decorating the bathroom comes a long way down
   my list of . . . . There's a lot more
   important things to do.

   guests   ingredients   names

4. The list of . . . . included 400g of sugar and
   300g of butter.
5. I think we'd better draw up a list of possible
   . . . . for the wedding breakfast – just so
   that we have an idea of the problem!
6. The police need a list of . . . . of all those
   who witnessed the accident.

a loss of

1 Loss of + noun

Complete the sentences with these nouns:

earnings   *players*   *property*   *loved one*

1. Nothing can make up for the loss of a . . . .
. . . . Many people never get over it.

2. This club does not accept responsibility for loss
of members' personal . . . .

3. He is seeking compensation for loss of . . . .
caused by the accident which left him unable to
work for two years.

4. The team has been weakened by the loss of some
key . . . . through injury.

face   *privacy*   *sound*   *jobs*

5. I'm afraid that the loss of some . . . . is
necessary if the company is to survive. Reducing
the workforce is the only way forward.

6. We apologise for the temporary loss of . . . .
during that report from our correspondent in
India.

7. Loss of . . . . is one of the drawbacks of being
famous.

8. In certain cultures, loss of . . . . is a very
serious matter indeed.

2 Physical and mental loss

Complete the sentences with these nouns:

appetite   *blood*
confidence   *life*
memory   *sensation*

1. After the accident I suffered from a loss of
. . . . and could recall nothing of events leading
up to the crash.

2. Loss of . . . . is one of the classic symptoms of
the disease. The patient loses all interest in eating.

3. The explosion at the fireworks factory resulted in
a tragic loss of . . . .

4. Something is pressing on one of the nerves in
your arm and this is causing the loss of . . . .
in your fingers.

5. He was severely wounded and died from a
massive loss of . . . .

6. The actor suffered such a total loss of . . . .
that he couldn't go on stage.

a matter of

Matter of + noun

Complete the sentences with these nouns:

urgency   *dispute*
conscience   *interest*

1. It was very difficult for my grandfather to refuse
to join the army in 1939, but for him it was a
matter of . . . . He's been a pacifist all his
life.

2. It remains a matter of . . . . whether he did
the right thing. Some people believe his actions
have made the situation worse.

3. This is a matter of considerable . . . . to me,
so I'll gladly come to the meeting.

4. This case is a matter of the greatest . . . . to
us all and must have top priority — it could be a
matter of life and death.

concern   *weeks*
experience   *time*

5. Don't worry, you'll soon learn. Dealing with this
type of problem is all a matter of . . . .

6. Follow our crash-diet programme and you will see
a difference in a matter of . . . .

7. It's only a matter of . . . . before they go out
of business. They can't keep losing money at this
rate.

8. Local residents raised a number of matters of
. . . . about the siting of the new airport.

*"You'll see a dramatic difference in a matter of weeks
– if you follow this crash-diet!"*

a part of

1 Part of + noun

Complete the sentences with these nouns:

> bargain   blame   life   problem
> day   treatment   story   experience

1. Management will have to take part of the .... for the failure of the project.

2. We spent part of the .... in the art gallery, looking at their incredible collection of Picassos.

3. Going bungee jumping is all part of the .... of spending a gap year in New Zealand.

4. Yes, I'll lend you my car if you let me use your flat next month, but how do I know if you'll keep your part of the ....?

5. Voters feel they have only been given part of the .... They believe that the government is keeping vital information from them.

6. The doctor uses hypnosis as part of the .... for people who have a fear of flying.

7. I think part of his .... is that he finds it difficult to work as a member of a team.

8. He lived and worked in London for most of his career, but the early part of his .... was spent in Madrid.

2 Part of + noun

Complete the sentences with these nouns:

> ageing process   diet   speech   everyday life
> education system   job   team   growing up

1. Most people believe that sitting exams is a vital part of the ....

2. Computers and the internet have become part of .... nowadays.

3. Learning to take responsibility for yourself is an important part of ....

4. Fresh fruit and vegetables form an essential part of a healthy ....

5. Firefighters face danger every day, but they accept the risks as part of the ....

6. I'm part of the .... of scientists who are trying to find a cure for MS.

7. The gradual loss of memory is a normal part of the ....

8. Parts of his .... were excellent, but as a whole I didn't think much of it.

a piece of

Adjective + piece of

Use the following adjectives in these sentences:

> best   blank   clever   worst
> excellent   favourite   sensitive   incredible

1. What's your .... piece of music? Mine's the second movement from Mozart's Piano Concerto no. 21.

2. That's the .... piece of news I've heard for a long time! Congratulations!

3. A doctor just happened to be passing by as my baby choked on a sweet. She managed to save his life. It was an .... piece of luck.

4. I stared at the .... piece of paper. I had no idea how I was going to answer the question.

5. They managed to trace the killer from a very small amount of DNA evidence left behind at the crime scene. It was a very .... piece of detective work.

6. Her article on the misuse of public money by local councillors was an .... piece of investigative journalism.

7. The movement of the patient's eyes are recorded on a highly .... piece of equipment which gives extremely accurate readings.

8. This is the .... piece of writing I have ever read in my life. I think you'd better start again from scratch.

"It's all part of the job, Sir!"

a range of

1 Range of + noun

Complete the sentences with these nouns:

activities   options   products   issues
models   opinions   subjects   uses

1. For someone with your qualifications, there is a huge range of . . . . open to you. The careers advisory service are here to help you make the best decision.
2. Oil is a very important substance because it has a wide range of industrial . . . .
3. The speaker will deal with a broad range of . . . . affecting the teaching profession.
4. The La Manga complex offers a wide range of sporting . . . . for both children and adults.
5. Each student's ability is tested across a wide range of . . . .
6. There is such a broad range of . . . . on this issue that I can't see them reaching any kind of agreement.
7. Our company is introducing a new range of beauty . . . . later this year.
8. Ford offers a wide range of . . . . from small family cars to luxury limousines.

2 Verb + range of

Use the correct form of these verbs:

tackle   come   cover
meet   offer   stock

1. The council . . . . a range of services free of charge to those over 65.
2. The articles in this new men's magazine . . . . a broad range of topics, from sport to politics.
3. We . . . . a wide range of furniture and we're sure you'll find what you need in one of our stores.
4. I have to travel a lot, so I . . . . a broad range of people in my daily life.
5. The job has variety – you will have to . . . . a wide range of tasks.
6. The curtains . . . . in a wide range of colours and designs. Would you like us to send you our new catalogue?

a sense of

1 Sense of (feeling)

Complete the sentences with these nouns:

community   achievement
alarm   loss

1. Passing my driving test first time gave me a great sense of . . . .
2. We felt a growing sense of . . . . when my daughter had not returned home by midnight. She said she'd be home by 11.
3. There's a real sense of . . . . in this neighbourhood. Everybody is very caring and friendly.
4. He felt a deep sense of . . . . after the death of his wife.

outrage   importance
well-being   security

5. Helmets can give cyclists a false sense of . . . . They don't give riders as much protection as they think.
6. She is big-headed and has an exaggerated sense of her own . . . .
7. As the anaesthetic began to take effect, I had a great sense of . . . .
8. His racist remarks filled her with an overwhelming sense of . . . . She had to restrain herself from hitting him!

2 Sense of (ability)

Complete the sentences with these nouns:

balance   direction   humour
smell   taste

1. I'm sure he'll be able to find the house on his own. He has a pretty good sense of . . . .
2. He doesn't have much of a sense of . . . . He never laughs at my jokes!
3. I lose my sense of . . . . when I've got a cold, so I don't really care what I eat.
4. Gymnasts need a good sense of . . . .
5. Dogs have an acute sense of . . . . That's why they are used to search for hidden drugs and for people trapped in collapsed buildings.

a series of

1 Series of + noun

Complete the sentences with these nouns:

results   events   explosions   lectures
murders   strikes   reports   tests

1. We'll need to put you through a series of ....
   to discover what is wrong with you.

2. The police are trying to determine the series of
   .... that led up to the disappearance of the
   child.

3. Leeds City Football Club have sacked their
   manager after a series of disappointing ....

4. A series of unsolved .... in Berlin have
   raised fears that a serial killer is on the loose.

5. Professor Wilson will give a series of .... at
   Glasgow University this spring on contemporary
   Scottish poets.

6. The staff have voted to stage a series of one-day
   .... to express their opposition to the
   proposed job losses.

7. There was a series of ...., then the plane
   broke up and fell to the ground.

8. Tonight's is the last in a series of .... about
   what life is like for the ordinary people of Iraq.

2 Series of + noun

Complete the sentences with these nouns:

articles   attacks
crimes   disagreements
earthquakes   scandals

1. The company's reputation has been damaged by a
   series of financial ....

2. The explosion at the station was just the latest in
   an unending series of terrorist ....

3. *The Telegraph* is publishing a series of ....
   on healthy eating.

4. After a series of .... the singer and his
   song-writer have decided to end their partnership.

5. A series of .... struck Turkey, killing at least
   500 people, and destroying about 9000 homes.

6. He was arrested at Heathrow airport and he is
   expected to stand trial for a series of drug-related
   ....

a set of

Set of + noun

Complete the sentences with these nouns:

circumstances   keys   results   guidelines

1. She got a very poor set of .... in her
   recent examinations. I think she only managed a
   pass in mathematics and she failed the rest.

2. Given the right set of ...., I think he has
   a good chance of winning.

3. The Minister of Health issued a new set of
   .... yesterday on how doctors should
   treat patients who have recently returned from a
   country which have cases of this new flu.

4. I always leave a spare set of .... for my
   house with a neighbour just in case I lock myself
   out. So far, fingers crossed, I've never needed
   them!

golf clubs   teeth   problems   rules

5. I don't know what game he is playing. He seems
   to be using a different set of .... from
   the ones that I know!

6. I've always regretted not looking after my teeth
   when I was young. I had my first set of false
   .... when I was thirty.

7. I thought my life would become easier after my
   divorce, but as a single mother with a young child
   I had a new set of .... to deal with.

8. When we flew to Spain, we all had our normal
   luggage, plus a set of .... each. We were
   lucky we didn't have to pay excess baggage.

*"He'll be charged with a series of
drug-related crimes."*

a sign of

1 Verb + sign of

Use the correct form of these verbs:

find *see* *show*

1. The tyres on my car are beginning to ....
   signs of wear. I'll need to replace them soon.
2. We must stick to our original plan. Any change of
   policy will be ..*seen*.... as a sign of weakness.
3. The detectives searched the house from top to
   bottom, but they ....*found*. no sign of the
   stolen goods.

2 (Be) a sign of

Match the two halves of these sentences:

c
d
a
b
f
e

1. A fall in unemployment is one sign of
2. Spelling words incorrectly is a common sign of
3. A heavy, dark sky is a sign of
4. Admitting you've made a mistake is a sign of
5. Sore muscles and a headache are usually the first
   signs of
6. People say that being a good pool player is usually
   a sign of

a. rain.
b. strength, not weakness.
c. a growing economy.
d. dyslexia.
e. a misspent youth!
f. the flu.

3 Sign of + noun

Complete the sentences with these words:

having *improvement* *trouble*
times *giving in* *emotion*

1. She's such a cold fish. I have rarely seen her
   display any sign of ....*e*........ .
2. At last, her work is showing some signs of
   ..../......... .
3. The police have shown no signs of ...*g*....*n*.... to
   the kidnappers' demands.
4. I'm afraid she's showing the first signs of ..*h*.....
   the disease. We'll need to start treatment.
5. Make sure you call the police at the first sign of
   ..*t*........ .
6. Rising crime is just a sign of the ...*t*........!

a stage of

Stage of + noun

Complete the sentences with these nouns:

campaign *competition* *course*
development *disease* *journey*

1. By the time his relatives called the doctor, old
   Harry was in the advanced stages of the ...*d*...
   and there was little the doctors could do for him
   except make him as comfortable as possible.
2. All the British teams were eliminated in the
   knockout stage of the ...*comp*...?
3. Students are tested at the end of each stage of
   the ..*clou*... .
4. The children are at different stages of ...*dev*...
   so they have to be taught in small groups.
5. The last stage of our ..*j*........ was by
   helicopter from the small airstrip to a tiny island
   50 miles off the coast.
6. At the half-way stage of the election ...*cam*...,
   Bill Clinton had a clear lead over Al Gore.

project *process* *game*

7. My manager likes to get personally involved in
   every stage of the decision-making ...*proce*...
8. Juventus scored twice in the early stages of the
   ...*g*...... .
9. These plans outline the various stages of the
   building ...*proj*... .

"He's now in the advanced stages of the disease."

a supply of

1 Verb + supply of

Use the correct form of these verbs:

control	exhaust
have	provide

1. The new government has promised to .. _p....._ . _provide_ a reliable supply of clean water to all rural communities.
2. Make sure you .. _h......_ . an adequate supply of pens and pencils for the exam.
3. Within three weeks they had .. _e.....ed._ their supply of food and clean drinking water. Their supply of fuel had also run out, so they had to abandon the expedition.
4. The police are desperate to arrest the big dealers who .. _c.....c..._ the supply of drugs to young people in the area.

2 Common adjective collocations

Use the following adjectives in these sentences:

constant	free
fresh	good
inadequate	limited

1. If you don't want to miss a bargain, then hurry along to our stores today. We only have a .. _l........._ supply of these DVD players in stock.
2. The human body needs a .... _fr....._ . supply of vitamin C every day, so make sure you eat fruit every day.
3. The human brain needs a .. _con......_ supply of blood. Even a short disruption of the supply can cause serious problems.
4. There is an . _in........._ supply of skilled workers at the moment.
   > Yes, good people with the right qualifications are in short supply.
5. Many nuclear power stations are located on the coast so that they are near to a ... _good..._ supply of water.
6. Family planning clinics provide a .... _f......._ supply of contraceptives on request.

3 Good supply of

Complete the sentences with these words:

bad jokes	labour
drink	guns
money	oil

1. No, I can't pay for your holiday. I don't have an endless supply of .. _m......_ , you know!
2. Saudi Arabia is self-sufficient in energy. It has an abundant supply of .... _o....._ .
3. There was an unlimited supply of .. _d......._ at the party. No wonder so many people have hangovers this morning.
4. Many American companies build factories in the Far East where there is a plentiful supply of cheap .. _l........._ .
5. He seems to have an never-ending supply of .. _b.j......_ . I don't think I laughed once and couldn't wait to get away.
6. These people seem to have a limitless supply of .... _g......_ and ammunition, but no food! I can't understand it!

a waste of

Waste of + noun

Complete the sentences with these nouns:

talent	time	effort

1. Our meeting achieved absolutely nothing. It was a complete waste of .... _ti....._ .
2. She graduated from university with a first-class degree in music, but has been unable to get a job. What a waste of ... _ta....._ !
3. We spent days decorating the spare room – then a water pipe burst and flooded it. All our work was ruined. What a waste of .. _ef....._ .

resources	human life	money

4. Lots of people believe that the building of this statue is a scandalous waste of taxpayers' ... _m......_ .
5. There is growing opposition to the war and its senseless and tragic waste of .. _h..l......_ .
6. The report is critical of management and the department's waste of ... _r........_ .

Answer Key

ability

Ex 1: 1. assessing 2. doubted 3. affect 4. lost
5. showed 6. overestimated

Ex 2: 1. test 2. use 3. reflection 4. confidence 5. best
6. lack

Ex 3: 1. natural 2. mixed 3. considerable 4. proven
5. average 6. incredible

account

Ex 1: 1. listened to 2. keep 3. provide 4. accept
5. corroborated 6. differ

Ex 2: 1. conflicting accounts 2. blow-by-blow account
3. clear account 4. fascinating account
5. graphic account 6. full account

Ex 3: 1. faithful 2. eye-witness 3. hair-raising
4. humorous 5. sketchy 6. moving

action

Ex 1: 1. demanding 2. explain 3. put . . . . into 4. take
5. swing into 6. condone

Ex 2: 1. prompt 2. whatever 3. drastic 4. Disciplinary
5. joint 6. evasive

Ex 3: 1. need for 2. implications of 3. responsible for
4. plan of 5. result of 6. course of

activity

Ex 1: 1. organises 2. involved in 3. do 4. avoid
5. support 6. monitor

Ex 2: 1. worthwhile activities 2. pleasurable activities
3. outdoor activities 4. strenuous activity
5. frenetic activity

Ex 3: 1. leisure 2. political 3. extra-curricular
4. criminal 5. economic

Ex 4: 1. hive 2. variety 3. flurry 4. bouts 5. signs

advantage

Ex 1: 1. outweigh 2. had 3. weighing up 4. stress
5. give / gave 6. took

Ex 2: 1. main 2. mutual 3. added 4. unfair
5. distinct 6. great
additional = added (sentence 3)
considerable = great (sentence 6)
obvious = distinct (sentence 5)

Ex 3: 1. in / to 2. to / in 3. over 4. of 5. for

advice

Ex 1: 1. taken 2. give 3. ignore 4. welcome 5. turn to
1-I 2-T 3-I 4-G 5-T 6-G

Ex 2: 1. against 2. on 3. against 4. on 5. to 6. on

Ex 3: 1. professional advice 2. sound advice
3. contradictory advice 4. unsolicited advice
5. impartial advice 6. friendly advice

agreement

Ex 1: 1. sign 2. cancel 3. get 4. honour 5. reach
6. broke

Ex 2: 1. Verbal 2. tacit 3. amicable 4. general 5. binding
6. unanimous

Ex 3: 1. express 2. have 3. resolve 4. cause

aim

Ex 1: 1. clarify 2. achieving 3. pursue 4. support
5. have 6. sets out
fulfilling – sentence 2
sympathise with – sentence 4

Ex 2: 1. employment 2. awareness 3. dependency
4. relations 5. homelessness

Ex 3: 1. clear 2. laudable 3. long-term 4. broad
5. underlying 6. sole 7. common

answer

Ex 1: 1. receive 2. waiting for 3. demanded 4. give
5. need 6. was

Ex 2: 1. immediate 2. honest 3. final 4. short
5. detailed 6. correct

Ex 3: 1. knew 2. have 3. guess 4. come up with
5. provide 6. arrived at

Ex 4: 1. simple 2. long-term 3. wrong 4. only
5. obvious 6. definite

apology

Ex 1: 1. expect 2. owe 3. give 4. demanded 5. make
6. offered

Ex 2: 1. sincere 2. full 3. formal 4. belated 5. heartfelt
6. profound 7. public 8. abject

Ex 3: 1. letter 2. full 3. way 4. words

approval

Ex 1: 1. give 2. need 3. showed 4. win 5. seek 6. met
with

Ex 2: 1. full 2. official 3. grudging 4. unanimous
5. prior 6. widespread

Ex 3: 1. seal 2. roar 3. sign 4. nod

Ex 4: 1. for 2. in 3. without 4. on

Answer Key

area

Ex 1: 1. knows 2. touring 3. covers 4. policing 5. avoid 6. developing 7. destroyed

Ex 2: 1. into 2. over 3. off 4. in 5. in 6. to 7. from 8. outside

Ex 3: 1. deprived 2. surrounding 3. immediate 4. remote 5. built-up 6. restricted 7. disaster 8. rural

Ex 4: 1. special 2. reception 3. no-smoking 4. play 5. picnic 6. baggage reclaim

argument

Ex 1: 1. follow 2. support 3. put forward 4. accept 5. heard

Ex 2: 1. compelling (good) 2. feeble (poor) 3. telling (good) 4. strong (good) 5. woolly (poor)

Ex 3: 1. start 2. got into 3. settle 4. lose 5. listen to

Ex 4: 1. friendly 2. heated 3. massive 4. pointless 5. endless

attempt

Ex 1: 1. foiled 2. abandon 3. made 4. failed

Ex 2: 1. first 2. desperate 3. brave 4. half-hearted 5. unsuccessful 6. repeated 7. final 8. deliberate

Ex 3: 1-c 2-a 3-e 4-b 5-d

attention

Ex 1: 1. get 2. hold 3. have 4. need 5. pay
Giving attention: 1-pay; 3-direct to; 5-turn to
Getting attention: 2-attract; 4-caught

Ex 2: 1. undivided 2. close 3. insufficient 4. unwelcome 5. meticulous 6. immediate

Ex 3: 1. to 2. to 3. from 4. to 5. away 6. on

attitude

Ex 1: 1. shows 2. taken 3. typifies 4. shape 5. changed 6. hardened 7. understand

Ex 2: 1. negative 2. relaxed 3. right 4. aggressive 5. insular 6. patronising

Ex 3: 1. laid-back 2. devil-may-care 3. slap-dash 4. holier-than-thou 5. happy-go-lucky

ban

Ex 1: 1. imposed 2. defied 3. announced 4. lift 5. introduce 6. supported

Ex 2: 1. using e-mail 2. land mines 3. sale of handguns 4. tobacco advertising 5. human cloning 6. the trade in ivory
complete = total, blanket, outright, worldwide

Ex 3: 1. They've put a ban on the sale of alcohol at the match. 2. They've put a ban on the import of UK lamb. 3. They've put a ban on all flights into North Korea. 4. They've put a ban on the sale of pornography.

behaviour

Ex 1: 1. tolerate 2. affect 3. criticising 4. explain 5. apologised for 6. improved 7. change, change

Ex 2: 1. disgraceful 2. obsessive 3. violent 4. eccentric 5. good 6. anti-social

Ex 3: 1. standards 2. explanation 3. excuse 4. bounds 5. improvement 6. model

belief

Ex 1: 1. holds 2. share 3. stand up for 4. shaken 5. strengthen 6. clinging to

Ex 2: 1. mistaken 2. popular 3. unshakeable 4. firm 5. growing 6. genuine

Ex 3: 1. to 2. of 3. of 4. of 5. on 6. of

benefit

Ex 1: 1. brought 2. outweigh 3. include 4. derive 5. feel 6. outlining 7. reaping

Ex 2: 1. hard work 2. helmet 3. education 4. scheme 5. exercise 6. organic food

Ex 3: 1. child 2. unemployment 3. fringe 4. means-tested 5. housing 6. welfare

cause

Ex 1: 1. discovered 2. determined 3. establish 4. isolate

Ex 2: 1. likely 2. common 3. underlying 4. exact 5. main 6. real

Ex 3: 1. concern 2. alarm 3. complaint 4. optimism 5. celebration

Ex 4: 1-e 2-d 3-b 4-a 5-c

Ex 5: 1. for 2. of 3. to 4. for

challenge

Ex 1: 1. faced 2. accepted 3. provide 4. meet 5. pose 6. issued

Ex 2: 1. real 2. physical 3. new 4. biggest 5. unsuccessful 6. direct 7. legal 8. enormous

Ex 3: 1-d 2-e 3-f 4-c 5-b 6-a

Answer Key

chance

Ex 1: 1. give 2. had 3. miss 4. take 5. waiting for
6. improve 7. need 8. jump at
Ex 2: 1. second 2. better 3. rare 4. equal 5. last
Ex 3: 1. increase 2. ruined 3. stand 4. fancy 5. rate
Ex 4: a-4 b-1 c-3 d-5 e-2

change

Ex 1: 1. made 2. accept, resist 3.bring about
4. undergone 5. planning
Ex 2: 1. welcome 2. noticeable 3. last-minute
4. proposed 5. minor, sweeping
Ex 3: 1. of 2. for 3. of 4. to 5. of 6. for
Ex 4: 1. plan 2. attitude 3. address 4. venue 5. weather
6. the law

choice

Ex 1: 1. gave 2. make 3. restrict 4. have 5. influenced
6. left
Ex 2: 1. first 2. straight 3. obvious 4. difficult 5. free
6. deliberate
Ex 3: 1-c 2-d 3-b 4-a 5-e

circumstances

Ex 1: 1. investigating 2. depend on 3. knew 4. adapt to
5. change 6. died in
Ex 2: 1. exceptional 2. suspicious 3. present
4. unforeseen 5. exact 6. happier
Ex 3: 1. certain 2. no 3. any 4-e 5-c 6-b 7-a 8-d

comment

Ex 1: 1. have 2. made 3. invited 4. apologised for
5. appreciate 6. pass
Ex 2: 1. fair 2. further 3. nasty 4. passing 5. sarcastic
6. helpful 7. last 8. sad

complaint

Ex 1: 1. make 2. have 3. investigated 4. uphold
5. referred 6. received
Ex 2: 1. constant 2. common 3. official 4. justified
5. isolated 6. single 7. serious 8. preposterous
Ex 3: 1. of 2. for 3. of, with 4. for 5. of. 6. of

concern

Ex 1: 1. expressed 2. causing 3. appreciate 4. growing
5. share 6. override
Ex 2: 1. with 2. for 3. of. 4. over
Ex 3: 1-c 2-d 3-b 4-a
most important = major, overriding, primary, main

condition

Ex 1: 1. original 2. present 3. excellent 4. poor
5. showroom 6.reasonable
Ex 2: 1. improving 2. suffers from 3. requires 4. treat
5. aggravated 6. deteriorated
Ex 3: 1. difficult 2. cramped 3. adverse weather
4. driving 5. ideal 6. Living

consequence

Ex 1: 1. suffering 2. considers 3. understood 4. ignore
5. fears 6. realise
Ex 2: 1. disastrous 2. tragic 3. indirect 4. far-reaching
5. inevitable 6. unforeseen 7. long-term 8. likely

control

Ex 1: 1. taken 2. lost 3. keep 4. have 5. exercise
6. went out of
Ex 2: 1-e 2-f 3-a 4-c 5-b 6-d
Ex 3: 1. passport 2. birth 3. traffic 4.quality 5. remote
6. crowd 7. overall 8. air-traffic

cost

Ex 1: 1. cover 2. cut 3. calculated 4. depend on
5. claim …. back 6. spread
Ex 2: 1. at no extra cost 2. estimated cost 3. increased
costs 4. high cost 5. full cost 6. running costs
7. average cost 8. The cost is negligible
Ex 3: 1. idea 2. breakdown 3. grounds 4. details
Ex 4: 1. postage 2. borrowing 3. living 4. health care
5. damage

criticism

Ex 1: 1. resent 2. take 3. singled out for 4. aimed
Ex 2: 1. target for criticism 2. in response to criticism
3. sensitive to criticism 4. open to criticism
5. note of criticism 6. barrage of criticism
Ex 3: 1. received 2. come in for 3. attracted 4. run
into 5. come under 6. facing
The five adjectives are: strong, harsh, severe,
considerable, and fierce.
Ex 4: 1. unjustified 2. constructive 3. growing 4. mild

crowd

Ex 1: 1. disperse 2. attracted 3. disappeared into
4. avoid 5. mingled with 6. control
Ex 2: appear: gathered, collect, congregated
disappear: scattered, thinned, drift away
Ex 3: 1. cheering 2. angry 3. assembled 4. well-behaved
5. panic-stricken 6. capacity

Answer Key

danger

Ex 1: 1. realise 2. exposed to 3. reduce 4. flirt with
5. passed 6. face

Ex 2: 1-e 2-d 3-b 4-a 5-c

Ex 3: 1. to 2. of 3. to 4. of

Ex 4: 1. reminder 2. whiff 3. element 4. face 5. aware
6. possibility

Ex 5: 1. The world's rainforests are in danger of being
cut down. 2. The Leaning Tower of Pisa is in
danger of falling down. 3. The Polar Ice Cap is in
danger of melting. 4. Venice is in danger of flooding
/ being flooded.

date

Ex 1: 1. fix 2. confirm 3. brought forward 4. delayed
5. change 6. make

Ex 2: 1. earliest possible 2. expiry 3. later 4. completion
5. closing 6. sell-by date 7. firm 8. particular

Ex 3: 1. birth 2. general election 3. wedding
4. applications 5. meeting 6. manufacture

day

Ex 1: 1. other 2. some / one 3. these 4. a, one 5. any
6. all 7. very 8. every

Ex 2: 1. hard 2. long 3. big 4. nice 5. dying 6. lazy
7. lucky 8. 8-hour

Ex 3: 1. during 2. for 3. during 4. after 5. by 6. to

decision

Ex 1: 1. justify 2. influence 3. abide by 4. reverse
5. regret 6. put off 7. question 8. face

Ex 2: 1-b 2-c 3-e 4-d 5-a

Ex 3: 1. informed 2. tough 3. wise 4. joint 5. rash
6. controversial 7. courageous 8. final
We make / reach / arrive at / take decisions.

demand

Ex 1: 1. met 2. received 3. give in to 4. justify
5. renewed 6. made

Ex 2: 1. fallen 2. was 3. cope with 4. outstrips 5. risen
6. create

Ex 3: 1. time 2. police 3. parent 4. work 5. job
6. pilots

Ex 4: 1. in demand 2. on demand 3. demands on
4. demand for

description

Ex 1: 1. give 2. defied 3. issued 4. fitting 5. Write
6. contains

Ex 2: 1. detailed 2. vivid 3. apt 4. brief 5. accurate
6. vague

detail

Ex 1: 1. check 2. send 3. disclose 4. uncover
5. absorbing 6. go into 7. took 8. finalise

Ex 2: 1-c 2-d 3-f 4-e 5-b 6-g 7-a

Ex 3: 1. further 2. precise 3. personal 4. minor 5. gory
6. final

Ex 4: 1. in 2. about 3. into 4. on

difference

Ex 1: 1-c 2-d 3-e 4-b 5-a

Ex 2: 1. subtle 2. irreconcilable 3. real 4. striking
5. no 6. fundamental

Ex 3: 1-b 2-a 3-e 4-c 5-d

Ex 4: 1. between 2. in 3. to 4. with

difficulty

Ex 1: 1. get into 2. overcome 3. is in / has got into
4. caused 5. present 6. foresee

Ex 2: 1. technical 2. marital 3. main 4. financial
5. learning 6. current 7. unforeseen
8-b 9-a 10-c

direction

Ex 1: 1. looking in 2. ask for 3. take 4. gave 5. changed
6. heading in

Ex 2: 1. right 2. clear 3. opposite 4. clockwise
5. westerly 6. same 7. general 8. wrong

Ex 3: 1. every 2. each 3. all 4. one 5. both

disaster

Ex 1: 1. struck 2. averted 3. heading for 4. spelt
5. courting 6. ended in

Ex 2: 1. natural 2. utter 3. ecological 4. major
5. impending 6. nuclear

Ex 3: 1. of 2. into 3. for 4. of 5. of 6. for 7. of 8. for

doubt

Ex 1: 1. raised 2. removed 3. casts 4. having
5. confirmed 6. have

Ex 2: 1. No 2. some 3. any 4. my 5. no

Ex 3: 1. without doubt 2. in doubt 3. open to doubt
4. beyond all reasonable doubt 5. No doubt about
it.

Ex 4: 1. serious 2. slightest 3. niggling 4. lingering
5. growing 6. grave

Answer Key

effect

Ex 1: positive = 3,5,6   negative = 1,2,4,7

Ex 2: 1. opposite 2. profound 3. calming 4. deadening
5. noticeable 6. overall 7. combined 8. desired

Ex 3: 1-e 2-d 3-b 4-a 5-c

effort

Ex 1: 1. making 2. requires 3. rewarded 4. save
5. gone into 6. expending

Ex 2: 1. determined 2. extra 3. feeble 4. supreme
5. concerted

Ex 3: 1-e 2-a 3-d 4-b 5-f 6-c

Ex 4: 1. fund-raising 2. Relief 3. war 4. prize 5. waste

event

Ex 1: 1. mark 2. took part in 3. witnessed
4. sponsored 5. shook 6. cancelled

Ex 2: 1-h 2-e 3-i 4-a 5-b 6-d 7-c 8-g 9-f

Ex 3: 1. version 2. course 3. chain 4. summary

excuse

Ex 1: 1. run out of 2. made up 3. use him as 4. have
5. looking for 6. provided me with

Ex 2: 1. poor 2. good 3. old 4. convenient
verbs = give, think up, make, have

Ex 3: 1. lame 2. pathetic 3. feeble 4. not much of

expectation

Ex 1: A = 2, 8, 11   B = 1, 4, 6   C = 3, 5, 7, 9, 10, 12

Ex 2: 1. exceeded / surpassed 2. up to 3. fell 4. in line

Ex 3: 1. high 2. wildest 3. general 4. clear 5. unrealistic
6. different

Ex 4: 1. in 2. to 3. up 4. below 5. with 6. of 7. up
8. for

experience

Ex 1: 1. have 2. learn 3. gained 4. brings 5. share
6. based on

Ex 2: 1-e 2-d 3-b 4-f 5-a 6-c

Ex 3: 1-c 2-d 3-a 4-b

Ex 4: 1. traumatic 2. bitter 3. satisfying 4. memorable
5. fascinating 6. formative 7. exhilarating

explanation

Ex 1: 1. hear 2. gave 3. owe 4. demand 5. defies
6. think of

Ex 2: 1. a very detailed 2. The most likely, any other
possible 3. an immediate 4. no apparent
5. convincing 6. logical

Ex 3: 1. a word of 2. by way of 3. some sort of

Ex 4: 1-c 2-e 3-d 4-a 5-b

facts

Ex 1: 1. retain 2. gives 3. check 4. stick to 5. distorting
6. based on

Ex 2: 1. useless 2. interesting 3. necessary 4. well-
known 5. hard 6. disturbing

Ex 3: 1. of 2. in 3. for 4. of 5. from 6. despite

Ex 4: 1. get your facts right 2. face the facts 3. the facts
of life 4. a statement of fact

failure

Ex 1: 1.feel 2. criticised 3. ended in 4. blame 5. admit
6. put ... down to

Ex 2: 1-e 2-f 3-d 4-c 5-a 6-b

Ex 3: 1. history 2. Fear 3. risk 4. catalogue 5. sense

Ex 4: 1. crop 2. power 3. heart 4. business

fight

Ex 1: 1. put up 2. carry on 3. step up 4. is engaged in
5. give up 6. losing

Ex 2: 1. good 2. easy 3. tough 4. brave 5. fair

Ex 3: 1. to 2. against 3. over 4. with 5. for

Ex 4: 1-d 2-f 3-a 4-c 5-b (to be completed)

freedom

Ex 1: 1. restricting 2. give up 3. allow 4. fighting for
5. value 6. enjoy

Ex 2: 1. fundamental 2. complete 3. greater 4. new-
found 5. hard-won 6. artistic

Ex 3: 1. taste 2. land 3. sense 4. bid 5. symbol
6. struggle

Ex 4: 1. choice 2. press 3. movement 4. speech
5. individual

help

Ex 1: 1. appreciate 2. offered 3. use 4. ask for 5. get
6. seek 7. need 8. provides

Ex 2: 1. great 2. invaluable 3. professional 4. extra
5. individual 6. financial

Ex 3: 1-c 2-a 3-d 4-b

Ex 4: 1-b 2-d 3-a 4-c

hope

Ex 1: 1. gave 2. abandoned 3. pin ... on 4. hold out
5. have 6. raises 7. offers 8. clings to

Ex 2: 1-c 2-a 3-e 4-b 5-f 6-d

Ex 3: 1. high 2. only 3. new 4. best 5. faint 6. false

Answer Key

idea

Ex 1: 1. get across 2. considering 3. come up with
4. rejected 5. selling 6. go along with

Ex 2: a. dead against (D) b. receptive to (L) c. a lot of
resistance to (D) d. bitterly opposed to (D)
e. not wild about (D) f. in favour of (L) g. sold on
(L) h. hostile to (D)

Ex 3: 1. original 2. fixed 3. brilliant 4. funny 5. fair
6. faintest 7. vague 8. half-baked

image

Ex 1: 1. create 2. tarnished 3. improve 4. change
5. shed 6. project

Ex 2: 1. stereotyped 2. new 3. public 4. staid and stuffy
5. clean 6. right

Ex 3: 1. captured 2. appear 3. blot out 4. produces
5. conjures up 6. projected

impact

Ex 1: 1. have 2. make 3. minimise 4. assess 5. felt 6. lost

Ex 2: 1. major 2. detrimental 3. lasting 4. immediate
5. negligible 6. visual 7. huge 8. full

Ex 3: 1. survived 2. absorbing 3. withstand 4. took

impression

Ex 1: 1. got 2. create 3. formed 4. have 5. makes
6. came away with 7. giving 8. convey

Ex 2: 1. favourable 2. strong 3. wrong 4. initial 5. right
6. lasting 7. distinct 8. general

Ex 3: 1-e 2-c 3-b 4-a 5-d 6-a 7-c 8-b

improvement

Ex 1: 1. noticed 2. shown 3. made 4. bring about
5. suggest 6. been

Ex 2: 1-e 2-i 3-g 4-a 5-f 6-b 7-d 8-c 9-h

Ex 3: small improvement = marginal, minor, modest,
slight
large improvement = considerable, enormous,
huge, marked, massive, radical, real, remarkable,
significant, sharp, substantial, vast

Ex 4: 1. room 2. areas 3. signs 4. prospect 5. cost
6. number

incident

Ex 1: 1. witnessed 2. report 3. investigating
4. highlights 5. occurred 6. caused

Ex 2: 1. reports of 2. investigation into 3. wake of
4. knowledge of 5. account of 6. seriousness of

Ex 3: 1. whole 2. particular 3. serious 4. isolated
5. major 6. regrettable

influence

Ex 1: 1. calming 2. disruptive 3. positive 4. corrupting
5. pervasive 6. profound 7. undue 8. outside

Ex 2: 1-c 2-e 3-d 4-b 5-a

Ex 3: 1. had 2. fallen under 3. used 4. be under 5. lost
6. lingers on

information

Ex 1: 1. found 2. provide 3. take in 4. gather
5. withholding 6. share

Ex 2: 1. confidential 2. misleading 3. vital 4. reliable
5. further, latest

Ex 3: a. amount b. piece c. scrap d. mine e. access
1. a very interesting piece of information 2. access
to the information 3. a constant mine of
information 4. every scrap of information
5. a tremendous amount of information

instructions

Ex 1: 1. read through 2. follow 3. provides 4. hold on
to 5. repeat 6. understand

Ex 2: 1-c 2-d 3-b 4-e 5-a

Ex 3: 1. assembly 2. manufacturer's 3. safety 4. washing
5. cooking 6. payment

interest

Ex 1: 1. real 2. unhealthy 3. main 4. shared 5. passing
6. keen

Ex 2: 1. lose 2. aroused 3. show 4. share 5. hold
6. take 7-d 8-a 9-e 10-f 11-b 12-c

Ex 3: 1. places 2. source 3. lack 4. spark 5. building
6. site

issue

Ex 1: 1. cares, about 2. avoid 3. raised 4. resolve
5. addressed

Ex 2: 1-b 2-f 3-d 4-a 5-c 6-e

Ex 3: 1. emotive 2. real 3. complex 4. politically
sensitive 5. pressing 6. good 7. wide 8. sound
9. broad 10. growing

item

Ex 1: 1. missing 2. essential 3. main 4. valuable
5. important 6. bulky 7. next 8. faulty

Ex 2: 1-d 2-f 3-e 4-a 5-b 6-c

Ex 3: 1. each 2. single 3. particular 4. Individual 5. ten

Answer Key

judgement

Ex 1: 1-d 2-c 3-e 4-a 5-b
Ex 2: 1. reserve 2. form 3. confirmed 4. pass 5. trust
6. rely on
Ex 3: 1. a distinct lack of judgement 2. In my judgement
3. against my better judgement 4. an error of
judgement

knowledge

Ex 1: 1. denies 2. provides 3. broaden 4. live with
5. use 6. have
Ex 2: 1. common 2. working 3. general 4. prior
5. basic 6. wide 7. specialist 8. full
Ex 3: 1-b 2-d 3-c 4-a 5. not to my knowledge
6. secure in the knowledge 7. without my
knowledge

limit

Ex 1: 1. set 2. lowered 3. exceed 4. reached 5. impose
6. test 7. know
Ex 2: 1. spending limits 2. speed limit 3. time limit
4. age limit 5. credit limit 6. city limits
Ex 3: 1-f 2-h 3-a 4-b 5-d 6-g 7-e 8-c

look

Ex 1: 1. seen 2. gave 3. tell 4. spoil 5. like 6. has
Ex 2: 1-b 2-d 3-e 4-f 5-g 6-a 7-c 8-h
Ex 3: 1. had 2. took 3. get 4. sneaked
Ex 4: 1. distant 2. vacant 3. wild 4. filthy 5. curious
6. hurt

luck

Ex 1: 1. had 2. bring 3. believe 4. ran out of 5. trust
6. wished 7. holds 8. push
Ex 2: 1. bad 2. Good 3. hard 4. sheer 5. Better
Ex 3: 1. in luck 2. for luck 3. out of luck 4. your lucky
day 5. By a stroke of luck 6. a run of luck 7. with
a bit of luck

material

Ex 1: 1. use 2. made from 3. modify 4. treated
5. recycle 6. contain
Ex 2: 1. raw 2. inflammable 3. hard-wearing
4. recyclable 5. synthetic 6. hardest 7. radioactive
8. Waste
Ex 3: 1. publicity 2. classified 3. reading 4. indecent
5. copyright 6. fresh 7. valuable 8. relevant

matter

Ex 1: 1. discussed 2. be 3. look into 4. bring 5. settle
6. get
Ex 2: 1. delicate 2. serious 3. different 4. trivial
5. urgent 6. personal 7. easy 8. complex
Ex 3: 1-c 2-a 3-d 4-b
Ex 4: 1. light 2. advice 3. nothing 4. word 5. discussion

measures

Ex 1: 1. adopt 2. taken 3. introduced 4. considering
5. announced 6. needed 7. oppose
Ex 2: 1. unpopular 2. temporary 3. safety 4. security
5. desperate 6. preventative 7. precautionary
8. Half
Ex 3: 1. prevent 2. save 3. control
strong = tough, stringent, drastic

meeting

Ex 1: 1. held 2. chair 3. break up 4. attend
5. postpone 6. drag on
Ex 2: 1. public 2. chance 3. emergency 4. private
5. important 6. staff 7. first 8. well-run
Ex 3: 1. arrange 2. fix 3. pencilled in 4. set up 5. called
Ex 4: 1. called 2. started 3. appointed 4. excused
5. leave 6. adjourn

memory

Ex 1: 1. searching 2. commit 3. lose 4. jog 5. bring
back 6. blot out 7. etched 8. put ... behind
Ex 2: 1. terrible 2. fond 3. hazy 4. earliest 5. living
6. distant 7. painful 8. short-term
Ex 3: 1-c 2-b 3-d 4-a

method

Ex 1: 1. adopt 2. work 3. used 4. fails 5. devised
6. recommend
Ex 2: 1. traditional 2. infallible 3. popular 4. reliable
5. unorthodox 6. practical 7. effective
Ex 3: 1. transport 2. teaching 3. earthquakes 4. crowd
control 5. payment 6. pain control 7. birth
control 8. reaching agreement

mind

Ex 1: 1. made up 2. change 3. clear 4. train
5. broadens 6. has 7. crossed 8. springs
Ex 2: 1. one-track 2. sharp 3. enquiring 4. open
5. warped 6. suspicious
Ex 3: a. back b. frame c. peace d. clear e. doubt
1-c 2-e 3-b 4-d 5-a

Answer Key

mistake

Ex 1: 1. learn 2. made 3. realised 4. repeating
5. correct 6. point out
Ex 2: 1. common 2. understandable 3. fatal 4. stupid
5. occasional 6. costly 7. dreadful 8. genuine
Ex 3: a. refuse b. take c. apologise d. check
1. apologised profusely for 2. take the blame for
3. check over your work for 4. refuses to accept
responsibility for

moment

Ex 1: 1. have 2. lasted 3. take 4. spare 5. wait
6. dreading 7. choose 8. paused for
Ex 2: 1. bad 2. proudest 3. embarrassing 4. dreadful
5. key 6. quiet 7. anxious 8. brief 9. last 10. precise
Ex 3: 1-d 2-e 3-a 4-b 5-f 6-c
Ex 4: 1. from 2. in 3. to 4. at 5. for 6. after

movement

Ex 1: 1. restrict 2. co-ordinate 3. detect 4. retrace
5. monitor 6. allow
Ex 2: 1. graceful 2. rapid 3. restricted 4. slightest
5. sudden
Ex 3: 1. is heavily involved with 2. joined 3. weakened
4. sympathise with 5. ban 6. campaigning
Ex 4: 1. of 2. in 3. towards 4. against 5. away from
6. for

need

Ex 1: 1. illustrates 2. eliminate 3. stressed 4. meet
5. recognises 6. feel
Ex 2: 1. urgent 2. constant 3. growing 4. desperate
5. clear 6. pressing
Ex 3: 1. in 2. of 3. for 4. in
Ex 4: 1. special 2. basic 3. future 4. energy
5. individual 6. emotional

number

Ex 1: 1. occasions 2. reasons 3. changes 4. ways
5. factors 6. problems 7. times 8. advantages
Ex 2: 1. appalling / casualties 2. record / replies
3. alarming / complaints 4. increasing / cases
5. huge / convictions 6. total / votes 7. limited /
places 8. high / accidents
Ex 3: 1. risen 2. cut 3. has reduced 4. reach 5. fallen
Ex 4: 1. unlucky 2. Huge 3. exact 4. wrong
5. disproportionate 6. maximum

occasion

Ex 1: 1. dress 2. celebrate 3. used 4. forget
Ex 2: 1. special 2. suitable 3. serious 4. previous
5. memorable 6. festive
Ex 3: 1. this 2. one 3. more 4. particular 5. number
6. odd
Ex 4: 1. sense 2. spirit 3. keeping 4. sparkle

offer

Ex 1: 1. turned down 2. accepted 3. withdrawn
4. made / put in 5. put in / make 6. up
Ex 2: 1. special 2. tempting 3. final 4. kind 5. better
Ex 3: 1. help 2. support 3. work 4. lift 5. marriage
Ex 4: 1-d 2-c 3-b 4-a

opinion

Ex 1: 1. give 2. respect 3. formed 4. influence 5. revise
6. express 7. share 8. ask
Ex 2: 1-d 2-b 3-e 4-a 5-c
Ex 3: 1. strong 2. popular 3. second 4. honest 5. high
6. considered 7. Expert 8. personal

opportunity

Ex 1: 1. miss 2. take 3. gives 4. grab 5. comes up
6. denied
Ex 2: 1. possible 2. ample 3. rare 4. great 5. right
6. missed 7. golden 8. ideal
Ex 3: 1. every 2. much 3. an 4. only 5. no 6. this

order

Ex 1: 1. taking 2. disobeying 3. received 4. are under
5. came
Ex 2: 1-c 2-f 3-a 4-b 5-e 6-d 7-g
Ex 3: 1. strict 2. tall 3. marching 4. doctor's
Ex 4: 1. take 2. placing 3. sent 4. deal with 5. lost
6. cancel
Ex 5: 1. chronological 2. reverse 3. alphabetical
4. running 5. particular 6. pecking

person

Ex 1: 1. single 2. only 3. each 4. one 5. first 6. last
Ex 2: 1-f 2-h 3-g 4-a 5-e 6-c 7-b 8-d 9. right
10. average 11. easy, difficult 12. guilty 13. stupid
14. poor 15. reasonable
Ex 3: 1-c 2-e 3-a 4-d 5-b

Answer Key

place

Ex 1: 1. find 2. looking for 3. mark 4. saved 5. earn
6. change 7. holds 8. taking
a. country, town etc b. seats c. role
d. opportunity to study e. restaurant f. position
as part of a team

Ex 2: 1. come round to 2. get the feel of 3. get out of
4. turn … into

Ex 3: 1. right 2. conceivable 3. safe 4. quiet 5. public
6. unlikely 7. decent 8. uninviting

Ex 4: 1. interest 2. worship 3. birth 4. safety 5. work

plan

Ex 1: 1. make 2. change 3. scrap 4. wrecked
5. approved 6. announced 7. go ahead with, get

Ex 2: 1. detailed 2. crazy 3. contingency 4. original
5. future 6. audacious

Ex 3: 1. change 2. opposition 3. success 4. details
5. favour 6. beauty

position

Ex 1: 1. taken up 2. changing 3. occupies 4. jostled for

Ex 2: 1. applying for 2. held 3. strengthen 4. filled
5. abusing 6. risen

Ex 3: 1. reconsider 2. made 3. took 4. softening

Ex 4: 1. sheltered 2. upright 3. enviable 4. prominent
5. similar 6. vulnerable 7. awkward

possibility

Ex 1: 1. explored 2. exhausted 3. allow for 4. raises
5. rule out 6. avoid 7. examine 8. opens up

Ex 2: 1-C 2-R 3-C 4-R 5-C 6-R

Ex 3: 1-L 2-U 3-U 4-L 5-L

Ex 4: 1. one 2. any 3. various 4. endless 5. every

power

Ex 1: 1. have 2. used 3. falls from 4. returned to
5. seized 6. give

Ex 2: 1. abuse 2. trappings 3. rise 4. positions
5. hunger 6. balance 7. grip

Ex 3: 1. destructive 2. enormous 3. mysterious
4. sweeping 5. creative 6. absolute

Ex 4: 1. concentration 2. advertising 3. speech
4. positive thinking

problem

Ex 1: 1. having 2. fleeing from 3. solved 4. tackle
5. appreciate 6. ignore 7. wrestled with 8. poses

Ex 2: 1. growing 2. serious 3. basic 4. pressing
5. insurmountable 6. complicated

Ex 3: 1. root 2. answer 3. approach 4. extent 5. view
6. nature / extent

process

Ex 1: 1. repeat 2. developed 3. speeded up 4. reverse
5. streamline 6. begins

Ex 2: 1. painful 2. delicate 3. lengthy
4. complicated 5. gradual 6. natural

Ex 3: 1. manufacturing 2. decision-making 3. selection
4. peace 5. healing 6. democratic

progress

Ex 1: 1. discuss 2. made 3. followed 4. brought
5. monitored 6. holding up

Ex 2: 1. steady 2. rapid 3. slow 4. good 5. real
6. disappointing

Ex 3: 1. of 2. of 3. on 4. of 5. on 6. in 7. on 8. in
9. in
(In nos. 8 and 9 'in progress' means that
something was happening.)

promise

Ex 1: 1. making 2. have 3. keep 4. breaking 5. give
6. extracted 7. gone back on 8. hold to

Ex 2: 1. showing 2. full of 3. fulfil

Ex 3: 1. solemn 2. empty 3. big 4. broken 5. wild
6. rash

proposal

Ex 1: 1. put … forward 2. approved 3. ditch
4. consider 5. changed 6. back

Ex 2: 1. allow 2. work 3. met with 4. aimed at 5. went
ahead 6. backfired

Ex 3: 1. consideration of 2. support for 3. reactions to
4. concern over 5. in favour of 6. close look at

quality

Ex 1: 1. improved 2. affect 3. vary 4. test 5. suffered /
deteriorated 6. deteriorate / suffer

Ex 2: 1. for 2. in 3. on 4. in

Ex 3: 1c 2h 3e 4f 5b 6g 7a 8d

Ex 4: 1. variable 2. poor 3. superior 4. highest
5. addictive 6. unique

Answer Key

question

Ex 1: 1. answer 2. raise 3. expecting 4. repeat
5. misunderstood 6. invited 7. avoid 8. have
Ex 2: 1. straight 2. personal 3. open 4. unexpected
5. innocent 6. burning
Ex 3: 1. reply 2. barrage 3. series 4. kind

rate

Ex 1: 1. steady 2. own 3. tremendous 4. present
5. average 6. this
Ex 2: 1. going 2. concessionary 3. variable 4. flat
5. exchange 6. Interest 7. inflation 8. hourly
Ex 3: 1. success 2. dropout 3. crime 4. heart
5. survival 6. divorce 7. death 8. birth

reaction

Ex 1: 1. watch 2. affects 3. predict 4. get 5. gave
6. requires 7. been 8. varied
Ex 2: 1. favourable 2. angry 3. immediate / instinctive
4. mixed 5. natural 6. delayed 7. instinctive
8. violent
Ex 3: 1-d 2-a 3-e 4-c 5-b 6. knee-jerk 7. gut
8. allergic 9. chain 10. subconscious

reason

Ex 1: 1. have 2. see 3. give 4. know 5. explain
6. understand
Ex 2: 1. simple 2. particular 3. sentimental 4. valid
5. apparent 6. main
Ex 3: 1. for 2. why 3. to 4. for 5. for 6. why 7. to

record

Ex 1: 1. set 2. reached 3. held 4. broke 5. knocked
6. stood
Ex 2: 1. number 2. time 3. low 4. turnout 5. levels
6. audience 7. profits 8. temperatures
Ex 3: 1. dental 2. Accurate 3. confidential 4. official
Ex 4: 1. poor 2. track 3. criminal 4. safety 5. clean
6. past

relationship

Ex 1: 1. having 2. improved 3. work 4. building up
5. broke off 6. fell apart
Ex 2: 1. working 2. close 3. love–hate 4. stable
5. physical 6. lasting
Ex 3: 1-P 2-B 3-B 4-P 5-B
Ex 4: 1. strain 2. nature 3. breakdown 4. questions
5. details

report

Ex 1: 1. publish 2. deny 3. give 4. highlights
5. recommends 6. blame
Ex 2: 1. live 2. detailed 3. biased 4. eye-witness
5. damning 6. Unconfirmed
Ex 3: 1. recommendations 2. copy 3. contents
4. publication 5. touches 6. light
Ex 4: 1-c 2-a 3-b 4-e 5-d

request

Ex 1: 1. made 2. refuse 3. received / dealt with 4. met
with 5. dealt with 6. ignore 7. agreed to
8. granted
Ex 2: 1. repeated 2. last 3. reasonable 4. urgent
5. special 6. popular
Ex 3: 1. at 2. on 3. by 4. for

response

Ex 1: 1. positive 2. enthusiastic 3. initial 4. satisfactory
5. mixed 6. disappointing
7. a. a muted response b. an immediate response
c. a lukewarm response d. a favourable response
Ex 2: 1. criticism 2. appeal 3. complaints 4. pressure
Ex 3: 1-b 2-e 3-d 4-c 5-a

responsibility

Ex 1: 1. have 2. accept 3. claimed 4. assumed 5. deny
6. lies
Ex 2: 1. huge 2. overall 3. extra 4. equal 5. full
6. diminished
Ex 3: 1. range 2. position 3. sense 4. area
5. abdication 6. delegation

result

Ex 1: 1. predict 2. awaiting 3. depends on 4. see
5. had 6. know
Ex 2: 1. indicate 2. confirmed 3. exceeded 4. support
5. represent 6. prove
Ex 3: 1. direct 2. disastrous 3. end 4. inevitable 5. best
6. disappointing

right

Ex 1: 1. give 2. stand up for 3. know 4. abused
5. campaigned for 6. has 7-e 8-d 9-b
10-c 11-a
Ex 2: 1-d 2-e 3-b 4-c 5-a
Ex 3: 1. basic 2. automatic 3. equal 4. legal 5. every
6. human
Ex 4: 1. to 2. of 3. for 4. for 5. on 6. within

Answer Key

risk

Ex 1: 1. reduces 2. take 3. carries 4. pose
5. considered 6. outweigh
Ex 2: 1. real 2. calculated 3. potential 4. unnecessary
Ex 3: 1. small 2. prepared 3. worth 4. aware 5. own
Ex 4: 1-B 2-S 3-S 4-B 5-B 6-B

role

Ex 1: 1. opening 2. educating 3. removing 4. influencing
5. building up 6. campaigning for
Ex 2: 1. dual 2. minor 3. clear 4. peace-keeping
5. active 6. traditional
Ex 3: 1. take on 2. reversed 3. see 4. examines
5. playing 6. found

rule

Ex 1: 1. enforced 2. stipulate 3. come into effect
4. change
Ex 2: 1. set 2. violation 3. exceptions 4. adherence
Ex 3: a. follow, go by, abide by, comply with, stick to
b. break, flout, disregard, change, bend
Ex 4: 1. ground 2. present 3. hard and fast 4. strict
5. petty 6. first

safety

Ex 1: 1. guarantee 2. reached 3. compromise 4. improve
Ex 2: 1. in safety 2. to safety 3. for the safety of
4. from the safety of 5. for your own safety
Ex 3: 1. precautions 2. reasons 3. regulations 4. record
5. features 6. procedures
Ex 4: 1. concern about 2. reputation for 3. interests of
4. doubts about 5. place of 6. thought of

situation

Ex 1: 1. handled 2. comment on 3. depend on
4. misunderstood 5. improve 6. review
Ex 2: 1. impossible 2. delicate 3. current 4. desperate
5. difficult 6. Catch-22 7.ideal 8. volatile
Ex 3: 1. calls for 2. turn 3. deteriorating 4. continue
5. returned 6. arises
Ex 4: 1. gravity 2. advantage 3. side 4. facts 5. handling
6. misunderstanding

size

Ex 1: 1. in 2. to 3. in 4. into 5. on 6. to 7. in 8. up
Ex 2: 1. sheer 2. small 3. handy 4. maximum 5. normal
6. actual 7. good 8. manageable 9. standard
10. great
Ex 3: 1. collar 2. half 3. my 4. your 5. several 6. up to
7. take 8. French

space

Ex 1: 1. save 2. make 3. taking up 4. provided 5. make
better use of 6. staring into 7. find 8. clear
Ex 2: 1. extra 2. blank 3. confined 4. storage
5. enclosed 6. narrow 7. open 8. advertising
Ex 3: 1. amount 2. sense 3. plenty 4. shortage

standard

Ex 1: 1. maintain 2. reach 3. raise 4. sets 5. fallen
6. enjoy
Ex 2: 1. high 2. usual 3. same 4. falling 5. minimum
6. approved 7. low 8. modern
Ex 3: 1. care 2. hygiene 3. workmanship 4. living
5. behaviour 6. singing
Ex 4: 1. to 2. below 3. by 4. in 5. of 6. up

state

Ex 1: 1. fit 2. mental 3. untidy 4. financial 5. real
6. original 7. sorry 8. advanced
Ex 2: 1. poor state of repair 2. sad state of affairs
3. state of emergency 4. state of health 5. high
state of alert 6. state of total chaos 7. state of
decline 8. state of the economy
Ex 3: 1. shock 2. panic 3. fear 4. nervous exhaustion

story

Ex 1: 1. check 2. believe 3. make the story up
4. stick to 5. selling 6. read
Ex 2: 1. true 2. full 3. likely 4. gripping 5. complicated
6. same old
Ex 3: 1. point 2. side 3. moral 4. part
Ex 4: 1. success 2. cock-and-bull 3. hard-luck 4. real-
life 5. rags-to-riches 6. love

subject

Ex 1: 1. talk about 2. dropped 3. get onto 4. deal with
5. changed 6. came up
Ex 2: 1. taboo 2. cheerful 3. pet 4. touchy 5. chosen
6. complex 7. compulsory 8. favourite 9. core
Ex 3: 1. nothing 2. briefly 3. views 4. authority
5. information 6. holidays
Ex 4: 1. debate 2. discrimination 3. speculation
4. concern

success

Ex 1: 1. had 2. make 3. wish 4. owe 5. achieved
6. attribute 7. proved 8. guarantee
Ex 2: 1. degrees of 2. chance of 3. key to 4. measure
of 5. taste of 6. sign of
Ex 3: 1-c 2-e 3-a 4-f 5-b 6-d

Answer Key

suggestion

Ex 1: 1. make 2. have 3. agreed to 4. welcome
5. ignore / reject 6. reject
Ex 2: 1. better 2. serious 3. tentative 4. useful
5. bizarre 6. best
Ex 3: good suggestions = 3, 4, 6
bad suggestions = 1, 2, 5, 7, 8

system

Ex 1: 1. reform 2. works 3. introduced 4. devise
5. modelled on 6. broken down
Ex 2: 1. excellent 2. corrupt 3. current 4. complicated
5. inefficient 6. outdated 7. unfair 8. sophisticated
Ex 3: 1. injustices 2. advantages 3. overhaul 4. access

thing

Ex 1: 1. need 2. makes 3. washed up 4. Pack 5. think
6. accept 7. turn out 8. making 9. look at
Ex 2: 1-d 2-c 3-a 4-e 5-b 6-j 7-i 8-h 9-g 10-f
Ex 3: 1. see 2. miss 3. do 4. eaten 5. said
Ex 4: 1. good 2. slightest 3. bad 4. main 5. funny 6. last

thought

Ex 1: 1. hear 2. gather 3. Spare 4. had 5. go out to
6. occurred
Ex 2: 1. examination 2. eating meat 3. going home
4. dying 5. injection 6. meeting
Ex 3: 1. train of thought 2. freedom of thought 3. great
deal of thought 4. school of thought
Ex 4: 1. second 2. negative 3. secret 4. morbid
5. comforting 6. original

time

Ex 1: 1. take 2. spend 3. save 4. killed / spent 5. make
6. afford
Ex 2: 1. smashing 2. quality 3. spare 4. convenient
5. rough 6. ample 7. good 8. precious
Ex 3: 1. waste 2. amount 3. matter 4. length 5. course
6. space
Ex 4: 1. the whole time 2. some time 3. the first time
4. a specific time 5. next time 6. my usual time

trouble

Ex 1: 1. had 2. save 3. giving 4. asking for 5. storing up
6. got into
Ex 2: 1. share 2. amount 3. least 4. end
Ex 3: 1-d 2-e 3-b 4-c 5-f 6-a
Ex 4: 1. stir up 2. stay out of 3. want 4. broken out
5. look for 6. brewing

truth

Ex 1: 1. tell 2. distorting 3. face up to 4. expose
5. come out 6. hide
Ex 2: 1-c 2-e 3-a 4-d 5-b 6-f
find out the truth = discover, establish, realise
tell the truth = admit, reveal, speak
Ex 3: 1. honest 2. whole 3. sad 4. painful
Ex 4: 1. moment of truth 2. quest for the truth 3. ring
of truth 4. distortion of the truth 5. scant regard
for the truth

use

Ex 1: 1. lost 2. share 3. make 4. have 5. recommend
6. ban 7. introduce
Ex 2: 1. increase in the use 2. years of use
3. guidelines on the use 4. restrictions on the
use 5. range of uses 6. ease of use
Ex 3: 1. external 2. constant 3. full 4. further
5. improper 6. widespread 7. everyday
8. unlimited

value

Ex 1: 1. hold 2. offers 3. depend on 4. assess 5. fell
Ex 2: 1. sentimental 2. nutritional 3. novelty 4. shock
Ex 3: 1-b 2-a 3-d 4-c
Ex 4: 1. face 2. great 3. market 4. street 5. incalculable
6. original

view

Ex 1: 1. expressed 2. hear 3. taken 4. holds
5. represent 6. air 7. agree with 8. exchange
9. reflect
Ex 2: 1. personal 2. strong 3. outspoken 4. extreme
5. prevailing 6. opposing
Ex 3: 1-c 2-d 3-a 4-e 5-b
Ex 4: 1-c 2-a 3-d 4-e 5-b

violence

Ex 1: 1. resort to 2. stir up 3. condemned 4. condone
5. threatened 6. contain
Ex 2: 1. excessive 2. domestic 3. racial 4. widespread
5. gratuitous 6. mindless 7. endemic 8. sectarian
9. drug-related
Ex 3: 1. victims of 2. use of 3. outbreak of 4. scenes of
5. upsurge of 6. history of
Ex 4: 1. about 2. to 3. in 4. to

Answer Key

warning

Ex 1: 1. issued 2. ignore 3. given 4. shouted 5. heed
6. serve as
Ex 2: 1. health 2. final 3. advance 4. dire 5. written
6. clear 7. stern 8. prior
Ex 3: 1. without 2. of 3. to 4. for

way

Ex 1: 1. looking at 2. criticised 3. changed 4. see
5. admired 6. develop 7. lose 8. keep out of
9. made 10. push
Ex 2: 1. hard 2. various 3. efficient 4. novel 5. one
sure 6. proper
Ex 3: 1. possible 2. disgusting 3. meaningful 4. leisurely
5. shoddy 6. great

word

Ex 1: 1. looked up 2. saying 3. understand 4. find
5. sent 6. breathe 7. chose 8. exchanged 9. gone
back on 10. get a word in 11. took down
12. gets out
Ex 2: 1. quick 2. single 3. four-letter 4. own 5. exact
6. overused 7. kind 8. right
Ex 3: 1. a word of warning 2. word of mouth 3. words
of encouragement 4. words of apology 5. words
of comfort

work

Ex 1: 1. give up 2. find 3. done 4. face 5. completed
6. involves 7. check 8. made 9. get on with
10. go out 11. get off 12. put a lot of work into
13. gone into 14. getting down
Ex 2: 1. hard 2. monotonous 3. extra 4. skilled
5. back-breaking 6. hard day's
Ex 3: 1. search of 2. piles of 3. rewards of 4. standard
of 5. backlog of 6. pressure of

Of Section

an act of

1. mercy 2. generosity 3. revenge 4. terrorism
5. treason 6. faith 7. desperation 8. God

an amount of

Ex 1: 1. drank 2. do 3. stored 4. spends 5. needs
6. get through 7. cost 8. making
Ex 2: 1. Excessive 2. average 3. generous 4. maximum
5. total 6. limited

a copy of

Ex 1: 1. Free 2. well-thumbed 3. unauthorised 4. poor
5. true 6. back 7. Advance
Ex 2: 1. make 2. keep 3. enclose 4. signing 5. get
hold of 6. printed

a great deal of

1. controversy 2. concentration 3. time and effort
4. soul-searching 5. work 6. publicity 7. truth
8. trouble

a feature of

Ex 1: 1. landscape 2. life 3. elections 4. building
Ex 2: 1. striking 2. safety 3. key 4. redeeming
5. familiar 6. special

a lack of

Ex 1: 1. practice 2. facilities 3. sleep 4. understanding
5. progress 6. experience
Ex 2: 1. investment 2. self-confidence 3. exercise
4. enthusiasm 5. respect 6. privacy 7. interest
8. people

a level of

Ex 1: 1. reached 2. requires 3. reduce 4. measure
Ex 2: 1. fitness 2. violence 3. frustration 4. pollution
5. expertise 6. anxiety 7. unemployment
8. difficulty

a list of

Ex 1: 1. make 2. find 3. memorise 4. publishes 5. left
6. crossed
Ex 2: 1. complaints 2. candidates 3. priorities
4. ingredients 5. guests 6. names

Answer Key

a loss of
Ex 1: 1. loved one 2. property 3. earnings 4. players
5. jobs 6. sound 7. privacy 8. face
Ex 2: 1. memory 2. appetite 3. life 4. sensation
5. blood 6. confidence

a matter of
1. conscience 2. dispute 3. interest 4. urgency
5. experience 6. weeks 7. time 8. concern

a part of
Ex 1: 1. blame 2. day 3. experience 4. bargain 5. story
6. treatment 7. problem 8. life
Ex 2: 1. education system 2. everyday life 3. growing up
4. diet 5. job 6. team 7. ageing process 8. speech

a piece of
1. favourite 2. best 3. incredible 4. blank 5. clever
6. excellent 7. sensitive 8. worst

a range of
Ex 1: 1. options 2. uses 3. issues 4. activities
5. subjects 6. opinions 7. products 8. models
Ex 2: 1. offers 2. cover 3. stock 4. meet 5. tackle
6. come

a sense of
Ex 1: 1. achievement 2. alarm 3. community 4. loss
5. security 6. importance 7. well-being 8. outrage
Ex 2: 1. direction 2. humour 3. taste 4. balance
5. smell

a series of
Ex 1: 1. tests 2. events 3. results 4. murders
5. lectures 6. strikes 7. explosions 8. reports
Ex 2: 1. scandals 2. attacks 3. articles 4. disagreements
5. earthquakes 6. crimes

a set of
1. results 2. circumstances 3. guidelines 4. keys 5. rules
6. teeth 7. problems 8. golf clubs

a sign of
Ex 1: 1. show 2. seen 3. found
Ex 2: 1-c 2-d 3-a 4-b 5-f 6-e
Ex 3: 1. emotion 2. improvement 3. giving in 4. having
5. trouble 6. times

a stage of
1. disease 2. competition 3. course 4. development
5. journey 6. campaign 7. process 8. game 9. project

a supply of
Ex 1: 1. provide 2. have 3. exhausted 4. control
Ex 2: 1. limited 2. fresh 3. constant 4. inadequate
5. good 6. free
Ex 3: 1. money 2. oil 3. drink 4. labour 5. bad jokes
6. guns

a waste of
Ex 1: 1. time 2. talent 3. effort 4. money 5. human life
6. resources